Debating Darwin

Debating Darwin

Two Debates: Is Darwinism True and Does it Matter?

GRAEME FINLAY, STEPHEN LLOYD,
STEPHEN PATTEMORE and DAVID SWIFT

MILTON KEYNES • COLORADO SPRINGS • HYDERABAD

First published 2009 by Paternoster
Paternoster is an imprint of Authentic Media
9 Holdom Avenue, Bletchley, Milton Keynes, Bucks, MK1 1QR, UK
1820 Jet Stream Drive, Colorado Springs, CO 80921, USA
Medchal Road, Jeedimetla Village, Secunderabad 500 055, A.P., India
www.authenticmedia.co.uk

*Authentic Media is a division of IBS-STL U.K., limited by guarantee, with its Registered Office at
Kingstown Broadway, Carlisle, Cumbria CA3 0HA. Registered in England & Wales
No. 1216232. Registered charity 270162*

British Library Cataloguing in Publication Data
A catalogue record for this book is available from the British Library

ISBN-13: 978-1-84227-619-8

Cover design by Matt Rees for Amplified Design (www.amplifiedcreative.com)
Typeset by Waverley Typesetters, Fakenham
Print Management by Adare
Printed and bound in Great Britain by J F Print Ltd., Sparkford, Somerset.

Contents

Responses

Author Profiles

David Swift has been primarily an independent/freelance researcher and writer for the past ten years. Much of his work relates to his desire to encourage Christians to engage in contemporary issues, especially those relating to the interface of science and religion, and ethical issues arising from biotechnological advances such as cloning and animal-human hybrids. He works for the Christian Medical Fellowship and is a member of the Scottish Council on Human Bioethics. David holds a BA (Natural Sciences) from Cambridge University and an MSc in water resources technology from the University of Birmingham, and has worked in the pharmaceutical and water research industries. He is married with three grown-up sons.

Graeme Finlay has a PhD in cellular immunology and is currently Senior Lecturer in General Pathology in the Department of Molecular Medicine and Pathology at the University of Auckland, New Zealand. He has also been working in the Auckland Cancer Society Research Centre for the past 28 years, which is involved in the development of novel anti-cancer agents and research into how these agents affect the cell division cycle, cell death pathways and the activity of the p53 tumour suppressor protein. He obtained a BTh by correspondence with the University of South Africa in 2000. Graeme has felt compelled to communicate some of the dramatic developments in evolutionary genetics and their theological implications to a wider (non-biologist) audience, and has published extensively on the subject, including three 2004 booklets titled *Evolving Creation, God's Books: Genetics and Genesis* and *A Seamless Web: Science and Faith*. In November 2007 Graeme delivered the Templeton Lecture 'Human Genetics and the Image of God' under the auspices of the Faraday Institute for Science and Religion, University of Cambridge. Graeme is married with a daughter and a son.

Stephen Lloyd is pastor of Hope Church, Gravesend, Kent, a position he combines with being a speaker and writer for Biblical Creation Ministries. Before entering the pastoral ministry Stephen was a Royal Society University Research Fellow in the University of Cambridge and a Junior Research Fellow at Trinity Hall, Cambridge, conducting research in electron microscopy of nanoscale materials. He has published over 50 research papers. His MA degree and PhD are also from the University of Cambridge. After leaving his research in Materials Science, Stephen obtained a Diploma in Theology and Religious Studies from the University of Cambridge. Stephen is married to Hannah and they have three young children.

Stephen Pattemore obtained an MSc in physics at Auckland University in 1977 with a thesis on wind power (before it was fashionable), then taught at high schools in New Zealand and India, completed a BD, and spent ten years in church planting and Bible translation in South Thailand. He completed a PhD degree through Otago University (2000), and his thesis has been published in two parts as *Souls under the Altar: Relevance Theory and the Discourse Structure of Revelation* (2003) and *The People of God in the Apocalypse: Discourse, Structure, and Exegesis* (2004). Stephen works for the United Bible Societies, training and supervising Bible translators in New Zealand, Papua New Guinea, Thailand and East Timor, and is editor of the journal *The Bible Translator – Practical Papers*. His other interests include the interface of science and faith, and the care of the earth. He married Raewyn in 1976 and they have four children and three grandchildren. He is an elder at Northcross Community Church on Auckland's North Shore.

Introduction:
The evolution of Neo-Darwinism

GRAEME FINLAY and DAVID SWIFT

The gentle pun in the title of this chapter is intended, because it is important to appreciate that the theory of evolution is not fixed, but has indeed evolved over the centuries. Such flexibility is a feature of science. Even though Charles Darwin is generally given the credit for formulating the theory – and undoubtedly he made the crucial contribution of recognising the role of natural selection – in fact the possibility of evolution had been contemplated long before him. And, following Darwin, the theory of evolution underwent a radical overhaul in response to the discovery of genetic mechanisms. The synthesis of Darwin's original theory with Mendelian genetics prompted its renaming to Neo-Darwinism. And the philosophical and theological perspectives which prompted resistance to the idea of evolution have their roots in the distant past. So the purpose of this chapter is briefly to sketch out what is meant by Neo-Darwinism and how it developed.

Before Darwin

Classical science

Although something of an over-simplification, it is reasonably fair to say that science – in the sense of a systematic investigation of the world around us – began with the classical Greek philosophers who lived around 600–300 BC. Two figures stand out in terms of their influence on the subsequent development of science, including biology, and – significantly – on the early Christian view of nature.

The first of these was Plato (c.428–c.347 BC) who, for philosophical reasons, decided that all of the various plants and animals are but imperfect temporal embodiments of unchanging perfect eternal 'Forms'. An important consequence of this view is that the association of organisms with these Forms provided an apparently sound rationale for why species were not observed to change, and could not in principle do so. This principle came to be known as the 'fixity of species', and automatically rules out any possibility of evolution.

The second was Aristotle (384–322 BC) who had a much more investigatory or observational approach to nature. This led him to appreciate something of the intricacies of living things and the way in which their various parts are so well adapted to one another. He was convinced that living things must have been designed – with their end purpose in mind; this is called a teleological view.

The early church

To the early church fathers, such as Augustine, it was axiomatic that the whole of nature had been designed and created, and they were more than happy to have support for this from the classical Greek philosophers. Along with this they adopted the view that species had been created substantially in their present forms and could not change. As a result, the principle of the 'fixity of species' became part of Christian doctrine.

Although Archbishop Ussher, who lived in the seventeenth century, is usually given the credit for it, in fact it was early church scholars such as Eusebius who first calculated an age for the earth based on the Old Testament genealogies. They concluded that the earth must have been created about 4,000 to 5,000 years BC, and this became the orthodox Christian view.

It was also about this time that it was first suggested that fossils may have been deposited in the course of the Genesis flood.

The scientific revolution

An important stimulus to the scientific revolution, especially where biology was concerned, was the voyages of discovery – particularly to the New World and the Far East – which revealed immensely more species than had previously been imagined.

The huge number of different species led to the challenge of classifying them, and various biologists attempted this. A pioneer of the project to systematise the vast diversity of living things was the English clergyman John Ray. It was he who, for example, was the first to distinguish between bats and birds. Eventually the Swedish scientist Linnaeus came up with the basis of the system that we use today, with each species named by reference to its genus. The close similarities of some species within a genus made even Linnaeus, although he was a staunch believer in the creation of fixed species, begin to wonder if in such cases the species might have been derived from a common stock. This was one of the first indications that perhaps species could change or evolve or even diverge from a common ancestor.

A further indication came from homology. As early as the second century AD the physician Galen had noted the similarities of the skeletons of humans and monkeys, and later scientists (including Leonardo da Vinci) compared the human skeleton with those of other vertebrates such as horses and birds. Interestingly, it was Erasmus Darwin, the grandfather of Charles, who suggested that the similar skeletons may indicate a common ancestry; and in due course Charles Darwin included homology such as this as evidence for his theory of evolution.

Another development that helped pave the way for the theory of evolution, based largely on a reinterpretation of the fossil strata, was a recognition by many that the earth may be considerably older than the traditionally held age of just a few thousand years.

Along with this, scientists increasingly felt free to base theories exclusively on their observations and no longer found it necessary to align them with what the Bible says.

Natural theology

On the other hand, as has often been pointed out, many of the pioneers of the scientific revolution were devout Christians, who very much saw their scientific investigation as a godly enterprise. To them it was an expression of worship.

Kepler, for example, who worked out that the planets follow elliptical orbits, commented that in doing this he was 'thinking God's thoughts after him'. And Robert Hooke, who did much pioneering microscopy, saw clear evidence of God's handiwork in the intricate details of, for example, an insect's legs. 'And can any be so sottish [foolish],' he wrote, 'as to think all those things the productions of chance? Certainly, either their Ratiocination [reasoning] must be extremely depraved, or they did never attentively consider and contemplate the Works of the Almighty'.[1]

Perhaps the clearest – certainly the most well-known – presentation of the case that nature must have been purposefully designed and fabricated by a Creator was penned by the Rev William Paley, Archdeacon of Carlisle, in his *Natural Theology, or evidences of the existence and attributes of the Deity collected from the appearances of nature* (1805). He pointed out that no one would doubt that a watch, with all of its intricate and interacting parts, must have been purposefully designed and manufactured by a watchmaker. And he argued that as we discover similar intricacies in nature, especially the ways in which, time and again, biological functions depend on the co-operation of multiple parts, it is no less evident that nature must also have been purposefully designed and brought into being by a Creator.

Evolution in Darwin's time

In Germany, following von Goethe, the developing stages of an embryo were seen to reflect the hierarchy of forms that were found in nature. In France, Buffon, Lamarck and Saint-Hilaire promoted evolutionary ideas. Lamarck argued that organisms acquire variations (or new characteristics) through their environment or way of life, and that these can be inherited (this is known as the inheritance of acquired characteristics), so that over many generations substantial changes could accumulate.

Evolutionary concepts were widespread also in England. Reference has already been made to Charles's grandfather, Erasmus Darwin, whose ideas were expressed in *Zoonomia* (1790s). Erasmus believed that all warm-blooded animals are descended from a single ancestor. The newly formed University College London became known from the 1820s for its promotion of the concept of human evolution. Robert Chambers captured the public imagination with his grand scheme of evolutionary development in *Vestiges of the Natural History of Creation* (1844).

The philosopher Herbert Spencer from the 1850s used embryological and Lamarckian ideas to argue for human and social evolution. It was he, not Darwin, who coined the phrase 'survival of the fittest', and did much to popularise evolutionary ideas.

Darwin and *On the Origin of Species*

While at university, Darwin accepted both of the prevailing beliefs that (a) species are fixed, and (b) they were designed. But then he went on his voyage of discovery on board *HMS Beagle* during which he observed the diverse, yet in some cases quite similar, species, such as the various finches on the Galapagos Islands. It seemed incredible to Darwin that any creator, no matter how 'bountiful', would make so many separate species, yet with so little difference between them, and far more likely that they had been derived from a common ancestor.

Some of his predecessors, such as Buffon and Lamarck, had had similar speculations; but the problem they had all faced was: How? Darwin's invaluable contribution was to propose a plausible mechanism through which progressive change might occur.

Natural selection

Domestic breeding, which has been carried out for thousands of years, involves selecting those individuals that have desirable characteristics and using these to breed the next generation, so that over several generations substantial improvements can be achieved in the desired characteristic. For example, farmers have bred cereals to produce larger seeds; and dog breeders have selected greyhounds to optimise their running speed.

Darwin saw how a somewhat comparable process could occur in nature: although nature cannot 'choose' an arbitrary characteristic in the same way as might a human breeder, selection occurs naturally in the sense that those individuals that survive better will generally have more offspring. Darwin needed two important concepts to come to his theory of natural selection:

- *Naturally arising variation.* Individuals within a given species are not all the same, but there are minor variations between them. Some variations confer an advantage: for example, an individual may be faster, so it can catch more prey; or perhaps it is better camouflaged, so it evades predators more successfully. That is, some individuals, because they have an appropriate variation, survive better and will generally have more offspring; so that, on average, the desirable variation(s) will be passed on preferentially and will be a little more common in the next generation (analogous to domestic breeding). One of Darwin's major contributions was his proposal that variations between organisms could arise, not through some innate capacity to respond to need, but through random means.

- *Competition.* Darwin was impressed by the Rev Thomas Malthus's *An Essay on the Principle of Population* in which he argued that the human population will always be limited by naturally available resources. Darwin came to see that competition for survival in nature is unavoidable because organisms have the capacity to reproduce to numbers that far exceed the capacity of the environment to sustain them.

That is, natural selection is the inevitable outcome of there being variation among the individuals of a species and competition between those individuals to survive and reproduce in the face of limited natural resources. Stated simply, in any generation parents are a selected population.

There are two significant potential outcomes from the cumulative action of natural selection:

(i) adaptation and / or specialisation; and
(ii) diversification which can lead to the formation of new species.

Adaptation and/or specialisation

First, it is possible for a species to adapt to its environment and / or lifestyle. Here is an example of natural selection that has occurred in human populations since the development of farming several thousand years ago: In many populations the gene for lactase (an enzyme that breaks down milk sugar) is turned off following weaning. But populations associated with dairy farming (a practice that originated about 7,000 years ago) possess a simple mutation in the control region of the lactase gene that allows the enzyme to be made in adulthood. When DNA from ancient human remains was studied for the lactase gene mutation, it was not detectable. It appears that the development of dairying led to selection for a rare genetic variation that is now frequent. In some cases, two species can adapt to each other – called co-evolution – such as some orchids and the bees that pollinate them.

As an extension of this progressive adaptation or specialisation Darwin suggested that new structures such as eyes and wings could have arisen gradually through a series of advantageous intermediate stages. For instance, it is thought by many that eyes probably evolved from a patch of light-sensitive cells through a series of gradual modifications (advantageous variations which arose naturally and were retained by natural selection because they offered some small improvement in the performance of the rudimentary eye) until, over many generations, complex eyes had developed.

Diversification and speciation

Where a species is fairly small in number and confined to a limited geographical area, individuals within the species are likely to be able to breed freely with one another and any evolutionary change will generally affect all of the individuals of the species.

However, some species have large numbers of individuals, and the populations of such species may be spread over a wide and diverse geographical area. Where this is the case, it could be that different individuals within such species face quite different challenges such that what is a beneficial variation to individuals in one area will not necessarily be advantageous to others in a different area. That is, different variations will be preferred in different parts of the species' geographical range. If the different groups of individuals are sufficiently separated (especially if there is a physical barrier such as a mountain range, or if the populations are on different islands), so that individuals generally breed with others from their own area rather than further afield, then the preferences for different variations in different areas can lead to the species diversifying; that is, the different groups of individuals could become quite distinct. And if this process of diversification continues, then it can lead to the original single species splitting up into two or more.

Consequently, the theory of evolution through natural selection undermines both the fixity of species and the concept that they were specifically designed. As Darwin put it:

> The old argument of design ... as given by Paley, which formerly seemed to me so conclusive, fails, now that the law of Natural Selection has been discovered. There seems to be no more design in the variability of organic beings and in the action of natural selection, than in the course which the wind blows. Everything in nature is the result of fixed laws.

And the continued operation of these processes – of adaptation and splitting (speciation) – is thought to explain how, over a long period of time, the current wide variety of plants and animals has arisen from a common ancestor.

Mendel and genetics: Neo-Darwinism

Although variations were key to his theory, a major drawback for Darwin was that he did not know how they arose or how they were propagated. In the absence of anything better, to a large extent he followed Lamarck's idea of the inheritance of acquired characteristics. As it happens, work that would lead to a better explanation of how variations occur and are inherited was being carried out by the Augustinian monk Gregor Mendel at about the same time as Darwin's *On the Origin of Species* was being circulated; but it did not come to the attention of the scientific community until 1900.

Mendel's experiments

Mendel carried out a wide range of breeding experiments with various strains of pea plants that differed in characteristics such as height, colour of flower, or whether the peas were smooth or wrinkled. What he showed was that the characteristics resulted from the inheritance of discrete hereditary units (which came to be known as genes). That is, rather than the individual's environment or way of life affecting its heritable characteristics, the characteristics result from the inherited genes – which is the opposite of the inheritance of acquired characteristics.

Each individual has two copies of a particular gene, and passes on just one to each of its offspring (which also receives a copy from its other parent, giving it a total of two). Further, each gene may occur in (at least) two forms – one dominant and one recessive. If a gene is dominant then the individual will display its corresponding characteristic even if it has only one copy of that gene; whereas both of its genes would need to be of the recessive type in order for it to have the corresponding characteristic.

Population genetics

Once this fundamental understanding of how inheritance operates had been worked out, great advances were made in the early decades of the twentieth century in the science of genetics. These included explaining evolutionary changes in terms of altering the distribution or frequency of gene variants in the populations comprising a species.

A notable example was the development of melanism (dark wings) in the peppered moth. Before the nineteenth century this moth had been known only as having pale wings; but then progressively more of them occurred with dark wings, until by the end of that century almost all of them had dark wings, especially in industrial areas. It appeared that before the industrial revolution the pale-winged form had offered better camouflage from preying birds against pale-coloured lichen-covered tree trunks, whereas the darker wings were better against the darker tree trunks.[2] It was shown that melanism was due to a single gene variant which had been very rare before the industrial revolution. But once the dark form offered a selective advantage, those with this variant survived better than those without, and gradually it became more common within the moth species.

This example not only demonstrated the reality of natural selection taking place but, because of the clear change in the species population (from having predominantly pale to having predominantly dark wings), it was also seen as illustrating and substantiating the theory of evolution as a whole.

Through the succeeding decades of the twentieth century many other cases were demonstrated of natural selection in action – where there had been a change in genetic composition as a result of environmental pressures. For example, an enzyme called amylase helps us to digest starch. Human populations with a high starch diet (arising from the availability of starchy food derived from crop cultivation) have accumulated more copies of the amylase gene than populations that depend on fishing and pastoral practices. The random generation of extra gene copies provided a selective advantage by allowing people to digest their food more efficiently. Those people could produce more children, and so the frequency of people with extra amylase gene copies progressively increased.

In addition, there were many examples of diversification: such as the various species of Galapagos finches which appear to have adapted to different habits and foods; and a range of species of the herb *Achilea* that grow at different altitudes in the Sierra Nevada of California, each adapted to the growing conditions at that altitude.

By the middle of the twentieth century there was no doubt that evolution – in terms of both diversification and specialisation – occurred.

Advances in biochemistry

We take it for granted now, but in fact it was nearly the middle of the twentieth century before biologists realised that the material that carries the genetic information is DNA (rather than protein, as had been thought previously). This discovery was rapidly followed by the discovery of the double helical structure of DNA by James Watson and Francis Crick in 1953. DNA comprises a backbone of alternating sugars and phosphates, and attached to each sugar is a chemical group called a base. The combination of phosphate + sugar + base is called a nucleotide, which is the basic unit or building block of DNA. (See Figure 1.) There are four types of base – represented by A, C, G and T – which are the information-bearing 'letters' of the genetic alphabet: it is the sequence of these bases that encodes the genetic information.

Many genes have the vital role of encoding the information required to make proteins. Proteins themselves are composed

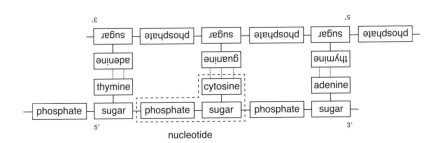

Figure 1   Structure of DNA

The basic unit of DNA is a nucleotide which comprises a phosphate, a sugar (deoxyribose), and a base of which there are four types (adenine, cytosine, guanine and thymine). Each strand of DNA consists of a series of nucleotides which are joined by linking their phosphate to the sugar of the preceding nucleotide. This results in a backbone of alternating sugar and phosphate, with the base that is attached to each sugar protruding to the side. The strand is directional due to the relative attachments of the up- and downstream phosphates on the sugar molecule (indicated by 3' and 5' which refer to specific carbon atoms of the deoxyribose); it is constructed and 'read' in the 5'⇨3' direction. Two strands associate via the bases, somewhat like the rungs of a ladder; each base must pair with its appropriate complement: adenine with thymine, cytosine with guanine; and the strands are oriented in opposite directions.

of linear sequences of units called amino acids, and they perform a vast range of functions in the body. In order to make a protein, the sequence of bases that defines a gene is copied into a messenger RNA molecule which is transported into the cytoplasm to structures called ribosomes where the protein is made.

When proteins are assembled, the base sequence present in RNA is read off in groups of three, with each triplet specifying a particular amino acid (of which there are 20 different types). One could think of the base triplets as three-letter words, with the words identifying the appropriate amino acid. Some base triplets have other functions such as 'start' and 'stop' which mark the beginning and end of the protein. The relationship between the triplets and amino acids – known as the genetic code – was figured out in the 1960s.

Now that we understand how the genetic information is encoded, we also appreciate in biochemical terms what constitutes a mutation. At its simplest, a mutation can be just replacing one base by another, which, for example, could change an amino acid in the resulting protein. Much more dramatic changes can result from the insertion or deletion of one or more bases, because this corrupts all of the subsequent base triplets within the gene. At times, large segments of DNA composed of thousands or millions of bases can be rearranged.

Although the process for copying DNA is remarkably good, in fact most naturally occurring mutations arise through occasional miscopying.

Biochemical support for evolution

As scientists have uncovered the biochemical and genetic mechanisms at the heart of biology they have provided further support for evolution, or common descent.

Most notable is that the genetic code – the way in which the base triplets present in DNA specify the amino acid sequences of proteins, and the mechanisms for implementing this code when proteins are made – are almost the same throughout all forms of life.

There is also much similarity in the biochemical reactions and pathways that make up the basic metabolic processes that are essential for life, such as those for extracting useful energy from nutrients.

What is more, for many of the proteins involved in these core metabolic processes it has been found that, in general, organisms that had already been considered closely related from an evolutionary point of view tend to have similar sequences; whereas those that were already considered distant relations have relatively more dissimilar sequences. Indeed, it is possible to construct a kind of family tree – linking the different proteins on the basis of their degree of similarity or difference – which bears a good resemblance to the conventional family trees based on morphological similarities.

In recent years we have also found that some of the genetic mechanisms that underlie embryological development in quite different organisms are remarkably similar. A notable example of this are the Hox genes which, at a very early stage, demarcate the overall body plan from which the rest of embryological development proceeds, and occur in flies, fish, birds and humans.

All of these substantial genetic and biochemical similarities in the mechanisms that have a fundamental role in living things are believed to support the case for evolution from a common ancestor: it would seem incredible that such similarities would have occurred if the vast variety of organisms had arisen independently from different sources.

Summary of Neo-Darwinism

Evolution involves three processes which are substantially distinct and can be summarised as follows:

1. *Production of new genetic material*

Genes are fundamental to evolution, because they are the basic units of inheritance. It is proposed that genes have arisen and have been subsequently modified essentially by mutation. Most commonly, this is through miscopying of DNA in the course of reproduction from one generation to the next, resulting in changes in the sequence of bases. Mutations may occur not only in the sequences that code for end products such as proteins (called structural genes), but also in the 'control sequences' which control when and how the structural genes are used. So, as mentioned above, the changes may range from very minor (having little or no effect on the production or amino acid sequence of a protein) to substantial (affecting the genetic mechanisms involved in embryological development).

2. *Production of variations*

Reproductive mechanisms, notably the production of sex cells (during the process of meiosis) and fertilisation in the course of sexual reproduction, segregate and mix the available genes in an enormous number of different ways. This mixing of genes means that no two individuals are identical, and there are variations between the many individuals that make up a species.

3. *Natural selection*

When individuals have variations that confer some survival or reproductive advantage then they are likely to produce more offspring than those lacking those variations. As a result, the genes and/or gene combinations that are responsible for the advantageous variations are preferentially passed on to the next generation. It is important to note that the production of new genetic material by mutations, and the production of variations by the mixing and segregation of genes, are essentially random – there is no mechanism for causing favourable genes or favourable gene combinations to arise (or even of 'knowing' what would be favourable). In contrast, natural selection is not a chance process, but a logical consequence of there being variation and competition in nature, such that advantageous variations are preferentially perpetuated.

The interaction of the above three processes can be summarised as follows: The random processes of producing and mixing genes result in genes and gene combinations that confer varying degrees of 'fitness' in a particular environmental context. Natural selection weeds out the harmful and retains the beneficial – potentially providing a stepping stone to further advances.

A corollary of natural selection preferentially retaining favourable gene variants is that less favourable ones tend to be lost from the gene pool of a population. This results in a decrease in the number of available gene variants; it is assumed that genetic variability is restored by further mutation. Finally, many variations can appear and vary in frequency within populations by random drift, in which natural selection plays no perceptible role.

References

Burger, J., M. Kirchner, B. Bramanti et al. 'Absence of the lactase-persistence-associated allele in early Neolithic Europeans', *Proc Natl Acad Sci USA* 104 (2007), p. 3736.

Patin E. and L. Quintana-Murci, 'Demeter's legacy: rapid changes to our genome imposed by diet', *Trends in Ecology and Evolution* (2008), p. 59.

Perry, G.H., N.J. Dominy, K.G. Claw et al. 'Diet and the evolution of human amylase gene copy number variation', *Nature Genetics* 39 (2007), p. 1256.

Waller, J., *Fabulous Science: Fact and Fiction in the History of Scientific Discovery* (Oxford: Oxford University Press, 2002).

Notes

[1] *Micrographia* (1664).
[2] There is debate now about whether this is the correct explanation, but the precise reason for the change in selection is not important in this context.

1

Christian Theology and Neo-Darwinism are Incompatible: An Argument from the Resurrection

STEPHEN LLOYD

The resurrection of Jesus Christ makes Neo-Darwinism incompatible with Christianity. Accommodating Neo-Darwinism leaves the biblical story, centred on the resurrection, incoherent, as it creates a story in which the hero Jesus, through his resurrection, defeats an enemy (1 Cor. 15:26) of his own making.[1]

This is a bold opening statement, not least because I am claiming that the Bible has something to say about a modern scientific theory. Given that the Bible is anything but a scientific textbook,[2] how can it comment upon, let alone reject, scientific models developed millennia later? No one turns to the Bible to evaluate the merits of theories like electromagnetism, molecular orbital theory or defect strengthening in metals. Nor does the Bible reflect any knowledge of genetics, biochemistry or palaeontology in their modern technical form. Hence it is understandable that a prominent theistic evolutionist like Denis Alexander would argue that the religious significance of evolution is minimal.[3]

If Neo-Darwinism were merely a theory about how organisms can change over time as determined by current observations and experiments, this chapter should be as short as one on, say, the biblical view of theories of brittle fracture. But Neo-Darwinism is more than an evaluation of mechanisms of variation. It is a story, a narrative, for the history of life on earth. What makes Neo-Darwinism so compelling and influential is the way it provides such an elegant narrative to make sense of something as complex and messy as the history of life on earth. Neo-Darwinism is one of the few grand narratives that even radical post-moderns still insist upon.[4]

The Bible has no argument with the reality that organisms can change, be that the reality of the variations in the finches Darwin observed on the Galapagos Islands, or bacterial drug resistance. It has no argument with these specifics, because it does not address them directly and they are well supported scientifically.[5] What the Bible does question is the larger narrative of which these sorts of changes are cited as evidence: the big story of amoeba to man evolution (for want of a better phrase) through an unbroken chain of descent by entirely natural processes. For the purposes of this chapter we can drop the *Neo-* in *Neo-Darwinism*, since the original Darwinism and its later developments share this same big story. The details of the possible mechanisms involved are not a concern of this chapter.

My opening statement is also bold because it is claiming that this discussion about the 'big story' of Neo-Darwinism is anything but a peripheral matter for Christians. It is not a hobby horse for single-issue fanatics obsessed with questions of origins, but something that takes us to the heart of the Christian message. Why? Because the gospel is also a story.

The importance of the storyline of the Bible is being increasingly recognised in theology. This story does not function as a 'filler' for the 'nuggets' of timeless, abstract truth about God and salvation. It is not merely a convenient narrative framework into which to fit the theology, as if a completely different story would do just as well. Rather, the story is the *basis* for the theology and itself provides an important hermeneutical framework. For example, the person and work of Christ are properly understood only in the light of the Old Testament history of Israel.[6]

In their document 'Theological vision for ministry' the recently formed Gospel Coalition helpfully summarise two ways of expressing the gospel: 'God, sin, Christ, faith' and 'creation, fall, redemption, restoration'.[7] The two expressions are not in opposition to each other, but rather emphasise different aspects of salvation, namely its means and its purpose respectively. The former expresses our personal story of salvation while the latter brings out God's story for the whole of creation. There has been an increasing recognition in the church of the importance of presenting this larger story in evangelism because it provides the framework in which our personal story of salvation makes sense.[8] In days of greater biblical literacy many non-Christians were aware of the broad framework of the story of the Bible, but this is no longer true in the West today. Why is this relevant to Darwinism? My argument is that Darwinism is incompatible with the big storyline of the Bible. As that storyline is stressed, particularly in evangelism, the urgency of assessing its compatibility with Darwinism is increased.

So why do I insist that the storyline of the Bible is incompatible with Darwinism? Some brief explanation of my methodology is necessary. Too often we come with our modern questions and issues and ransack the Bible for anything (preferably 'proof texts') that seems remotely relevant. That approach creates the danger of asking the Bible questions it is not interested in addressing, with the result that the content and intent of particular Bible passages are distorted. We must come to the Bible not so much to get our questions answered as to get our answers questioned.

My method here is not to start with scientific questions and then ask what the Bible says about them. Instead I want to hear the Bible on its own terms (in so far as that is possible) about three particular doctrines, each of which functions as a crucial element of the story of the Bible, each of which is required to make the resurrection coherent in the Bible's story.[9] I am deliberately using the term *doctrines* because these are main-stream biblical truths taught from many passages in the Bible. They are not fringe beliefs derived from a particular reading of one passage of scripture. Their close relationship to the plotline of the Bible is a useful safeguard to ensure that we hear these teachings in the way they actually function in scripture. Only once I have sketched the broad exegetical basis of these doctrines will I then ask about the *minimum* implications that these doctrines might have for theories of origins, and for Darwinism in particular. Other less well-established biblical teaching may suggest more far-reaching implications, but I want to focus on the outer parameters that these three foundational doctrines define for a story of origins that is consistent with the biblical story. Although necessarily limited, together these three doctrines provide a robust basis to argue that Christian theology and Darwinism are incompatible.

Doctrine 1: Adam as a historical individual from whom the whole human race is descended[10]

Luke 3:38 and Jude 14 refer to Adam without apology, embarrassment or caveat as in the same category as other individuals who are indisputably regarded as historical.

Other teaching explicitly presupposes the historicity of Adam, for example Jesus' use of the creation accounts in Matthew 19:4–6. The teaching[11] in 1 Timothy 2:11–14 assumes a number of historical details in the Genesis accounts. As Carson notes, if the writer is merely alluding to some cultural 'myth' we have the problem of explaining of what this myth consists. It can hardly be argued that it is a general truth that males are created before females or that females are intrinsically more susceptible to deception. The teaching makes sense only if the writer is arguing on the basis of a particular historical event.

1.1 Adam and the storyline of the Bible

The passages already discussed are both clear and significant, but on their own they do not provide a case for saying that a historical Adam is integral to the story of the Bible. However, if we look at how the fact of a historical Adam *functions* in Pauline theology it appears that to remove Adam as a historical individual would make Paul's argument about the work of Christ incoherent.

In 1 Corinthians 15:20–27 Paul teaches that Christ is the beginning point of resurrection life. The parallels in vv. 21–22 are crucial: 'For since death came through a human being, the resurrection of the dead has also come through a human being; for as all die in Adam, so all will be made alive in Christ.'[12] Resurrection life was not a feature of mankind generally, but came through one man individually. To maintain this parallel means sin did not come through man in some general way (as an empirical fact that we all sin), but through the actions of a specific individual.

Thus the doctrine of Adam defines (in part) the mission of Christ, including the resurrection.

In 1 Corinthians 15:44–49 Paul draws the parallel between the 'first Adam' and 'last Adam'. Christ is clearly a historical figure who acts as a representative head. He is the antitype of Adam, an earlier historical figure (cf. Lk. 3:38).

In Romans 5:12–21 Paul's argument (however the details of that argument are understood) requires a historical Adam. The mention of the period between Adam and Moses (vv. 13–14) presupposes Adam as historical and the period as a definite, real period in history in which there was no (Mosaic) law, during which sin existed and death reigned. The emphasis on 'one trespass', committed by 'one man' (vv. 17–18) before which there was no sin assumes the account of Genesis 3. Adam is the representative sinner just as Christ is the representative righteous man.

In each of these three passages Paul does not merely *happen to believe* Adam is a historical individual; his argument – concerning no less a doctrine than the saving work of Christ – *requires* it. A line of history is involved in all these passages. Christ appears at a particular point in that history, as the turning point of salvation history. The logic of the story breaks down if the coming of Christ is a historical event, but the reason for that coming (the fall of the individual Adam), or its outworking (the restoration of creation) is not. Carson summarises what is at stake with respect to the reality of a historical Adam:

> I suggest therefore that if Paul's insistence on the historicity of Adam, on his individuality and representative status, on the nature and consequences of the fall, on the links between these things and the person and work of Christ, and on their typological place with respect to the new creation, – if this all be allowed to tumble into disarray, the foundations of *Christian* theology (not just *Pauline* theology) are threatened.[13]

The point of concern in the above has been the *historicity* of Adam. Many theistic evolutionists accept this, but would question the claim that Pauline theology is insistent on the *physical descent* of the whole human race from Adam.

Paul does not explicitly state that Adam is the father of all human beings, but arguably that is because he simply assumed it. His speech to the Athenians points strongly in this direction (Acts 17:26). It is a matter of common sense that any population must go back to a single pair and it is incredible to maintain that Paul could have identified that pair as, for example, ancestors of *Homo sapiens* dating back 200,000 years rather than Adam and Eve. For his argument to the Athenians to have any force, this ancestor Adam must be their ancestor (and the ancestor of any other group Paul came across).

Alexander claims that Adam is a federal head of humanity, not the genetic ancestor.[14] But this is a false dichotomy. One does not have to adopt a realist view of imputation or argue that sin is physically inherited to maintain that physical descent from Adam is part of the rationale of our identity and connection with him. Federal headship does not involve arbitrary decree. Adam was our legal head precisely because he was our natural head. Physical descent is explicitly in view in Romans 5:14, suggesting that our relationship with Adam (Rom. 5:12) includes physical descent.

The Bible treats physical descent as something very important – just think of the amount of space given to genealogies in the Old Testament. Luke also saw it as important to trace Jesus' physical descent back to Adam.[15] Could Jesus have been a descendant of a *Homo sapiens* out of Adam's line? In the new covenant, descent is just as important, but it is now *spiritual* descent. Our status in Christ as our federal head is not a legal fiction because of real spiritual descent. We are children of God by spiritual birth (Jn. 1:12–13).

1.2 Scientific implications of a historical Adam

Darwinism claims that there is a continuous, seamless chain of descent between modern humans and prehuman hominids. Belief in a historical Adam requires that story to be challenged at some point, whichever scientific model of Adam is adopted.

At one extreme is the position that Adam is an entirely separate special creation discontinuous in descent with other primates. If that is the case, genetic similarities (including apparent genetic mistakes) between humans and primates do not imply a common ancestor. However, if the relevance of that genetic evidence for establishing lines of descent (rather than, say, similarities of design) is challenged in the case of human evolution, logically it should be challenged in the rest of the evolutionary story.[16]

At the other extreme is a scenario in which a biological chain of descent between modern humans and prehuman hominids is maintained, but there is a definite point at which a single individual (namely Adam) is made fully human, in the image of God, a morally responsible spiritual being with an eternal destiny. His parents would not be fully human in that sense, although anatomically identical. This scenario conflicts with the Darwinian story, because a historical Adam requires that there should be something qualitatively different and *discontinuous* between humans and prehuman creatures. Our 'image-of-God-ness' is not something that emerges gradually (or else you could not specify a particular individual as the first to display this) and it is a step that involves an intervention of God. Although theistic evolutionists usually find talk of 'intervention' unpalatable, this particular instance does not cause any concern, since it is not scientifically detectable.[17] Atheistic evolutionists, too, are undisturbed, since the foundational evidential basis for Darwinism is unchallenged; it is merely a disagreement over the significance and uniqueness of man that makes no practical difference scientifically. However, once a date for Adam is specified, any harmonisation of the evolutionary and biblical stories is more problematic.

I will now examine two positions at opposite ends of the spectrum of potential dates for Adam.

The most recent that anyone would want to date Adam is of the order of 6,000 years ago. But even if dated to 10,000 or 20,000 years ago a serious difficulty is raised with what we are discovering of the lifestyle of what would then be pre-Adamic man. For example, Neanderthals who are thought to have become extinct around 25,000 years ago wore clothing and showed many signs of culture. They buried their dead with artefacts and flowers – as if they believed in an afterlife.[18] If that is not evidence of these people being spiritual beings made in the image of God, what sort of evidence would be needed? In addition, a recent date for Adam means that he cannot be the physical ancestor of many peoples in the world. For example, Aboriginal tribes are thought to have been in Australia for at least 40,000 years. This has very practical implications in evangelism. In an evangelistic Bible study examining the book of Romans, I would want to explain that what the Bible taught about Adam was relevant to all of us because of the historical reality that he was our physical ancestor. If Adam postdated Aboriginals, I could not say that to an Australian Aborigine who happened to be in the group.

These difficulties with pre-Adamic man are avoided if Adam is placed much further back – say 100,000 to 200,000 years ago. But then it becomes much harder to sustain Adam as a historical individual in the sense maintained by the biblical writers. No one questions that genealogies can contain gaps, but one imagines that both Luke and Jude would be surprised at the suggestion that potentially thousands of names were missing from their genealogies.[19] If a date for Adam 200,000 years ago is not considered problematic for the biblical chronology then it is hard to see how the Bible provides any limit to when Adam could have existed.

An enormous number of practical and theological perplexities arise from *any* harmonisation of a historical Adam with the Darwinian story. I will take Alexander's preferred model of human origins as an example.[20] In this model Adam existed around 6,000 to 8,000 years ago. God chose to reveal himself to Adam out of the whole population of *Homo sapiens*, thus making him spiritually alive in 'God's image'. He becomes '*Homo divinus*' and he is constituted the federal head of all humanity so that all other *Homo sapiens* are also in God's image (whether this applies retrospectively to *Homo sapiens* who had lived before Adam is not clear). When Adam (rather than one of the other *Homo sapiens* who were now also in God's image) subsequently sins, his fall similarly affects all humanity.

Alexander recognises that the mechanism for the global transmission of the 'image of God' and the global transmission of the sinful nature following Adam's disobedience, across *Homo sapiens,* are problematic. But these represent just the beginning of the questions raised by his model, which he readily admits is not required by the Genesis text.[21] Could Adam's first act on receiving the image of God have been to eat his parents, since as animals they would be a legitimate source of food? Similarly, the day before Adam was made spiritually alive, he could presumably rape, murder and lie (since he had broadly similar physical, mental and emotional faculties to those we possess, yet he was not morally accountable).[22] The day after, all of these actions would constitute sin for Adam, and for all those for whom he was the federal head. Did Adam stop wearing clothes (Gen. 2:25) the day he became *Homo divinus*?

Perplexities are part of Christian theology, so in and of themselves they should not count as arguments against a particular view, but there comes a point at which challenging the Darwinian story is less novel than dealing with the increasingly bizarre questions that are raised through trying to accommodate it.

Doctrine 2: A global flood

Few would dispute that Genesis 1 – 11 is foundational to the story of the Bible. The flood story comprises over a quarter of this material, yet it often receives very little attention – despite being crucial to any assessment of the compatibility of Darwinism and the Bible.[23]

2.1 *Textual arguments for a global flood*

There is no shortage of strong arguments for a global flood.[24] The whole account in Genesis 6 – 9 lays repeated stress on the universality of the flood. Genesis 7:19–23, for example, is worth quoting in full to feel the force of this emphasis:

> The waters swelled so mightily on the earth that all the high mountains under the whole heaven were covered; the waters swelled above the mountains, covering them fifteen cubits deep. And all flesh died that moved on the earth, birds, domestic animals, wild animals, all swarming creatures that swarm on the earth, and all human beings; everything on dry land in whose nostrils was the breath of life died. He blotted out every living thing that was on the face of the ground, human beings and animals and creeping things and birds of the air; they were blotted out from the earth. Only Noah was left, and those that were with him in the ark.

This is no casual statement that everything was killed or that the earth was flooded. The writer repeats himself, itemises the casualty list in different ways (cf. v. 21 and v. 23), and expresses the same truth in both positive and negative ways (*all* human beings were killed and *only* Noah and those in the ark were saved). It will not do to respond that words of universality like *all* do not always mean 'all without exception'. To cite other places (e.g. Gen. 41:57) as examples in which universal language is not absolute is not an adequate reason to conclude that the same applies in the story of the flood. What in the context of the flood story provides grounds for arguing the language is not as universal as it at first appears? In fact, I would want to ask what else the writer could have said if he wanted to make it clear that the flood was indeed universal? If the flood was not global we have to face the problem of a text that is, at best, misleading.

Further arguments support a global, rather than a local, flood. Why bother with taking years to build an ark if you could escape the flood through migration? Migration could be given equal symbolism. Why were birds taken on the ark? The promises that such a flood would never be repeated (Gen. 9:15; Is. 54:9) are difficult to reconcile with merely a large local flood.[25]

Other arguments rest on some basic scientific consequences from the text that would be well understood by people of ancient times. For example, if the waters cover the mountains (even if only the mountains visible to Noah) they must flood a region far beyond the tops of these mountains. Even if these mountains were only a few hundred metres high you could not escape a global deluge unless you argue that the laws of physics were suspended as well as the water.

To propose a local flood raises many questions which need to be engaged with, unless it is merely a device to solve an apparent conflict between Genesis and geology. How local would such a flood have been? Ten miles? Hundreds of miles? Even allowing a large amount of hyperbole it is hard to see how a flood of only a few miles could fit the extravagant language of Genesis 6 – 8, or be consistent with the promises cited above. If, on the other hand, a more substantial deluge is argued for, there is the problem of the evidence left by this flood: the bigger the flood, the more significant its geological effects and its geological explanation. For example, where did all the water come from, and how can the year-long time scale of the flood be accounted for? It is not only supporters of a global flood that face geological difficulties.

The questions are not merely geological. A local flood, just as much as a global flood, has to explain the logistics of the ark. For example, how many animals were on the ark? (Its enormous size suggests a large number.) How were they looked after by eight people? How did these eight people manage such niceties as the problem of the smell from the manure?[26] The geology and logistics of a *local* flood deserve a comprehensive contemporary treatment.

2.2 *Universality of the post-flood promises*

Apparently universal language is not confined to the account of the flood itself. In Genesis 9 God makes a new covenant and uses the same universal language with the same categories as in chapters 6 – 8. This covenant is with 'every living creature of all flesh that is on the earth' (9:16). Crucially the covenant is made between Noah and his descendants (9:9). If it is argued that the language of the destruction of the flood is not universal, then the same must apply to these post-flood promises, since they are framed in the same terms. But this then raises further difficulties. If the flood was local, within the last, say, 20,000 years, then the descendants of peoples who were not wiped out by the flood are in a different category from those descended from Noah. Our presentation of the Bible's message would need to distinguish promises that apply to these two groups, much as some might distinguish promises made to Israel and those made to other nations.

Noah is explicitly said to be the father of all the peoples of the earth (9:19). The universality of this statement is supported by the way Noah is portrayed as the new Adam commanded to 'Be fruitful and multiply, and fill the earth' (9:1,7) and to have dominion over creation (9:2). Noah is portrayed as a man of obedience (6:22; 7:5), but, like Adam, he later disobeys. Just in case we missed the point: as the introduction to another story, that of Babel, which again uses universal language (Gen. 11:1), the author reminds us in Genesis 10:32 that the nations came from Noah's sons.

The stories in Genesis 1 – 11 follow a pattern of sin, judgement and grace. God's intervention at Babel preserves humanity from destroying itself, but the answer of grace appears in Genesis 12:3 only with the promise to Abram. God promises him that 'in you all the families of the earth shall be blessed'. If the language of the flood and Babel is understood universally as covering all nations, then it makes sense that this promise to Abram is similarly universal – a promise that brings hope to all peoples, wherever they might be located over the globe.

However, if the flood is only local, the post-flood promises are local; if Babel describes the origin of only some languages, on what basis is it appropriate to take the promises to Abram as universal in the sense of applying to all people groups over the whole globe?

It could be argued that since the writer of Genesis had no knowledge of peoples beyond the Ancient Near East (ANE) we would be importing modern concerns and questions to press the text of Genesis 12:3 to be a genuinely universal promise. In fact, the same arguments could be used of the creation story itself in Genesis 1. It could be consistently argued that this passage is talking of a local creation – how God created the world as experienced by people of the ANE. The dominion given to mankind in Genesis 1:28 over 'every living thing that moves upon the earth' could be read as a dominion over a small subsection of creation. The implications of this sort of reasoning extend to the New Testament. On what basis do we take the mission of Jesus to 'all nations' (Matt. 28:19) as extending to the entire planet, or that Jesus is the only way of salvation for each and every person (Acts 4:12)? As far as we are aware, the New Testament writers had no knowledge of peoples in Australia, for example.

My argument here is not for formal consistency that arbitrarily requires all statements of apparent universality to be understood in the same way. The consistency I am wanting is that driven by the narrative itself in which the apparently universal commands, promises and events in the early chapters of Genesis are linked together so that the framework of the story breaks down if they are not understood in the same way.

2.3 The flood in the storyline of the Bible

How does the flood *function* in the storyline of the Bible?

My argument is that the flood is not merely an account of something that happened, but a crucial part of the 'plot' of the Bible, without which the rest of the story becomes incoherent. N.T. Wright helpfully describes the history of salvation as a drama in several acts.[27] In his scheme Genesis 1 – 2 is the first act, Genesis 3 – 11 is the second act, Israel to the Messiah is the third act, the story of Jesus is the climactic fourth act, and we are currently in the fifth act. The drama makes no sense if any of those acts is missing. What I am arguing is that the flood is significant enough to merit being a separate 'act' following on from the 'fall' in act two.

The flood is a great turning point in the story of the Bible. Before the flood sin and violence are multiplying out of control. Instead of blessing flowing from the multiplication of mankind, this multiplication leads to a spiral of self-destruction. Despite signs of hope in Genesis 4:26, by the time of the flood only eight righteous people remain. The godly line is almost wiped out. After the flood sin is still present, but violence is curbed (Gen. 9:6). A new humanity is created from the descendants of Abraham, from whom Jesus, the 'second man', would come. He would become the head of a people that is a 'multitude that no one could count' (Rev. 7:9), who fill the earth and begin the work of transforming the earth.[28] While grace was not absent before the flood, after the flood it is grace that abounds more than sin. An era of grace is inaugurated. This is most strikingly demonstrated when Genesis 6:5–7 and Genesis 8:21 are compared. Before the flood mankind's wickedness was the reason to bring judgement, while after the flood the same wickedness is the reason for grace. The change is linked to sacrifice (Gen. 8:20).

It is fitting that such a climactic moment in salvation history should be marked by a flood that is described in the language of 'un-creation' and re-creation.[29] This post-flood creation is one that has been dismantled and reassembled to better suit a world of sin (for example, a world with shorter life-spans limits the trouble any one individual can cause[30]) and to prepare for a final new creation at the parousia.[31] 2 Peter 3:4–7 (echoing Jesus' words in Matt. 24:37–39) explicitly makes the link between creation, flood and re-creation such that the counterpoint to the re-creation at the parousia is the re-creation of the flood. Such thinking is also behind the writer's use of Noah as an example in 2 Peter 2:5. Noah is there cited as an example of someone made for a new world (after the flood), but who for a time lived in the old world, warning of its demise. That, according to 2 Peter, is a parallel of the situation of the Christians he wrote to (2:9), who were people of the world to come but who lived in the old world awaiting destruction.[32]

When the flood is understood in this framework it is far harder to understand it as a local event. The un-creation/re-creation descriptions in Genesis fit most naturally with a judgement that is as extensive as the original creation (in line with 2 Pet. 3:4–7). If creation and re-creation are global events, on what basis can we say that the flood is not similarly global? The flood cannot function as a climactic turning point in the Bible's story without its being a global event affecting all humanity. The warning in 2 Peter has force precisely because the writer is arguing that the flood is something that affected everyone. There are many other historical judgements he could have cited, but the flood was the only universal one – the only proper parallel to the cataclysm of the second coming.

It is the connections between the flood and new creation that lead to the doctrine of the resurrection. Firstly, the flood and new creation define crucial turning points in the Bible's plotline, of which the cross and resurrection stand at the defining moment (Fig. 1, p. 25). Secondly, the resurrection marks the entrance of the new world into our age, a foretaste of the transformation to be completed at the parousia. The re-creation brought about by the flood, I have argued, is the precursor to the new creation.[33] According to 2 Peter 3:6–7 it is the 'present' world which is re-created, a world that is different from the original creation that existed before the flood.

2.4 The flood and geology

To say that a year-long global flood has geological implications is something of an understatement. Assuming water was not miraculously created to flood the world, the existing water on the earth could do so only if the flood also involved a major change in the topography of the earth's crust. This would make the geological implications even more severe, to the extent that the flood becomes the defining framework for geology, not a large catastrophe to be fitted into an existing framework. This would be true even had Darwin never proposed his theory.

Some would dispute that a global flood must have had geological implications. The idea of a 'tranquil' global flood has a long history, but as harmonisations go it is difficult to imagine a more unattractive one. While it is consistent with the central argument that the flood was global it does not explain the suddenness of the flood, or where the water came from to flood the world. It proposes an idea that conflicts with conventional geology (in insisting on a global deluge), but confronts that conventional geology with an alternative that has no explanatory power because it is an event that leaves no evidence. It is impossible to disprove, but for the same reason deeply dissatisfying scientifically. Theories that can be tested against evidence are to be preferred.

The details of the geological implications of a global flood are not determined by Scripture. There is, in fact, no consensus among geologists who accept a global flood concerning which rocks should be attributed to the flood, or how the order of fossils in the various rock layers is to be explained. This is not so much a weakness in a mature global flood model, as an area that has lacked the sophisticated, expert attention that it requires in a model that is still in the early stages of construction.[34] But it is worth noting that few proponents of a global flood would attribute the entire fossil record to the flood. And some would argue that certain portions of the geological column record genuine evolutionary sequences (in the sense of recording morphological change in organisms over time).[35] These are questions that can be addressed only by scientific investigation.

Doctrine 3: 'No-agony-before-Adam'

The final doctrine I want to consider is the origin of, and deliverance from, suffering and physical death in both human beings and animals.[36]

We need to be careful with the terminology here. First, the word *suffering*, or even *pain*, is a little vague, and in limited circumstances some pain is not always a bad thing. So I want to confine my discussion to the more extreme case of agony: pain far beyond the need to inform of danger. A good example would be the pain of childbirth, something that is explicitly referred to in Genesis 3:16. My arguments may also apply to less extreme pain, but this would make very little difference to the scientific conclusions I reach. Where I use the word *suffering* here, I mean it in the more extreme sense of 'agony'.

Secondly, when I refer to animals I am talking about 'higher' animals rather than microbes. It is the suffering and death of creatures that can experience severe pain, such as apes, dogs and antelopes, that concern us here. It is sufficient for my argument to concern myself only with these more obvious examples of higher animals. Where the line should be drawn between these and the microbes at the other end of the spectrum is not something that can be addressed directly from the Bible. It is a scientific question that I am not competent to answer. Plant death or cell death is certainly not in view.

3.1 Human physical death as a consequence of sin

The Genesis accounts are less ambiguous than is sometimes claimed in depicting the physical death of human beings as a punishment for sin, although the punishment certainly includes more than physical death. Physical death is suggested by the references to Adam returning to 'dust' (Gen. 3:19), and to 'living forever' (Gen. 3:22) as a contrast to Adam's fallen state. In Genesis 5 the repeated refrain *and he died* is hard to read except as an emphatic statement that physical death was an anomaly following Adam's disobedience. The mention of Enoch not dying (Gen. 5:24) in the context of his godly life is, then, an astonishing reversal of this new pattern. No one would dispute the physical nature of the death brought by the flood, and in keeping with the preceding narrative the destruction of the flood is directly attributed to human sin (Gen. 6:5–7).

The New Testament is even clearer in teaching that physical death is a consequence of sin. We have already seen how Christ's physical resurrection is contrasted with physical death through Adam in 1 Corinthians 15:21. Paul is explicit in saying that 'death came through sin' (Rom. 5:12) and v. 14 makes it clear that Paul is referring to physical death. Most importantly the discussion of death in Romans is in the context of Christ's *physical* death. And his death is also linked to suffering (e.g. 1 Pet. 3:18; cf. Is. 53:3–9; Phil. 3:10). In Jesus' own words, he had to suffer *and* to die (e.g. Mk. 8:31). It was not enough for him to suffer and then come from the cross alive, or to die in some painless way. Suffering *and* death were required to deal with human sin.

If suffering and death were part of the punishment or the consequence for sin it is hard to see how they could have been present before sin. If sin brought only spiritual death to mankind, why should not the solution have been Jesus undergoing some period of spiritual death? While this was undoubtedly part of the punishment, the New Testament also lays great emphasis on the physical nature of Jesus' sufferings (e.g. 1 Pet. 4:1).

Not only is physical death a punishment for sin, it is also presented as a terrible monstrosity – not a natural counterpoint to life. It is the 'last enemy' (1 Cor. 15:26), something held in the devil's power, and its fear leads to slavery (Heb. 2:14–15). Even more striking is Jesus' response to the death of Lazarus (Jn. 11:33,38). His anger is not due to the loss of a friend – he was about to raise him back to life – it was an intense reaction to the existence of death because of sin.

Death is not always spoken of so negatively. Abraham can die 'an old man and full of years' (Gen. 25:8); Paul can look at his own death as something to be welcomed (Phil. 1:21–23); and the death of believers is described as 'falling asleep' (1 Thes. 4:13). But these are examples of those who have hope even in the face of death because its 'sting' has been removed (1 Cor. 15:56). Physical death itself is the inevitable end to a process that is not viewed so positively: the body is 'wasting away' (2 Cor. 4:16). The fact that death can be a source of rejoicing for a believer does not make it something good, any more than rejoicing in suffering makes suffering good.

3.2 *Animal suffering and death as a consequence of sin*

The Genesis narrative gives a number of indicators that animal suffering and death are not present until after the fall. Diet is an important topic in these chapters, with both vegetarian and meat-eating options mentioned. It is a vegetarian diet for both man and animals in Genesis 1:29–30 and for man in Genesis 2:9,16, while by Genesis 9:3 it now includes meat with an explicit contrast being made to the more restrictive diet existing previously. Readers of Genesis knew that many animals were carnivorous, so they would conclude that this was not the case with the initial creation. If the writer was merely expressing the fullness of God's provision, his point would be weakened if he did not mention the nutritious meat that God had also given if the diet was not, in fact, exclusively vegetarian.

There is no hint of fear or dread between Adam and the animals in Genesis 2:19–20, whereas this is explicitly mentioned in Genesis 9:2, as is the possibility of being killed by an animal (Gen. 9:5). After the fall, death of animals is also required for clothing (Gen. 3:21) and offering (Gen. 4:4).

The flood story gives the clearest picture that animal and human suffering are linked together. God is 'sorry' about having made both man *and animals* (Gen. 6:7), because he sees corruption and violence (6:11–3) in both man and this same group of animals (described as 'all flesh', e.g. 7:15,16,21). Animals are also included in the post-flood covenant (Gen. 9:12, 15–17) and death penalty (Gen. 9:5–6). If violence in animals is part of the original creation, why is God so grieved over it that an appropriate response is the destruction through the flood?

Further connections between animal death and human sin are found in many parts of the Old Testament, only a few of which can be briefly mentioned here. The sacrificial system presupposes such a connection. Animals were included in the Passover judgement and protected in Israelite homes (Ex. 12:12, 29). The fate of the animals of Nineveh is tied to the response of its people (Jon. 3:7–8; 4:11).

Why should amoral animals suffer for our sin? Sin is the ultimate absurdity, and part of its horror is the way it creates a world of injustice where animals and other humans suffer for sins that are not their own. Physically, our biological interconnectedness requires it.

The connection between animal suffering and sin that I have described is in line with our instinctive abhorrence of animal suffering. If animal suffering is morally neutral (i.e. neither good nor bad, just a fact of creation that is as morally insignificant as the tides), why should we seek to minimise it? Why should we be concerned about the conditions in which animals are transported, chickens are farmed or the suffering caused by vivisection? Why, for that matter, should vets use anaesthetics?

3.3 Agony, death and the storyline of the Bible

Any reader of the Bible, ancient or modern, lives in a world of suffering that prompts the question, 'Why?' Is suffering a 'brute fact' we have to accept, like gravity? Did God make a world of suffering? The story of the Bible addresses these questions – the Bible's treatment of origins is, among other concerns, a theodicy.[37]

The biblical story is explicit in Romans 8:19–23, in which the creation–fall–redemption–restoration 'time-line' of the Bible is clearly in view. There was a point in time when creation was 'subjected to futility' and there is the promise of a future point in time when creation will be 'set free from its bondage to decay'. These verses are complex and disputed, but many theistic evolutionists would agree that the 'creation' spoken of is the created order *excluding* human beings, because v. 23 introduces humanity as a separate group. They would also agree that the one who subjected creation to 'futility' was God and that the point in time at which the change occurred was the fall. However, many would argue that the futility Paul speaks of is not some change in creation itself (for example the introduction of disease, carnivores and death), but the futility subjected on creation by mankind's sinful exercise of the dominion over the creation he was originally charged to care for (Gen. 1:28).[38] (I will call this the 'bad steward' reading.) In other words, creation is out of harmony with man since man is out of harmony with God. This is undoubtedly correct, but I am not convinced that, in the light of the whole biblical story, it exhausts all that Paul means by the 'futility' of creation.[39]

Crucial to the first 'act' in the Biblical story is the repeated emphasis on the goodness of creation in Genesis 1, summed up with the statement that it was 'very good' in v. 31 as something to be admired. This is understood in a number of ways by those who adopt a 'bad steward' reading. For example, Lucas argues that *good* (which has a wide semantic range) in this context means creation was well crafted: it was fit for purpose.[40] God is pictured as a master craftsman. He argues that objects of creation (except man) are amoral, hence cannot be 'good' in any moral sense. The difficulty is that gas chambers and cluster bombs are also amoral, yet we regard them as things that are bad. They can display exquisite craftsmanship and be perfectly 'fit for purpose', but they are bad because of the evil intent of those who made them. Cancer is very 'fit for purpose' for killing people and animals in a lot of pain.[41] Reading *good* as *fit for purpose* destroys any theodicy.

Others go further, insisting that if God says this world is good, then it *is* good, whatever our perception.[42] Disease, pain and death are then part of the 'package deal' of biology,[43] a necessary entailment of life, and they must be good since God says they are. While this position displays an admirable willingness to submit to an unpalatable reading of Scripture, it is pastorally impossible. For example, adopting this position I would need to explain (with appropriate pastoral sensitivity) to a cancer victim that cancer was part of a world pronounced good. It may not seem good, but if God says it is, you must believe it is good, because to question this would be to deny God's word. If, however, diseases such as cancer are not part of the original good creation, then my counsel could be different. I could explain that cancer is something terribly bad; it is something that stems from the curse in the world introduced by sin, but as a Christian I can trust that God has a good purpose to bring out of even such a bad thing as cancer. A lot hangs on how *good* is understood.

Fortunately, the narrative flow of Genesis provides some reassurance for pastors. In addition to the arguments concerning human and animal suffering discussed earlier, Genesis 3 provides evidence of physical changes in creation as a result of the fall. The statement that the woman's pain would 'increase greatly in childbearing' (3:16) is problematic for the 'bad steward' position, because even if some pain was present before[44] something has happened, that makes the pain far greater as a result of the fall. A marred relationship with an unsupportive husband could make childbirth even more difficult, but it is hard to see how it could account for the *greatly* increased pain. Similarly I do not understand how a broken relationship with God or fellow human beings (as suggested by the 'bad steward' reading) makes farming intrinsically more difficult (3:17–19). Lamech's words in Genesis 5:29 also reinforce the idea that people understood it was the ground itself which was cursed.[45]

The link between devastation in the natural world and human sin is commonplace throughout the Old Testament (e.g. Is. 13:9–13; 24:1–23; Jer. 4:22–28; 23:10; Hos. 4:1–3; Zeph. 1:2–3). Many of these descriptions are poetic, some apocalyptic, but however symbolic the language, they use that language to refer to something real in creation. Some devastation can be directly attributed to human action such as war or acts of greed, but to see it all in these terms is to overestimate the power of mankind and to read modern environmental concerns into the text. Mankind cannot create earthquakes and withhold rain. Passages such as Isaiah 11:6–9 and 65:17–25 are complex, but at the very least they indicate something non-ideal about a violent and predatory world which can hardly be attributed to bad stewardship. These and many more passages are part of the broad sweep of biblical material that is hard to integrate into a 'bad steward' reading.

The 'bad steward' reading perhaps comes into the greatest difficulty in keeping the coherence of redemption and restoration in the biblical story. I have already discussed how the suffering and physical death of the cross are a distraction from the real issue of spiritual death if physical death predates Adam. Similarly, Jesus' sweat in the garden and his crown of thorns in the passion narratives would be reflections of the world as it was created, not symbolic of the curse from which it is about to be rescued. The healing miracles of Jesus would not undo the effects of sin, but would be akin to a bad architect trying to undo his original design. And what of the resurrection, which is most basically a victory over physical death (1 Cor. 15:54–57)? We have a very strange story if at its centre we find that Jesus came to *conquer* something he had originally created. Matthew 12:25 comes to mind.

The restoration of creation raises more questions. For the biblical narrative to be coherent there must be some connection between the problem and the solution. Hence if the problem with creation is bad stewardship, surely the solution is merely good stewardship. All that is needed are transformed tenants, not a new building. Why is re-creation necessary? Why should the new creation be set free from features of creation that have not originated from bad stewardship, such as the existence of carnivores, earthquakes and parasitic worms that live only in the eyeballs of human beings?[46] If these worms were not introduced in their current form because of the fall, why should they be absent as part of a restored creation?

The first instalment of re-creation is the resurrection of Jesus, in which believers will one day share. Romans 8:23 indicates that our bodies need 'redemption', and the transformation of our bodies is explicitly stated to be a parallel to the deliverance of creation. If disease and suffering are part of the created state of our bodies, why should they be absent in a resurrected body? There is a real tension here in insisting that the new creation (and Jesus' resurrection body) is something physical yet suffering-free, when it is also claimed that pain and disease are necessary entailments to physical life. Since Jesus ate food after his resurrection (Lk. 24:41–43) his resurrection body must have been ageing, according to the table that Alexander uses to illustrate the 'package deal' of biological life.[47] If, in fact, it is possible to have physical life without these negative parts of the 'deal' in the new world, then there is no reason to discount the same possibility in the original creation.

In response to these objections it could be argued that the New Testament explicitly teaches that the new world will be different. But surely passages such as Revelation 21:1–4 need to be interpreted with as much caution as the early chapters of Genesis? If similar principles of interpretation that advocates of the 'bad steward' position adopt for Genesis were used for this passage, I would conclude that freedom from suffering is only an unlikely possibility in the new world. Revelation 21:3–4 is poetic and it is enmeshed in a highly symbol-laden passage.

It should not be read as a scientific textbook that gives details of the functioning of a new world – after all a 'literal' reading is completely incompatible with the future of the universe as predicted by cosmologists. Verse 4 could be understood as teaching the absence of spiritual death (a major concern in Revelation) and the missing tears and pain are the fruit of the sinful actions of people. The passage says nothing about the absence of disease or of a transformed nervous system that frees us from pain.

If we balk at that interpretation I suggest it is time to reconsider the 'bad steward' reading. It is a reading that creates a different story: God is not the hero who cleans up our mess, but one who decides to make a world including bad things and then later decides to make a similar world excluding them. That is a story, but one with an absurd plotline.

3.4 Scientific implications of 'no-agony-before-Adam'

The biblical arguments for human physical death postdating Adam are sufficient to make Darwinism and the Bible incompatible.[48] Animal suffering also postdating Adam only adds to the conflict. Yet scientifically speaking it is hard to see how the two can be separated. Disease and other decay processes cross the animal-human divide. Similarly, if human suffering and death are seen as something bad, surely suffering and death in an anatomically near-identical prehuman ancestor must also be bad?

If animal suffering and death were absent in the original creation the scientific implications are more immense than a conflict with Darwinism. Fossil-bearing rocks bear witness to a colossal level of animal death and suffering, so these rocks must postdate Adam's fall. Even with the most ancient Adam that anyone might want to posit, this creates a massive conflict with the dates conventionally given to these fossil-bearing rocks.[49]

From the doctrines that I have discussed, the conflict with Darwinism is not about change through descent – even so-called 'macro-evolution' is not ruled out.[50] The conflict is over the sequence and time scale of those changes. Essentially, it is a conflict over the age of fossil-bearing rocks.

4. Concluding reflections

I have tried to sketch in a very preliminary way a framework with which to assess the compatibility of Darwinism and the story of the Bible. My argument is that the resurrection becomes a quirk of history – a stunning, but isolated miracle – unless its purpose and significance is elucidated by the wider biblical story, in part defined by these three doctrines that conflict with Darwinism. They are necessary (though not sufficient) to provide a coherent doctrine of the resurrection. The relationship between Christ and a historical Adam unpacks the relevance and significance of the resurrection for all humanity: Jesus is the head of a new humanity. The physical resurrection is the antidote to the very physical suffering and death introduced by the first Adam. The new creation inaugurated by the resurrection is the antitype of the re-creation brought in by the flood.

In short, the Darwinian story cannot exist as a symbiotic guest within the story of the Bible. If Darwinism is true, the Bible's story unravels into incoherence.

It might be objected that this conclusion is too stark because all the passages I have considered could be read in another way. Of course, *any* text can always be *read* in another way, but whether that reading is a good interpretation, revealing the author's intention, is another matter.[51] Particularly important for the issues addressed here is that our interpretation must make sense of the story of Scripture.[52]

That said, I recognise there is much work to be done to develop the arguments I have presented – exegetically, and at the levels of biblical and systematic theology. Despite its long history as the mainstream understanding of the church, the position I have presented is rather underdeveloped theologically. However, I would argue that the same is true for theistic evolution. There is not space to interact with the responses that exist to some of the many questions I have raised about theistic evolution, but I have pressed these questions because they focus the debate in the areas I believe to be of crucial importance in our articulation of the Bible's message. I have highlighted only some of the apologetic and theological difficulties entailed by those who want to make Darwinism and the Bible story compatible. But these are sufficient to make theistic evolution in its various forms a deeply unattractive, as well as a novel, position for both a pastor and an apologist.

Finally, if the Bible's story is as I have narrated it, then we need a scientific alternative to the Darwinian story. An alternative will not be found by poking holes in Neo-Darwinism, but by constructing a wide-ranging model that takes account of as much of the available data as possible and that brings coherence to that data in a more compelling way than any alternative.[53] It is a project that is enormously exciting, innovative and enriching to science. Rather than being an old project that has been tried and has failed, it is one that has barely begun.

But that is another story.

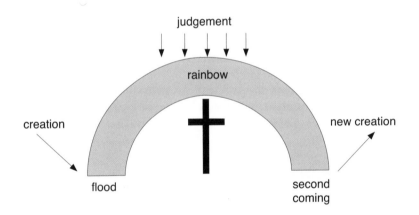

Figure 1   The flood in the storyline of the Bible
The rainbow is the symbol of the Noachide covenant that preserved the earth from future destruction by a flood.

Notes

[1] I am grateful for comments on an earlier draft from M. Fryer, P. Garner, A. McKitterick, J. Smith and P. Williams.

[2] Ironically, Darwin appears sometimes to have treated the Bible in this way. In a letter from 1844 he says, 'I am almost convinced

(quite contrary to the opinion I started with) that species are not (it is like confessing a murder) immutable.' Quoted in M. Denton, *Evolution: A Theory in Crisis* (Bethesda: Adler & Adler, 1986), p. 34. Here, Darwin made the mistake of equating a modern scientific technical word, *species*, with the Bible's word *kind*. Modern followers of Darwin sometimes treat the Bible as an anthropological textbook. For example, R.J. Berry can write: '... Adam was a Neolithic farmer. (This is a statement from Genesis, not my embellishment ...)' (*Science & Christian Belief* 12 (2000), p. 169).

[3] Denis R. Alexander, *Does Evolution have any Religious Significance?* (Pitlochry: Christians in Science, 1998).

[4] P.E. Johnson, *Reason in the Balance* (Downers Grove: IVP, 1995).

[5] Recent research by a scientist who dissents from Neo-Darwinism has also defended the validity of Darwin's conclusion that these finches derived from a common ancestor. See T.C. Wood, *A Creationist Review and Preliminary Analysis of the History, Geology, Climate and Biology of the Galápagos Islands. Center for Origins Research Issues in Creation No. 1.* (Eugene: Wipf & Stock, 2005). Also see www.bryancore.org/issues/volumes.html.

[6] N.T. Wright, *The New Testament and the People of God* (London: SPCK, 1992).

[7] Available from the website: www.thegospelcoalition.org.

[8] D.A. Carson, 'Christian witness in an age of pluralism', in *God and Culture* (eds D.A. Carson and J.D. Woodbridge; Carlisle: Paternoster, 1993), pp. 31–66.

[9] In framing my argument around the resurrection I am not for a moment suggesting that Christian supporters of Darwinism question this core biblical teaching (or a number of other core teachings I discuss), only that there is an inconsistency in their position.

[10] This section draws heavily on D.A. Carson, 'Adam in the epistles of Paul', in *In the Beginning: A Symposium on the Bible and Creation* (ed. N.M. de S. Cameron; Glasgow: Biblical Creation Society, 1980), pp. 28–43.

[11] I am not concerned to draw out what that teaching might be. One controversy is quite sufficient for this chapter!

[12] All biblical quotations are taken from the New Revised Standard Version.

[13] Carson, 'Adam', p. 41.

[14] D.A. Alexander, *Creation or Evolution. Do we have to Choose?* (Oxford: Monarch, 2008), p. 238.

[15] See A. Hayward, *Creation and Evolution: The Facts and the Fallacies* (London: SPCK, 1985), p. 198.

16 For a brief discussion of the cogency of arguments for descent based on 'shared-errors' see W.A. Dembski and J. Wells, *The Design of Life* (Dallas: Foundation for Thought and Ethics, 2008), pp. 133–6.

17 R.J. Berry stresses that his model is not open to scientific scrutiny at this point (*Science & Christian Belief* 11 (1999), p. 37).

18 B.J. Hayden, 'The cultural capacities of Neanderthals: a review and re-revaluation', *Human Evolution* 24 (1993), pp. 113–46; M. Balter, 'Dressed for success: Neanderthal culture wins respect', *Science* 306 (2004), pp. 40–41.

19 However, the existence of gaps in some genealogies does not mean there must be gaps in all genealogies.

20 Alexander, *Creation*, pp. 236ff.

21 Alexander, *Creation*, pp. 238, 241, 275.

22 I am using these moral categories for an amoral *Homo sapiens* since to an observer these actions would be indistinguishable from those of the anatomically identical, but morally accountable, *Homo divinus*.

23 Alexander, *Creation*, pp. 242–3 deals with the flood in a single paragraph.

24 Some have distinguished between arguments for a global flood in the sense of water covering the entire globe, and a flood that had the effect of wiping out the whole human race except Noah and his family. For the latter to be distinguished from the former requires that the human race was confined to a relatively small local area at the time of the flood. But given the arguments considered above concerning ancient man it seems difficult to maintain this view consistently. Hence I will take arguments for an anthropologically universal flood as also being arguments for a global flood.

25 Psalm 104:9 appears to contradict this point if it is assumed that it is talking about the creation week. However, as Wilcock rightly observes, this psalm is a description of how creation works now (i.e. a post-flood world). See his *The Message of Psalms 73–150* (Nottingham: IVP, 2001), p. 122.

26 These questions have been actively pursued in both the present and the past by those who want to take the historicity of the flood seriously. See J. Woodmorappe, *Noah's Ark: A Feasibility Study* (Santee: Institute for Creation Research, 1996) and the recent translation of Johannes Buteo's 1554 work, *The Shape and Capacity of Noah's Ark* (transl. T. Griffith and N.H. Monnette), *Center for Origins Research Issues in Creation No. 2* (Eugene: Wipf & Stock, 2008).

27 Wright, *People of God*, p. 141.

[28] The final 'reversal' of Babel awaited the NT church. The church is a people to be scattered from one point over the world to spread the knowledge of God (Acts 1:8) rather than idolatry.

[29] D. Clines, 'Noah's flood: 1: The theology of the flood narrative', *Faith and Thought* 100 (1972–3), pp. 128–42.

[30] The rapid decline in life-span after the flood is something very hard to explain if it were not global.

[31] This concept of 'preparation' for the new creation is implicit in the language used by Jesus of earthquakes being 'birth pangs' of the new world (Mt. 24:7–8). If a recent alternative model of earth history is correct, earthquakes have existed only since the flood and are 'aftershocks' of the tectonic upheavals associated with the flood. (See S.A. Austin, J.R. Baumgardner, D.R. Humphreys, A.A. Snelling, L. Vardiman and K.P. Wise, 'Catastrophic plate tectonics: a global flood model of earth history', in *Proc. 3rd Int. Conf. Creationism* (ed. R.E. Walsh; Pittsburgh: Creation Science Fellowship, 1994), pp. 609–21). This would support my argument that the flood was not just a judgement, but also the precursor to the new creation.

[32] R.J. Bauckham, *Word Biblical Commentary: Jude, 2 Peter* (Nashville: Thomas Nelson, 1983), p. 250.

[33] This is in contrast to Alexander, who argues that the *original* creation was made to anticipate the new creation – see *Evolution*, p. 34).

[34] For an introduction to how the latter problem might be fruitfully tackled, see K.P. Wise, 'The pre-flood floating forest: a study in paleontological pattern recognition', in *Proc. 5th Int. Conf. Creationism* (ed. R.L. Ivey Jr; Pittsburgh: Creation Science Fellowship, 2003), pp. 371–81.

[35] For example, D.P. Cavanaugh, T.C. Wood, and K.P. Wise, 'Fossil Equidae: a monobaraminic, stratomorphic series', in *Proc. 5th Int. Conf. Creationism* (ed. R.L. Ivey Jr; Pittsburgh: Creation Science Fellowship, 2003), pp. 143–53.

[36] The argument in this section draws heavily on an unpublished manuscript by P.J. Williams.

[37] N.M. de S. Cameron, *Evolution and the Authority of the Bible* (Exeter: Paternoster, 1983), pp. 63ff.

[38] E.g. R.J. Berry, 'This cursed earth: Is "the Fall" credible?', *Science & Christian Belief* 11 (1999), pp. 29–49; J.J. Bimson, 'Reconsidering a "Cosmic Fall: *Science & Christian Belief* 18 (2006), pp. 63–81.

[39] In addition to the arguments I cite below, the 'bad steward' reading is difficult to reconcile with Alexander's view of Adam considered earlier. If creation's futility began when Adam fell, who was keeping

it from futility previously – for example, before any *Homo sapiens* were around? Once they appeared did they display perfect dominion over creation? If so, why did Adam need to be made in the image of God when his forebears were already doing a good job?

40 E.C. Lucas, 'A "good" creation?', *Science & Christian Belief* 19 (2007), pp. 185–6.

41 My examples are emotive, but they are the everyday concerns of any pastor.

42 Berry, 'This cursed earth', p. 30; 'A cosmic fall?', pp. 78–80.

43 Alexander, *Creation*, p. 279.

44 This is in fact a misreading of the Hebrew. The word translated 'increased' does not imply that there was already pain before. See H. Blocher, *In the Beginning* (Leicester: IVP, 1984), p. 180.

45 F.A. Schaeffer, *Genesis in Space and Time* (Downers Grove: IVP, 1972), p. 95.

46 The latter example is frequently cited by David Attenborough in numerous popular articles.

47 Alexander, *Creation*, p. 279.

48 Cameron, *Evolution*, p. 65.

49 Strictly speaking a 'no-agony-before-Adam' position requires only that rocks containing fossils of higher animals capable of suffering intense pain be young. It does not require the rest of the earth or the cosmos to be young. Scientifically, these are more difficult to separate, since similar dating methods are used for each.

50 There are, however, strong *scientific* arguments against the ability of Neo-Darwinian mechanisms to account for the evolution of all life, e.g. W.A. Dembski, *No Free Lunch* (Lanham: Rowman & Littlefield, 2002). Alexander insists that Dembski's information arguments do not apply to biology (Alexander, *Creation*, p. 310) – a position that seems as strange as insisting that biology is exempt from gravity or quantum mechanics.

51 For example, groups such as the Jehovah's Witnesses claim to accept the authority of Scripture, yet argue that texts that seem to attribute divinity to Jesus should be read another way.

52 N.T. Wright, *Scripture and the Authority of God* (London: SPCK, 2005).

53 An introduction to building an alternative model can be found in K.P. Wise, *Faith, Form and Time* (Nashville: Broadman & Holman, 2002).

2

Christian Theology and Neo-Darwinism are Compatible

GRAEME FINLAY and STEPHEN PATTEMORE

Great are the works of the LORD, studied by all who delight in them (Ps. 111:2).

These words, inscribed (in Latin) above the doors of the Cavendish Laboratory in Cambridge University, are testimony to a truth strongly believed by many scientists throughout the history of the Western scientific enterprise: Biblical faith, based on God's revelation in history (as recorded in the Bible), and scientific knowledge, based on tested research, are naturally and deeply compatible. This *must* be so since both aspire to understand truth about a single reality – the universe – and is no less true of evolution as science than it is of any other branch of scientific knowledge.

Yet there is often thought to be conflict between science and the Christian faith, particularly when it comes to questions of origins – of the universe, of life, and of species, including human beings. This perception is at least partially illusory. The image of 'conflict' has been cynically engineered by the opponents of Christianity for reasons that have nothing to do with the essential nature of science and Christian faith. De Fontenelle in France[1] and T.H. Huxley in Britain,[2] for example, deliberately created the illusion of conflict with the express purpose of transferring to secular scientists the prestige (and funding) once possessed by clergyman–naturalists. This crusade is still fanatically pursued by their spiritual descendants, such as Richard Dawkins.

On the other hand, there are times when Christians have used Scripture as a source of data with which to oppose the findings of science. The opposition of the Roman Catholic Church to Galileo is often cited as a classic example (although in this case Scripture was cited in support of the Aristotelian view of the solar system).[3]

But it is undeniable that dispute over evolution has often divided the Church. Some Christians are engaged in very public and polarised conflict over evolution with scientists and educators. We have no wish to engage in these polemics. However, we do want to address what underlies the discomfort felt by many sincere Christians about current scientific understanding of the origins of the universe and of life on earth. The problem is simply that they understand Scripture to exclude categorically the possibility of, for example, the evolution of species in general and of humanity in particular. Faced with an apparent choice either to believe the Bible or to believe the scientists, Christians with a high regard for Scripture often choose to believe the Bible. However, there are also many people who start from the same Christian commitment, become convinced of the weight of evidence for evolution, and then abandon their regard for Scripture, and often the faith itself. This choice is based on misunderstandings – of science and of Scripture – and we will seek in this chapter to demonstrate the ultimate consistency of scientific knowledge and biblical faith.

We will begin by exploring how we come to know truth about our world, and the relationship between knowledge derived from Scripture and from nature. We will go on to examine key portions of Scripture, from both testaments, to see how contemporary scientific understanding (especially of evolution) is compatible with them. And, finally, we will attempt to face some of the more difficult obstacles to holding the two together.

First, however, it is essential to define our terms and to make some important distinctions so that everyone is very clear on what we are talking about.

Evolution as science is that branch of research that seeks to describe in mechanistic terms the processes by which life has developed. The scientific way of thinking limits itself to describing physical and biological phenomena. Science therefore lacks the power to include personal categories in the story it tells. Science cannot tell us of value and purpose or God's personal activity. In contrast, *evolutionism as religion* is that system of metaphysical belief that interprets evolutionary science through dogmatic atheistic eyes. To the devotee of evolutionism, material process is all there is. Anyone whose life has been formed by encounter with the living God, made known in Christ, is free to study physical process, but rejects evolution*ism* as a caricature of the real world.

The distinction between *evolution* and *evolutionism* has been stressed by many Christian writers.[4] If only people could discriminate between evolution and the many philosophies that have been imposed upon it, the public understanding of science would be improved beyond recognition.

The evangelical theologian Charles Hodge of Princeton (died 1878) stated that Darwinism was atheism. This has provided a rallying cry for people opposed to evolution. But Hodge was rejecting an understanding of evolution *that entailed the denial of purpose* (that is, philosophical evolutionism). Christians, then, are free to accept evolution if it is seen to be an expression of God's creative purpose – as Hodge explicitly acknowledged.[5] An openness to *evolution as science* characterised leading evangelical theologians of a century ago (A.A. Hodge, James McCosh and B.B. Warfield, a main architect of the concept of the inerrancy of Scripture),[6] and still does so today (J.I. Packer, J.R. Stott and Michael Green).[7]

1. How do we know truth?

For many Christians the answer is simple. We know truth because it is in the Bible. But this statement needs to be qualified – it is not sufficient in itself. In particular, we have to ask how the knowledge we gain from Scripture relates to the knowledge we gain from other sources, such as from science. There are two related questions we must address: Does the study of nature lead to the knowledge of truth about the world *independent of* the revelation of Scripture? And if it does, what should we do when the 'truth' revealed by science appears to conflict with the 'truth' revealed in Scripture?

The first question can be answered immediately: Yes! Scripture says nothing whatever about kiwis, for example. Yet we would accept that the study of the biology and ecology of kiwis leads to a knowledge of truth. And we can take this a step further, to areas of research not open to simple visual observation, like the structure of matter. Once again, the Bible has nothing to say about these topics. And yet we readily accept that responsible, testable, peer-reviewed science has revealed truth about electrons, protons, quarks and other subatomic particles, and the fundamental forces of nature. Not *ultimate* truth, because by its very nature the results of science are tentative. But truth nevertheless. Truth which can lead to prediction and the design of both helpful and harmful technology, superconductors and atomic bombs.

But we need not simply trust our intuition. Scripture itself affirms the validity of knowledge derived from study of the natural world:

> For what can be known about God is plain to them, because God has shown it to them. Ever since the creation of the world his eternal power and divine nature, invisible though they are, have been understood and seen through the things he has made. (Rom. 1:19–20)

> The heavens are telling the glory of God;
>   and the firmament proclaims his handiwork.
> Day to day pours forth speech,
>   and night to night declares knowledge.
> There is no speech, nor are there words;
>   their voice is not heard;
> yet their voice goes out through all the earth,
>   and their words to the end of the world. (Ps. 19:1–4)

These are but two of the many passages where the wonders of the world of nature are affirmed as not only valid in themselves, but as testimony to the ultimate truths about God himself. And from the suggestions in Proverbs of studying the ants, rock badgers and lizards (Prov. 6:6; 30:25–8) to Jesus' invitation to consider the birds and wildflowers (Mt. 6:26–34) Scripture often urges us to delight in knowing the natural world and to shape our own lives on the basis of that knowledge.

The more difficult question is the second one. What do we do when science and Scripture appear to conflict? We can react instinctively and say, 'Of course, Scripture takes priority, and the science must be wrong!' But what we are really saying is, 'My *interpretation* of Scripture takes priority over your *interpretation* of science.' At the heart of the matter, what is at issue is the interpretation of Scripture.

Take, for example, the question of the movement of the earth and sun, the issue over which the medieval Church convicted Galileo of heresy. The Bible is full of statements about the sun 'rising' and the sun 'going down'. But so is our everyday language today. We have no difficulty in accepting that this is figurative, or at least *relative*, language. It corresponds to our local, earth-bound experience. It can be true simultaneously with the scientific fact of the earth's rotation and movement around the sun. So far not even the medieval Church had a problem. But note that already we have accepted that Scripture must be *interpreted*. We have allowed that Scripture is true *even though the literal form of words used is strictly not true*. So we cope easily with statements about the sun running joyfully across the sky (Ps. 19:4–6). This is clearly poetic language, and we accept its truth even though its literal meaning is not true. But what about Psalm 104:5: 'Thou didst set the earth on its foundations, so that it should never be shaken'? Poetry again? Yes, certainly. And yet it equally certainly represents the view of the structure of the universe held by the psalmist, and by many since his day, which is, in its literal sense, simply not true.

Still more difficult is the passage in Joshua 10:12–13 where the narrator, writing under the inspiration of the Holy Spirit, makes a plain statement of fact: 'The sun stood still and the moon stayed.' Our point is not to dispute that a miracle took place. But if the statement was *literally* true it would not have accomplished the miracle. For the sun somehow to stop its movement around the centre of our galaxy would not lengthen Joshua's day. That requires an adjustment to the rotation of the earth.

We have long adjusted our understanding of Scripture to allow for the scientific truth that day and night are caused by the rotation of the earth on its axis, and that the earth moves around the sun, not vice versa. This example shows that when there is a conflict between the apparent truth uncovered by science and the apparent truth of a statement of Scripture, we have a responsibility not simply to reject the science, but to test both the interpretation of the scientific data and our interpretation of

Scripture. And underlying that is the willingness to adopt a stance of humility towards our current understanding of Scripture. Science does not provide ultimate truth, but nor does our present understanding of Scripture.

2. The nature of biblical language

The Bible affirms that God speaks. From the first chapter of Genesis, where God's creative activity is accomplished by words, through his revelation on Sinai (Ex. 20:1), to his communication through the prophets (Amos 3:8), supremely in Jesus (Heb. 1:1–2), and ultimately from the throne of heaven (Rev. 20:5–8), God has spoken. And God has spoken in human languages, through the normal modes of human communication.

The study of linguistics provides evidence of the tremendous power of human language. Communication involves much more than simply encrypting abstract ideas in some verbal or written code. Rather, when we communicate we (like God in Genesis 1) *do things* with words, we *use* words to *mean* something. And we *establish networks* of social relationships with other people. Going beyond sound systems and grammatical rules, contemporary linguistics focuses on *pragmatic* aspects of our language in which the context of the act of communication is of vital importance.

Speech Act Theory[8] argues that by our speech utterances in specific contexts we accomplish varieties of tasks within our social network, and ultimately change the world. To properly understand a statement it is important to grasp what the author of the statement is *doing* with his words. In our immediate natural environment, in our native language, we do this instinctively at a subconscious level. When we try to understand acts of communication from a distant time and place (such as the Bible), the task of interpreting is more complex and self-conscious.

Relevance Theory[9] argues that our communication acts are strongly inferential (that is, we are expected to infer a wider meaning than that expressed in the words themselves) and are governed by a tendency to optimise relevance. This means that we provide our listeners (or readers) with words which are clues to our meaning, clues that will lead them to that meaning without undue mental effort, based on our estimation of the common understanding (of the world, of history, of language) that we share. Correspondingly, listeners (and readers) always interpret everything they hear or read, based on the best possible context available to them at the time. When we are close to the context, communication is usually successful. The further we are from the context, the less certain we can be of automatically picking the right context for interpretation.[10]

Understanding the way language works has important implications for the way we understand the Scriptures. Firstly, whenever we hear or read something, we engage in interpretation. There is no understanding without interpretation – language does not have intrinsic meaning in a vacuum. Someone uses language to mean something to someone in some situation. Secondly, the context of a communication is not merely helpful, it is centrally important to understanding it. And thirdly, a 'literal' interpretation has no inherent priority over a non-literal one. In ordinary, everyday language we nearly always say less than we mean, and often say things which are *pointers* to the meaning we intend rather than being *containers* of that meaning.

These results affirm the importance of historical-critical exegesis in biblical scholarship, involving the careful reconstruction of historical, social, geographic and cognitive contexts within which biblical texts were written. They underline the importance of understanding the *genre* or type of language of a particular text, and the original setting in which that genre found its place. But they also affirm the importance of the reader in the task of interpretation, because we always bring to a text *our own* most readily accessed assumptions, so that who we are influences how we read. In particular, when Christians sometimes assume that a strictly literal interpretation should be the first or preferred way to approach a biblical text such as Genesis 1 – 3, *they have themselves brought that assumption to the text*; they have not found it in Scripture. It is part of their view of how language works, and it is not an assumption that is supported by modern linguistics.

A priority of biblical faith, then, is to understand those passages of Scripture that describe how God relates to his creation, taking account of both the ways by which authors sought to communicate and the very active role that we ourselves play as readers.

3. Ways of reading Scripture

Throughout history, people have approached Scripture in many different ways. The early church theologian Origen of Alexandria (died c.254 AD) absorbed many of his assumptions about the nature of reality from the Greek philosopher Plato. This led him to favour allegorical readings of Scripture. The application of allegorical approaches provided readers with highly imaginative interpretive schemes and allowed them to perceive in a text any meanings they were predisposed to find.

Origen's approach hugely influenced the way by which the medieval theologians interpreted Scripture. They sought to extract four senses of meaning from the text (the *quadriga*):

1. historical (or literal): the direct meaning, taken at face-value
2. allegorical: the spiritual meaning
3. tropological (or moral): ethical guidelines
4. anagogical: pointers to the ultimate Christian hope.

Scripture and the world were seen as rich resources of symbols, the spiritual meanings of which could be inferred by the use of allegorical strategies. When we read the early chapters of Genesis, we need to safeguard ourselves from similar flights of fancy. We could read the creation stories (Gen. 1:1 – 2:3 and 2:4–25) as allegories or as myths (an approach that became popular in the nineteenth century), and mine them for symbols that we would arbitrarily transmogrify into spiritual truths, abstracted from any context in the real world. Alternatively we could approach them as 'literal' prosaic history.

None of these approaches is acceptable.[11]

For example, an *a priori* commitment to a literal interpretation cannot be sustained. We come across statements that have to be figurative. We are told that God breathed into man's nostrils, planted a garden, walked in the garden, and made clothes of skin (Gen. 2:7,8; 3:8,21). If God is Spirit, he does not have physical lungs and limbs. These statements are anthropomorphisms, descriptions of God *as if* he were a human being. We have to accept that in these cases, the text uses pictorial, figurative language. We should be alert to the likelihood that the surrounding text also uses various forms of graphic imagery to convey its message. The Reformers of the sixteenth century were renowned for their 'literal' reading of Scripture. Does the call to accept figurative language in the earliest chapters of Genesis represent a betrayal of what those Reformers lived and died for? N.T. Wright explains what the Reformers meant by 'literal':

> Many churches, including my own, have retained the Reformers' emphasis on the 'literal' sense of Scripture, not in the sense of 'taking everything literally' but in the sense of 'discovering what the writers meant' as opposed to engaging in free-floating speculation.[12]

Thus to the Reformers, the 'literal' sense of Scripture was the sense that the text itself demanded, and that may be perceived only with careful attentiveness to the way the text is written. Such a 'literal' sense would require us to eschew a wooden literalism if it is apparent that the text is rich is metaphorical language.

4. Are the Genesis creation stories science?

Bible readers throughout history have approached Genesis on the basis of their culture-bound presuppositions. These are deep, unexamined assumptions about the nature of reality. We unconsciously and inevitably absorb our presuppositions as we grow up, and they affect the way we see the world. One particular influence about which we are not aware is the all-prevailing science and technology that conditions our outlook on reality.

Gordon Wenham warns us that questions such as, 'When did the world begin?' or 'Where did life originate?' or 'How did life develop?' are inspired by the scientific attitudes that pervade our culture, but in all probability they never occurred to the writer of Genesis. 'We should therefore be cautious about looking for answers to questions he was not concerned with.' Our assumptions about the world are completely different from those of the second millennium BC. When we read Genesis, we tend to look for points that were irrelevant to the author of Genesis and we all too easily overlook points that were fundamental.[13] Scientific questions were foreign to the minds of the ancient Israelites. We should heed the warnings of the *Wycliffe Bible Commentary*:[14]

> If a student expects to find in Genesis a scientific account of how the world came into existence ... he will be disappointed. Genesis is not an attempt to grapple with or answer such technical questions. It deals with matters far beyond the realm of science. The author seeks to bring us in touch with the eternal God.

Evangelical biblical scholars have emphasised repeatedly that the aims, content and language of Genesis are completely different from those of science (Table 1).[15] In fact, science is an intellectual pursuit that became established in human thinking only in the scientific revolution of seventeenth-century Europe.

Table 1   Differences between science and Genesis

	Natural science	Genesis
Aims	probes the observable world	seeks to discern the unobservable; the relation between God and man; addresses what cannot be known by science
Overall approach	answers questions of 'what' and 'how'; is descriptive	primarily answers questions of 'why' and 'what ought to be'; is prescriptive
Content	is concerned with the forces of nature; proximate causes	is concerned with God; ultimate causes; to specify that creation is the result of God's creative acts
Literary style	is dryly factual	needs the whole range of literary genres to do it justice
Language	uses mathematics and technical terminology; specific	is imprecise, uses the language of appearance; is rich in cultural idiom; everyday speech, and non-technical terminology

To J.I. Packer, the creation stories should not be read as factual descriptions of the empirical world. They are not a source of scientific data. Rather, the language of the creation accounts is pictorial and their purpose is theological. Packer makes five key points about the relationship between the Genesis creation story and science.[16]

1. The narrative is a celebrating of the fact of creation and of the Creator's wisdom, power and goodness, rather than an observational monitoring of stages in the creative process.
2. The story focuses not on the cosmic system as a system, but on the Creator apart from whose will and word it would not at this moment exist.
3. The narrative method is imaginative, pictorial, poetic and doxological [expressing worship] rather than clinically descriptive and coldly prosaic in the deadpan scientific manner.
4. The Earth-centredness of the presentation reflects not scientific naivety about the solar system and outer space, but theological interest in man's uniqueness and responsibility under God on this planet.
5. The evident aim of the story is to show its readers their own place and calling in God's world, and the abiding significance of the Sabbath as a memorial to creation, rather than to satisfy curiosity about the details of what happened long ago.

For example, Genesis 1:16 simply states that God made the stars. It is not interested in the physical processes by which stars form. The behaviour of gas clouds under the influence of gravity is the legitimate business of physicists. The assertions 'God made the stars' and 'stars form in vast clouds of gas and dust' are not incompatible kinds of statements.

5. Ancient authors, readers and genres

We can take important steps to avoid the mistake of reading our expectations into Scripture and to protect ourselves from fantastic interpretations. As a starter, Packer urges people to conduct their Bible reading in the context of their heritage of Christian theology. If this is not done, they run the danger of becoming arbitrary in their interpretations.[17] According to historian Mark Noll, a major weakness of some expressions of Christianity is their strikingly individualistic approach to the Bible.[18] The danger is that an 'every man for himself' approach to the Bible results in the proliferation of cults.

The next step is to place ourselves, as much as is possible, in the world of the biblical authors. They wrote in the language, culture and historical situation of their times. They addressed practical issues of existential relevance to their lives. Accordingly, the *intentions* of the original authors should be ascertained as far as is possible: 'the universally applicable meaning of the text is related primarily to its *originally intended* meaning'.[19] If we want to find the enduring importance of the Genesis creation stories for us in the twenty-first century, we should reconstruct (as much as we can) the significance of their message in the particular religious and social conditions of the ancient world. Postmodern thinkers have lost interest in the concept of 'authorial intention', but it remains a valid consideration for readers of the Bible, because the clues to the author's intentions are often found embedded in the text itself.[20]

In addition, an urgent priority is to discover the impact of a text on its original readers. Of course, this may not be easy. Genesis was first read by people whose language, culture and concerns are greatly removed from ours. But only when this spadework has been done are we fully equipped to discover what the text has to say to us.

Readers of the Bible must understand the genre of the particular piece of literature with which they are engaged – whether it is history, law, poetry, social critique or parable. This must be determined empirically, by examining the literature on its own terms and on the basis of its content. One thing must be established as 'given' for all Christians: the Old Testament, including Genesis, is the inspired and authoritative Word of God to us because it was so for Christ and his disciples. It follows that the actual genre cannot affect the status of the text as divinely inspired. We emphasise that the Bible is for us the inspired Word of God, authoritative in all matters of faith and conduct, even as it is inevitably written in the languages of human beings.

6. The content of Genesis 1

The Bible starts with a prologue consisting of the first 11 chapters of Genesis. These chapters constitute a primeval history, and provide a context for the beginning of Israel's story. The first chapter contains a creation narrative, in which God is the one speaker and agent. It has a symmetrical structure, consisting of an eight-fold repetition of God's creative acts, given in six days.[21]

Day 1	light separated from darkness
Day 2	sky separating the waters under it from those above it
Day 3	act 1: seas gathered from land act 2: land producing all kinds of vegetation
Day 4	lights set in the sky
Day 5	all kinds of sea creatures and birds
Day 6	act 1: all kinds of land animals act 2: people
Day 7	rest

The eight creative acts each have the general structure of a four-line poem. This marks the text as a carefully composed and stylised piece of writing, and emphasises the orderliness of creation.

1. And God said
2. And it was so
3. And God saw
4. And there was evening and there was morning

How should Christians approach such literature when they accept it as authoritative but recognise that it was composed in a cultural setting totally different from their own? Old Testament scholars bring out surprising things that are not obviously apparent to the ordinary reader:

1. There is a poetic quality about Genesis 1. 'We are meant to experience the orderliness of God's activity through the sensuality of the language and through the particular way in which the text speaks.' Much of this language is lost in translation.[22] The text is marked by a rhythmic quality, which arises from the repetition of words and phrases; by its symmetry; and by the use of symbolism, especially the symbolism of numbers.

2. The text contains symmetrically arranged structures (chiasms) which attest to careful attention to form. For example, the creation of the sun and moon are described in chiastic form.

   A   lights … to separate the day from the night (14a)
   　　B   to mark seasons and days and years (14b)
   　　　　C   and let them be lights (15)
   　　　　　　D   the greater light to govern the day (16a)
   　　　　　　D′ the lesser light to govern the night (16b)
   　　　　C′ to give light (17)
   　　B′ to govern the day and the night (18a)
   A′ and to separate light from darkness 18b

   By focusing attention on the central pair of statements (DD′) this device points to God's sheer authority over his creation and emphasises that the heavenly lights are there to perform a function, not to be venerated as objects of worship.

3. The narrative starts with a picture of chaos, in which the earth is described as being without form (*tohu*) and empty (*bohu*). It concludes with rest, the rest of the seventh day. Between the states of chaos and rest, Genesis 1 is laid out as a duplicated triad. The first three days are days of 'preparation', in which God provided *form*. He separated light from darkness, the waters above the sky from the waters below it, and the sea

from the dry land. The second group of three days are days of 'population' or adornment, in which the *empty spaces were filled* with their respective inhabitants. The sources of light were put in place (linking days 1 and 4), the sea and the sky were filled with fish and birds (linking days 2 and 5), and the dry land was populated with animals and people (linking days 3 and 6).

Table 2   The form of Genesis 1

Chaos	
'The earth was without form (*tohu*) ...'	'... and void (*bohu*)'
God gives form: acts of separation	God fills the voids: acts of populating and adornment
days 1–3	days 4–6
Day 1 light separated from darkness	Day 4 lights set in the sky
Day 2 sky separating the waters under it the from those above it	Day 5 all kinds of sea creatures and birds
Day 3 act 1: seas gathered from land act 2: land producing all kinds of vegetation	Day 6 act 1: all kinds of land animals act 2: people
'thus the heavens and earth were created ...'	'... in all their vast array'
Day 7: rest	

This symmetry (complete with a double action on days three and six) is widely recognised by biblical scholars. The arrangement of Genesis 1 is not *chrono*logical but *theo*logical. We are off the mark if we ask how light (day 1) or morning and evening (days 1–3) preceded the existence of the sun (day 4).

The Genesis story should be read with an eye to the literary devices used. In particular, woodenly *literal* approaches should be rejected in favour of perceiving the manifest artistic *literary* composition of the text. Old Testament scholars have variously described the Genesis prologue as semipoetic, a literary representation of creation in anthropomorphic language, a theological work in narrative form, a skilfully composed work conveying a complex of deeply meditated ideas, theology in pictures. This story presents something more urgent than mere descriptions of the natural world. It is time to make that vital 'something' explicit.

4. The word *God* dominates the chapter (34 times between 1:1 and 2:4a). There can be no question of asking *how* God created. The issue is simply *who* created everything and *what* he is like. The interest is not *geo*logical and *bio*logical but *theo*logical. The urgency of presenting the nature of Israel's God may be more clearly understood when we consider the nature of the gods of Israel's neighbours.

7. Understanding Genesis: clues from Israel's neighbours

For almost its entire history, the tiny confederation of Israelite tribes was overshadowed by militaristic superpowers. Israel's faith as proclaimed by the prophets of God was diametrically opposed to the all-prevailing animism, astrology and polytheism of those culturally dominant neighbours. Israel's uniqueness is illustrated strikingly when we compare the biblical creation accounts with the creation stories of Sumeria, Babylonia and Assyria, that have been discovered on cuneiform tablets. Israel's creation stories, genealogies and flood stories show both interesting parallels and striking contrasts with those of her neighbours. Most biblical scholars see the first 11 chapters of Genesis as a response to this animistic, astrological, polytheistic challenge (as Table 3 shows):

Table 3   Genesis and Mesopotamian creation stories

Subject	Myth	Culture and century BC	Biblical parallel
Creation	Enuma Elish	Old Babylonian (Sumerian), 1100	Genesis 1 – 2
Creation	Akitu, New Year Festival	Old Babylonian	Genesis 1 – 2
Genealogy	King List	Sumerian, 1600	Genesis 5
Flood	Ziusudra Myth (Eridu Genesis)	Sumerian, 1600	Genesis 6 – 9
Flood	Gilgamesh epic	Akkadian, 2000–1600	Genesis 6 – 9
Flood	Atrahasis Epic	Old Babylonian, 1600	Genesis 6 – 9

The faith of Israel emerged from her liberating encounter with God in history. This experience of deliverance was written up using literary forms widespread in the ancient world. It appears that Israel took the crude myths of her neighbours and gave them radically new content, as a means of proclaiming her revolutionary understanding of the nature of God, the world, and humanity. The true significance of the Genesis creation stories is thus to be found by seeing them as striking challenges to paganism (Table 4).

The monotheistic faith of Israel is contrasted with polytheistic religion. Israel's God is eternal, allowing no creaturely speculation as to his origins. The other gods supposedly arose from a pre-existing primeval world. Israel's creation story thus has one great omission that distinguishes it from the others: there is no word on the origin of God.[23]

Israel's God is supreme over (and distinct from) the world; the other gods are part of an organismic, animistic, magical system. In Genesis, the world is not divine: it is de-deified, stripped of personality. This revolutionary biblical insight was foundational for the development of science.[24] Only Israel's God is good, just and powerful. In terms of essential nature, 'God' is simply not the singular of 'gods'.[25]

Genesis uses restrained language to present a cosmogony: a statement of the ultimate source of the universe. The creation stories of Israel's neighbours were, rather, theogonies and theomachies (describing the origins and squabbles of the gods). *God* brings the world into being by creation; *the gods* do so by procreation. In Genesis the 'deep' was under God's control. To Israel's neighbours, the waters of chaos were personified as gods that could overwhelm the world.

The writer of Genesis saw the celestial bodies and the sea monsters as God's creatures; Israel's neighbours saw them as gods. In Genesis, human beings are creatures formed entirely of earth, but imbued with God's breath and accorded a special responsibility, and the climax of creation; Babylonian mythology presents humanity as a mixture of earthly and heavenly material, earth and the blood of the gods, and an afterthought of creation.

Table 4 The purpose of Genesis

	The faith of Israel	The religions of the empires
Deity	monotheistic	polytheistic
	one eternal God	gods arise from the waters of chaos (one version)
	God is distinct from the world	gods are part of the (animistic) world
	God is good	gods may be evil
	God is just, powerful	gods are capricious, and have limited power
Origins	cosmogony	theogony and theomachy: how the gods are born and fight
	by creation	by procreation
	the whole universe is created	matter existed before the gods' creative work

	The faith of Israel	The religions of the empires
Primeval waters of chaos	power of God moves over the waters from the beginning	waters themselves personified as gods – Apsu and Tiamat
	creation is not repeated in the annual new year ritual	waters of chaos annually threaten to overtake reality
World	sun, moon, stars are creatures, mere lights, not even named	sun, moon, stars are gods; the sun god is personified as Marduk
	the sun and moon serve people	people serve the sun and moon
	sea monsters are magnificent creatures of God	sea monsters are gods, representing the powers of chaos
	the world is good	the world works against spiritual enlightenment
Human beings	creatures made of earth, like the animals but with God's breath, and bearing God's image as the very representative of God	a mix of the earthly and heavenly: human beings are made partially from the blood of gods
	the climax of creation	an afterthought of creation
	all bear the divine image	only the king bears the divine image
	God provides for humans	humans provide for the gods
	disobedient; pessimistic about man alone	wise; optimistic about man's future
Seventh day (Sabbath)	'Sabbath' is dedicated to God	'sabattu', the fourteenth and twenty-eighth days, considered unlucky

The message of Genesis is subversive, audacious, scandalous. It undermines the assumptions of polytheistic religion and engages in disguised mockery of the gods. It provides an alternative worldview. This vision of God was the ultimate revolution in the human understanding of reality.

As we discover the revolutionary impact of Genesis, we discern its meaning for us. Genesis allows us to glimpse God in all his majesty as the Lord whom we must serve – against all other conceptions of deity, and against animism, cosmic cycles, astrology, and the materialistic deification of matter. Genesis remains a challenge to the religious sensibilities of everyone who worships the material world – from the devotees of Marduk to those who deify the selfish gene – but proclaims no particular scientific world picture, evolutionary or otherwise.

Christians must not perpetuate the dichotomy that we either accept Genesis 1 as inspired literal prosaic history or reject it as primitive tribal myth. It is neither. It is a carefully written statement in narrative form that introduced humankind to the true God of Israel.

So is there any connection between Genesis (and the wider Hebrew understanding of reality) and science? There *must* be. Science can operate only in the context of a supportive (critically realist) worldview. Scientists tend to be oblivious to the metaphysical presuppositions that make their work possible. But the one worldview that provides such a metaphysical basis is the biblical one (Table 5). It is God who is the guarantor of truth in the universe, and of the lawfulness, consistency and goodness of matter.

Table 5   The character of God as a precondition for science

God is:	Therefore the world is:	Therefore science is:
Creator	God's handiwork	encouraged as an aspect of worship
Almighty	secure and will not degenerate into chaos	possible because the stability of creation is guaranteed, giving confidence to study it
Transcendent ('other' than creation)	de-deified	legitimate because people are free to explore creation as an elaborate mechanism, free from occult influences, astrology, magic; the heavens and earth obey the same laws (rejection of Aristotelianism)

God is:	Therefore the world is:	Therefore science is:
Faithful	consistent and lawful in its operation	possible because order and generalisations are to be expected
Rational	understandable	possible because the world is intelligible
Free	contingent (does not *have* to be the way it is)	required as the route to understanding: what is needed is observation and experiment (empirical approaches), not rationalistic deduction from first principles
Good	declared good	worthwhile because creation merits investigation; rejection of, or disengagement from, the world is inappropriate
Redeeming	the arena of God's activity; awaits future transformation	encouraged because time is directional (moves towards a goal); the physical world is of value
Loving	not hostile	well-founded, as people have the optimism to study the world because of God's caring commitment to it
Creator of humanity in God's image	amenable to study by the human mind	defensible as a valid human activity
Lord	subject to God; human authoritarianism is rejected	mandated because we ourselves are responsible for understanding the data of Scripture and of creation
At work and declares work to be honourable	is to be actively nurtured	desirable so that people may experiment on the world within prescribed moral constraints as part of their responsible stewardship

8. The content of Genesis 2 – 3

Before leaving Genesis we must note that it presents us with not one but two creation stories. The story narrated in Genesis 2:4b–25 (continued through the story of the fall in Gen. 3), is very different from the one in Genesis 1:1 – 2:4a. In fact, any thoroughgoing literalist interpretation of them must find them in direct contradiction to each other on a number of points, particularly on the order of creation. Whereas in Genesis 1 humankind (male and female together) is the final act of creation, in Genesis 2, man (as male) is the first of all the biosphere to be created, and everything else is described in relation to him. So the order is man, plants, animals, woman. Attempts to harmonise the two by translating, for example, the first part of Genesis 2:19 as 'God *had* formed every animal…' amount to special pleading since here the Hebrew verb is of the normal form used for a narrative sequence of events. The only reason for translating it as an English pluperfect is *in order* to try and harmonise the order with that of chapter 1.

It would surely be arrogant to assume that early authors and editors of Scripture could not perceive this difficulty. Yet the two accounts have been allowed to sit side by side from earliest times, illuminating both each other and the reality they describe. In contrast to the formal and structured account in Genesis 1 this second account is very relational. The man is at the centre of a circle of relationship: he is related to the inorganic stuff of the earth (v. 7), to God (v. 7), to the animals (v. 7, cf. 19 – both are *nephesh hayah*, living beings) and most intimately to the woman (vv. 21–5).

There is a fascinating tension within this story over the name of the first man. In v. 7 God forms the man (*ha-adam*) from the dust of the earth (*ha-adamah*) – reflecting the close relationship between this new creation of a living being and the non-biological substance from which it is formed. And throughout this story the man is always *ha-adam*, 'the groundling'. English versions struggle to know where to begin translating this as a proper name, Adam (NRSV and REB not until 4:25; GNT and CEV from 3:20; NLT and NIV from 2:19 or 20). The generic, representative groundling only gradually assumes a unique individual identity.

Perhaps the most vexed question relating to this second creation narrative is the entry of sin, and its relationship with death. Often Genesis 3 is seen as the definitive negation to an evolutionary understanding, because death is thought to be absent from the biosphere until the first human sin. This is not a tenable interpretation of this passage and we will return to discuss this in more detail when we have first examined some New Testament passages.

9. Other biblical witness

A theme running through the entire Bible is that God is the source of all reality. Regardless of which physical or biological phenomenon we look at, God is active as its author and sustainer. 'God has not wound the world up like a mechanical toy. He continues to be actively involved in its workings, changing night to day. He controls the sun, moon and stars, the rivers, and gives life to crops and animals,' writes John Drane.[26] Integral to the faith of Israel was the recognition that *every* natural process and phenomenon was the work of God (Table 6). In *every* case, science legitimately investigates the relationships between the components of a system, including the way they relate to time (i.e. develop or evolve).

Table 6   Compatibility of theological and scientific language

The language of creation	The language of science
The [Lord] created, stretched out, spread out, the heavens (Is. 40:26; 42:5; 48:13)	expansion of matter and space-time as described by cosmological models
God made the stars (Gen. 1:16; Ps. 148:5)	gravitational collapse of gas clouds, nuclear fusion
[The Lord] set the moon and the stars in place (Ps. 8:3)	variation in the distribution of matter in the cosmos; the effects of gravity
[The Lord] made the earth; laid the earth's foundation (Is. 45:12,18; Job 38:4)	accretion of matter orbiting the sun to form planets

The language of creation	The language of science
The Lord turns dawn to darkness (Amos 4:13; Job 38:12; Ps. 104:20)	daily rotation of the earth around its axis
God formed (forms) the mountains (Ps. 65:8; Amos 4:13)	plate tectonic and volcanic activity
The Lord creates the wind (Amos 4:13)	mass movement of gas molecules in response to pressure gradients
[The Lord] made the clouds (Job 38:9)	evaporation and condensation of water
God sends rain (Ps. 65:9–10; Acts 14:17)	uplift and precipitation of water vapour
[The Lord] makes grass grow (Ps. 104:14)	photosynthesis; morphogenesis
God gives crops in their seasons (Acts 14:17)	pollination, fruit set, biosynthesis
When [the Lord] sends his Spirit the sea creatures are created (Ps. 104:30)	biological reproduction and growth
It is [the Lord] who created mankind upon the earth (Gen. 1:27; Is. 45:12)	evolutionary change with population expansion
[The Lord] created my inmost being (Ps. 139:13)	fertilisation, cell proliferation and differentiation; embryonic development
God gives life and breath to everyone (Acts 17:25; 1 Tim. 6:13)	life arises from conditions supporting respiration and growth (oxygen, energy sources, metabolic substrates)

Even as Christians believe that God is the author of all physical reality, we recognise that the development and workings of that reality are wholly open to scientific investigation. Malcolm Jeeves's insight is fundamental: to the theist, God is the cause of everything, but scientifically the explanation of nothing.[27]

To Donald Mackay, 'any idea that God's being active in our world means that "there must be something science can't explain"

– about living bodies, or interstellar hydrogen, or whatever – is a complete *non sequitur*. The laws of nature we discover are not *alternatives* to divine activity, but only our *codification* of that activity in its normal manifestations'.[28]

The theologian B.B. Warfield termed this complementary relationship *concursus*. Holy Scripture is the Word of God; it is at the same time the words of human beings. There are no parts that are divine but not human, or human but not divine. The world around us exhibits exactly the same relationship. Every process exists by the will of God, and is created; and may be investigated scientifically as the interaction of matter and energy in time and space.

10. The theology of creation in the New Testament

The biblical teaching of creation is further clarified when we consider its use in the New Testament. Just as the Old Testament affirmed Israel's God as the true God by stressing his role as creator, so the New Testament presents Christ as Lord by identifying him as the creator.

In a letter to the church in the idolatrous city of Corinth, Paul emphasised the basis of Christ's Lordship – and indeed his divinity:

> There is for us only one God, the Father,
>   who is creator of all things,
>   and for whom we live,
> and there is only one Lord, Jesus Christ,
>   through whom all things were created,
>   and through whom we live. (1 Cor. 8:6)

The basis of Christ's unequivocal claim to be the one Lord of the Corinthian Christians was that he is creator – and therefore divine.

In Colossae the church was facing a cocktail of philosophical and religious ideas. Against this first-century New Age philosophy we read:

Christ is the visible likeness of the invisible God.
He is the first-born Son, superior to all created things.
For through him, God created everything in heaven and on earth …
God created the whole universe through him and for him.

(Col. 1:15–16)

The choice here was between a trendy New Age spirituality and the creator, in whom we are challenged (as in Genesis) to place our allegiance.

Jewish Christians were under pressure to choose between the Jewish religion (their former cultural, social and religious base) and Christ. They were urged to be faithful to Christ:

In these last days God has spoken to us through his Son.
He is the one through whom God created the universe. (Heb. 1:1–2)

The words 'through whom' do not imply that Christ is simply some sort of intermediary of God's creative work. The writer goes on to quote the Psalms in such a way as to identify Christ explicitly with God:

About the Son, however, God said,
'Your throne O God will last for ever and ever.' (Heb. 1:8)

To emphasise the divine authority of the Son, agency attributed to God in the Psalms is used of Christ: 'You Lord in the beginning created the earth' (Heb. 1:10). The biblical pattern is consistent: the concept of creation is introduced only that it may lead people to worship the one true God. And this true God has been made known in Christ.

Finally, John's Gospel universalises the place of Christ. The entire world is in darkness, but inextinguishable light shines in the darkness. This light comes from the Word who became a human being:

Through him God made all things.
Not one thing in all creation was made without him. (Jn. 1:1–5)

The New Testament writers declare Christ to be creator in the same way that the Old Testament writers declare Israel's God to be creator. The issue is the supremacy of Christ in the face of myriad alternative gods and philosophies. Christ is unique. He demands our utter commitment as one who is God together with the Father (and the Holy Spirit, as the early church soon recognised). But we are not told how the created world unfolded. This remains irrelevant to the purposes of the New Testament writers (who set out to show that Jesus is Lord), as it was to the Old Testament writers (who set out to show that Israel's God is Lord). Scientific stories are irrelevant to the biblical doctrine of creation, which 'must not be confused or identified with any scientific theory of origins. The purpose of the biblical doctrine, in contrast to that of scientific investigation, is ethical and religious'.[29]

11. The creation story in the New Testament

Surprisingly little use is made of the actual creation narratives in the New Testament, but the material presented is important for our understanding.

In the teachings of Jesus there are only two occasions where reference is made to Genesis 1 – 3. One is indirect and allusive – when Jesus tells his disciples in Luke 10:19, 'See I have given you authority to tread on snakes and scorpions.' Here the obvious allusion to Genesis 3:15, the crushing of the serpent's head, is strengthened by its equation with authority 'over all the power of the enemy'. There is nothing here which commits the New Testament reader to a particular view on human origins.

The other passage is Jesus' teaching on divorce (Mt. 19:4–5, Mk. 10:6–8). Jesus appeals to Genesis 2:25 to affirm the sanctity of marriage and to show that it precedes the Law of Moses. It goes back to the beginning, to God's creation of humanity. Moses' tolerance of divorce was a concession, but Jesus refers to the creation story to give the lifelong union of one man and one woman pre-eminence over *any and all* social constructions of relationships. Once again, this is valid under any theory of the origins of humanity. As long as humans have been humans, this has been the case. It would be pedantic literalism to push the teaching further, to suggest that here Jesus is defending or affirming the instant *ex nihilo* creation of morphologically distinct male and female humans. When Jesus says that at his second coming the angels will 'gather his elect from the four winds, from one end of heaven to the other' (Mt. 24:31 – cf. 'from the ends of the earth to the ends of heaven', Mk 13:27), we are not entitled to deduce that he gave his support to a flat earth, with the sky touching it on all sides. Whatever one's view on whether or not Jesus retained divine omniscience in his humanity (and there are scriptural data on both sides), he never violated the understanding of the natural world of those around him, or displayed anything like modern scientific or geographical knowledge. He had more important issues, like the nature of the Kingdom of God, on which to challenge the assumptions of his contemporaries. Here, as with any other passage of Scripture, we must seek the purpose of the author/speaker and the contextual assumptions embedded within each particular context.

St Paul makes more extensive use of the creation narratives, but space does not permit a full analysis here. First among the key passages, Romans 5:12, we will consider later when dealing specifically with the issues of sin and death.

In Romans 8:19–21 Paul affirms not only the createdness of the natural world, but the very evident frustration under which it exists, which we can assume includes the negative aspects of decay and death. Paul attributes this to the action of a merciful God whose activity with respect to his creation is past, present and future. Aspects of an evolutionary history which are often thought of as obstacles to its acceptance by Christians – particularly the long sequence of trial and error, death and predation, dead ends and extinctions – are placed under the sovereign guardianship of God whose purpose is restoration of relationship and a new creation. Humanity, whose special place – for good and evil – is emphasised in the creation narratives, is also the key to the renewal of creation.

In 1 Corinthians 11:2–16 Paul appeals to the creation narratives in his discussion of the place of men and women within the church. This is a passage whose interpretation is much controverted and we cannot begin to do it justice. It is clear, however, that although Paul refers to both creation stories, the one which governs his thought here is the second, Genesis 2:4b–25. Thus, although Genesis 1:27 says that both male and female are created in the image of God, for Paul's purpose he is content to say that the man is the 'image and glory of God' (v. 7) and to argue from the order of male and female creation in Genesis 2 for a distinction in the roles in the contemporary church. Once again we must be careful not to move away from Paul's purpose in this passage. We must not use it firstly to make statements about Paul's understanding of the mode of creation and then to make overarching claims about the literalness or otherwise of the Genesis narratives. Even when dealing with Paul's main purpose it is all too easy to make him say the opposite of what he does say. And when we try to move back behind that to his attitude to the Old Testament texts, we have to deal with the fact that he, like his Jewish contemporaries, often interpreted the Old Testament in allegorical and typological ways which we would be reluctant to follow today (see, for example, his treatment of the Hagar and Sarah story in Galatians 4). Paul was a man of his times, and shared many of the common assumptions of his contemporaries. He most likely assumed an actual literal interpretation of Genesis 2, but he does not argue for it. He uses the stories because their theology is authoritative.

Finally in Paul's writings we note his discussion of the resurrection in 1 Corinthians 15, where Adam features in vv. 21–2 and again in vv. 45–7. Here, as in Romans 5, Adam and Christ are depicted as the leaders of two streams of humanity. Adam functions as the primeval man, the 'man of dust' created from the substance of the physical universe. Though he 'became a living being' (from the Hebrew *nephesh hayah*) he and all who stand in his line are mortal, doomed to die. The new humanity in Christ is of an altogether different order. Our present Adamite humanity is physical, perishable, mortal. The new humanity in Christ is spiritual, imperishable, immortal. This argument works irrespective of whether Adam is seen as a unique individual (as Paul probably assumed), a representative individual, or a figure of the emerging human species. Our solidarity with Adam is not dependent on physical descent from him, any more than our solidarity with Christ is dependent on physical descent from him. We belong to Adam because we, too, have been born physical, biological, mortal beings.

12. Sin, death and Adam

We consider now issues that are frequently seen as forming the
deciding biblical argument against an evolutionary understanding
of the origins of life and of humanity, and we will examine them
against a range of scriptural evidence.

First is the vexed question of death and its connection with
sin and the fall. As Christians we accept the scriptural teaching
that humanity is fallen and sinful. But often there is an added
assumption that there was no death before the fall, and that death
with its precursors of disease, ageing, accident and predation are all
direct results of Adam's sin. This is then seen to rule out completely
evolution's long saga of struggle and death before humans appeared
on the scene. There are scriptural grounds on which this assumption
is based, and Paul's treatment of Adam and Christ in Romans 5 is
one of them. But before we turn to this passage we need to look
more closely at just what Genesis 1 – 3 affirms.

Firstly, the text of Genesis 1 – 3 nowhere states that there was
no death before the fall. God's statement, 'in the day you eat of
it you shall die' (2:17) was said only to the first human being
and had no relationship at all to any of the other animals. There
are enormous logical difficulties with the assumption that death
affected the world only after Adam sinned. What about plant
death – in both the digestion of animals and the reproduction of
plants themselves? What about cell death through the normal
life processes of animals? If, as is often suggested, all animals
were purely herbivores, then following the fall there would have
to have been an instant re-creation act, in which body chemistry
and behaviour patterns were changed. And were fungi, which
live on decaying matter, created only after the fall? *Nowhere* does
Scripture teach the radical re-creation that a sudden introduction
of death might imply.

So we come back to the rather more important issue of human
death. The assumption that biological death began only after
Adam sinned ends up turning the tables on God and the snake –
God becomes the liar and the snake the truth-teller. Because if God
meant that on the day Adam tasted the forbidden fruit he would
undergo biological death, then the snake was right. And this is

the only allowable hypothesis if we take a literal interpretation of God's words (including a literal interpretation of 'day') and add to it the assumption that God was talking about biological death. Adam didn't die that day, but lived a full life afterwards. We *must* conclude either that God was not talking about biological death, or that he was not intending to be taken literally when he said 'on the day you eat it ... ' And if God was not talking about biological death, then there is no statement in Genesis 1 – 3 about whether biological death was present before the fall or not. Even the curse (Gen. 3:19) is principally the toil which is required for subsistence living, not the physical death that ends it. 'Till you return to the ground' specifies the period of hard labour – the whole of life. The final line ('you are dust and to dust you shall return') is simply a statement of fact, perhaps underlining the conclusion that with the entry of sin, human death became simply a matter of physical decay without the prospect of continued relationship with God. N.T. Wright has described the effects of human sinfulness thus: 'The result is that death, which was always part of the natural transience of the good creation, gains a second dimension, which the Bible sometimes calls "spiritual death".' [30]

Now it is time to return to Paul. Does he make the absence of physical death before the fall a matter of doctrine? The answer is quite simply, no. If Paul understood God's prohibition, threat and punishment as referring to 'spiritual death', or 'relational death', or anything other than purely biological death, then everything Paul affirms is quite compatible with an understanding of biological death as a normal part of life independent of our fallenness. We are not here attempting to guess what Paul actually believed about the issue. The validity of Paul's theological arguments and affirmations cannot be held to depend on whether he held a scientifically verifiable view on the shape of the earth, or the movements of the solar system, or the origin of species, and the presence or absence of death prior to the fall. He was a man of his own day and we would expect that his assumptions were formed by the horizons of that day. But what he has recorded for us in Scripture is perfectly consistent with an understanding of the 'death' which came as a result of Adam's sin as being something like 'spiritual death', 'eternal death' or 'separation from God'. This is true of Romans 5, and it is true of 1 Corinthians 15. (For a discussion of 1 Cor. 11, see above. 1 Tim. 2:13–4 uses the story of Adam and Eve in a similar way.)

In Romans 5:12 Paul appears to base his argument about salvation through Christ on a unique event (the entry of sin, and subsequently death) into the human story, through one man, Adam. He makes the following statements in relation to death:

1. Death came into the world because of the entry of sin (v. 12). This is consistent with God's statement to Adam, and consequently with an understanding of 'death' here as spiritual death or separation from God.

2. Death spread to all men because all sinned (v. 12). There is no requirement that this spread is by genetic inheritance. Just as the effect of Christ's obedience and resurrection spread horizontally to the whole of believing humanity, so the effects of Adam's disobedience (eternal death, separation from the life of God) spread to the whole of disobedient humanity. Adam is the paradigm that established the pattern for all to follow.

3. Death ruled from Adam to Moses (v. 14) and beyond (v. 17). Certainly this *could* refer to physical death, but in the context of the above, and the whole chapter, could equally refer to eternal death.

4. All died as a result of the one man's sin (v. 15). But note that the contrast with the 'death' spoken of in this chapter is never ordinary biological life. Since all people by definition have that sort of life, it is irrelevant. The contrast is with 'the free gift of grace', 'the free gift bringing justification', 'the free gift of righteousness' and 'eternal life'. Death, here, is clearly separation from God, the state of being under condemnation and therefore having forfeited the life of God, spiritual or eternal death.

In 1 Corinthians 15, what is set in contrast to the death brought in by Adam is resurrection. Resurrection is not simply resuscitation of normal, biological life. It is participating in the eternal life of Christ. So once again, the focus is on death as that which separates us from the life of God. What is said in this chapter would be entirely consistent with a view which holds that the result of Adam's sin was the loss of eternal life, so that from then on death was simply a returning to dust, rather than being a passage to life with God. And that possibility of life with God is what Christ has restored – he has removed the sting from death, so that death once again functions as a prelude to resurrection to eternal life with God. This could be expressed another way, also deeply consistent with both 1 Corinthians 15 and the Genesis narrative: what Adam lost was the *possibility* of eternal life, a prospect that was represented by the tree of life, from which the first humans were now barred. And it is precisely this possibility that Christ's death and resurrection restores. As Paul puts it elsewhere, 'The gift of God is eternal life, in Jesus Christ our Lord' (Rom. 6.23). Humanity in Adam is inherently mortal, perishable, destined for dust, never having reached God's original purpose. Humanity in Christ puts on immortality, God's original purpose is restored, and death is defeated.

The issue of whether Adam was an individual or whether in the story he stands symbolically for humanity (and we have already seen that his name suggests that word play is not absent from the story) is not at issue here. There have been several attempts to locate Adam within evolutionary schemes – perhaps as a unique, representative human who lived at an early period of the emergence of *Homo sapiens*. Alternatively, the *name* Adam may be used as a generic term for a particular stage in emergent evolutionary development when the 'earthling' can first be described as being the image of his creator, or even as simply a name for earliest humanity composed of dirt but God-like in particular ways. Quite possibly Paul, within the horizons of the understanding of the natural world of his day, considered Adam to be a single historical individual. But as we have seen, what he affirms about us and our condition (past, present and future) is not dependent on that view being literally true.

13. God creates history

Consideration of the biblical message indicates that there is no reason why Christians should be uneasy about accepting the findings of evolutionary science. But we have provided no reasons why it is theologically important to do so. Biblical faith is unique because it is based on history; the Bible is an interpretation of history; Israel saw God as the creator of her history.[31] Indeed it is axiomatic for Christians that God is the God of history.

And biology is often called natural history. This is appropriate because evolution is a historical science. The concept of *evolution* cannot be considered to be an equivalent of (or alternative to) *creation*; *evolution* is one of a variety of *histories*. It follows that if God is the God of history, it is wholly appropriate that he is the God of evolution. Conversely, if we will not allow that God could be the Lord of evolution, then neither is he the Lord of history. Like Israel, we see God as the creator of our history – whether evolutionary or human. We must expect that the created order, endowed with the gift of freedom, has an evolving course, an authentic history.

The Cambridge historian Herbert Butterfield spoke of human history in terms of its process, structure, chanciness, tragedy, and progress. Biological history shares these same properties.[32] The chanciness and tragedies of evolutionary history, Israel's history, or our own personal histories arise from the freedom granted to creation. But in each case, God in his sovereign creative purpose has brought, and will bring, each phase of history to its purposed end. Evolutionary history (in all its genetic happenstance) climaxed in the advent of humanity, the image of God. Israel's history (with all its cataclysm and suffering) climaxed in the advent of Christ, the perfect Image of God. The history of the church (in all its failings) and of ourselves as members of it will climax in the conferral of Christ's perfect image on those who are redeemed.

Notes

[1] Ruth Barton, 'The creation of the conflict between science and theology', in *Science and Theology in Action* (ed. C. Bloore and P. Donovan; Palmerston North, NZ: Dunmore Press, 1987), pp. 55–71.

[2] John Waller, *Fabulous Science: Fact and Fiction in the History of Scientific Discovery* (Oxford: OUP, 2002), pp. 205–21.

3   Charles E. Hummell, *The Galileo Connection* (Downers Grove: IVP, 1986), pp. 151–2.

4   Donald M. Mackay, *The Clockwork Image* (London: IVP, 1974), pp. 52–5; Michael W. Poole and Gordon J. Wenham, *Creation or Evolution – a False Antithesis?* (Oxford: Latimer Press, 1997), pp. 11–14; Hummell, *Galileo*, pp. 240–41.

5   David N. Livingstone, *Darwin's Forgotten Defenders* (Grand Rapids: Eerdmans, 1987), pp. 100–105.

6   Livingstone, *Defenders*, ch. 4; David N. Livingstone and Mark A. Noll, 'B.B. Warfield (1851–1921): a biblical inerrantist as evolutionist', *Isis* 91 (2000), pp. 283–304.

7   Livingstone and Noll, 'B.B. Warfield'; John R. Stott, *Understanding the Bible* (London: SU, 1984), pp. 48–9; Michael Green, *You Must be Joking: Popular Reasons for Avoiding Jesus Christ* (London, Sydney, Auckland: Hodder & Stoughton, 1991), p. 27.

8   J.L. Austin, *How to Do Things With Words* (Oxford: OUP, 1962); John R. Searle, *Speech Acts: An Essay in the Philosophy of Language* (Cambridge: CUP, 1969). For application to the study of biblical text see Anthony Thiselton, *New Horizons in Hermeneutics: The Theory and Practice of Transforming Biblical Reading* (Grand Rapids: Zondervan, 1992); Kevin Vanhoozer, 'From Speech Acts to Scripture Acts: The Covenant of Discourse and the Discourse of the Covenant', in *After Pentecost: Language and Biblical Interpretation* (eds Craig Bartholomew, Colin Greene and Karl Möller; Grand Rapids: Zondervan, 2001), pp. 1–49.

9   Dan Sperber and Deirdre Wilson, *Relevance: Communication and Cognition* (Oxford: Blackwell, 2nd edn, 1995); Robyn Carston, *Thoughts and Utterances: The Pragmatics of Explicit Communication* (Oxford: Blackwell, 2002).

10 For the application of this theory to the understanding of biblical text see Stephen Pattemore, *The People of God in the Apocalypse: Discourse, Structure, and Exegesis*. SNTSMS 128 (Cambridge: CUP, 2004), pp. 22–50.

11 A. Konig, *New and Greater Things: Re-evaluating the Biblical Message on Creation* (Pretoria: UNISA, 1988), pp. 35–8.

12 N.T. Wright, *Scripture and the Authority of God* (London: SPCK, 2005), pp. 99, 65–6.

13 Poole and Wenham, *Creation*, p. 22; G.J. Wenham, *Word Biblical Commentary, Genesis 1–15* (Nashville: Thomas Nelson Publishers, 1987), pp. liii, xlv.

14 C.F. Pfeiffer and E.F Harrison, eds, *The Wycliffe Bible Commentary* (London: Oliphants, 1962), p. 2.

[15] Stott, *Understanding*, p. 11; Derek Kidner, *Genesis: an Introduction and Commentary* (London: Tyndale Press, 1967), pp. 26–7; Ernest Lucas, *Genesis Today* (London: Scripture Union, 1989), pp. 49–50, 55f; B.K. Waltke and C.J. Fredricks, *Genesis: a Commentary* (Grand Rapids: Zondervan, 2001), pp. 74–5.

[16] James I. Packer, *God's Words: Studies of Key Bible Themes* (Fearn, Ross-shire: Christian Focus Publications, 1998), pp. 59–60.

[17] James I. Packer, 'Theology and Bible Reading', in E. Dyck, ed., *The Act of Bible Reading* (Downers Grove: IVP, 1996), pp. 65–6.

[18] Mark A. Noll, *The Scandal of the Evangelical Mind* (Grand Rapids: Eerdmans, 1994), pp. 61–2, 75.

[19] Gordon D. Fee, 'History as Context for Interpretation', in Dyck, *Act*, p. 14.

[20] For a robust treatment of the importance of authorial intentions to communication see Raymond W. Gibbs, *Intentions in the Experience of Meaning* (Cambridge: CUP, 1999).

[21] The next two sections have been informed by biblical scholars, including Henri Blocher, *In the Beginning: the Opening Chapters of Genesis* (Leicester and Downers Grove: IVP, 1984); Victor P. Hamilton, *The Book of Genesis Chapters 1–17* (Grand Rapids: Eerdmans, 1990); Kidner, *Genesis*; Konig, *New and Greater*; Lucas, *Genesis*; Poole and Wenham, *Creation*; W.S. Towner, *Genesis* (Louisville etc.: Westminster John Knox Press, 2001); L.A. Turner, *Genesis* (Sheffield: Sheffield Academic Press, 2000); Waltke and Fredricks, *Genesis*; John H. Walton, *Ancient Israelite Literature in its Cultural Context* (Grand Rapids: Zondervan, 1989); Wenham, *Genesis 1–15*; Gordon Wenham, *Exploring the Old Testament Volume 1: The Pentateuch* (London: SPCK, 2003).

[22] E. Fox, *In the Beginning: A New English Rendition of the Book of Genesis.* (New York: Schocken Books, 1983), p. xiv.

[23] Fox, *Beginning*, p. xxxiii.

[24] Harold Turner, *The Roots of Science* (Auckland: DeepSight Trust, 1998).

[25] C.S. Lewis, *Reflections on the Psalms* (Glasgow: Collins, 1961), p. 71.

[26] John Drane, *Old Testament Faith* (Tring: Lion, 1986), p. 68.

[27] Malcolm Jeeves, quoted in C.F.H. Henry, ed., *Horizons of Science* (San Francisco: Harper & Row, 1978), p. 29.

[28] Mackay, *Clockwork*, p. 60.

[29] J.D. Douglas, ed., *Illustrated New Bible Dictionary* (Leicester: IVP, 1980), 332.

[30] N.T. Wright, *Surprised by Hope: Rethinking Heaven, the Resurrection, and the Mission of the Church* (New York: Harper Collins, 2008), p. 95.

[31] A. Konig, *Here Am I!* (Grand Rapids: Eerdmans, 1982), pp. 4, 6, 37, 88, 95.

[32] Herbert Butterfield, *Christianity and History* (London and Glasgow: Fontana, 1957).

3

Why We Disagree:
a Response to Finlay and Pattemore

STEPHEN LLOYD

There is much that I can affirm in the chapter by Graeme Finlay and Stephen Pattemore (to whom, for the sake of convenience, I will refer to as F&P). I wholeheartedly share their conviction that biblical faith and scientific knowledge are 'naturally and deeply compatible' (p. 31). I concur with their concerns that we should recognise genre and literary artistry in our interpretation of Genesis. It is also right to insist that Darwinism be assessed independent of its use (or abuse) in support of different ideologies. There is nothing inherently atheistic about the mechanisms of Darwinism. Belief in God as the 'sustainer' (p. 53) of the world is affirmed equally by Christians sceptical of Darwinism. Theistic Darwinists do not hold a monopoly on the doctrine of God's providence. Similarly, it is axiomatic for all evangelicals that God is the 'God of history' (p. 64).

My difficulty is that I do not understand why any of these points are arguments for the compatibility of Darwinism and Christian theology. For example, the unity of biblical and scientific truth is more a reason to be sceptical of Darwinism than to accept it. Darwinism is no more consistent with a 'God of history' than any other story of origins. Furthermore, my position with respect to the three doctrines I highlighted in my chapter takes better account of the 'heritage of Christian theology' (p. 42).

What is striking about our respective chapters is that there is little overlap in the material we cover. F&P do not mention the flood at all but rather devote a large proportion of their chapter to

Genesis 1. I deliberately did not even mention the 'days' or literary structure of Genesis 1 because I believe these are something of a distraction in assessing the compatibility of Darwinism and Christian theology, as I will explain further in a moment.

I will focus my response around an examination of F&P's statement that 'At the heart of the matter, what is at issue is the interpretation of Scripture' (p. 35). I want, first, to challenge some key assumptions they adopt in their approach to the interpretation of the early chapters of Genesis and then to question whether 'interpretation of Scripture' is, in fact, the decisive issue. To understand why we disagree is perhaps the most helpful strategy to promote a greater measure of sympathetic engagement, if not agreement, in the future.

Interpretative methodology

A large proportion of F&P's chapter is taken up with issues of interpretation relating to literary structure and genre. I find myself in agreement with many of their observations about the nature of the text – the early chapters of Genesis are replete with literary structure and artifice. I too, delight in the 'sensuality of the language' of these chapters (p. 44)! What I question are the conclusions that F&P draw from these observations. They bring assumptions to the text that are pervasive in the writings of theistic Darwinists, but that are as unjustified as an assumption that a 'literal' interpretation should be the default way to approach a text, an assumption which they rightly criticise (p. 37).

The essence of F&P's argument in the first part of their chapter is that the literary features of the early chapters of Genesis imply the possibility of a greater diversity of interpretation than a 'literal' approach would suggest, while at the same time excluding a category of interpretations that could in principle be supplying information relevant to constructing a scientific model of earth history. In the words of J.I. Packer that they paraphrase (p. 41), 'The creation stories should not be read as factual descriptions of the empirical world. They are not a source of scientific data. Rather, the language of the creation accounts is pictorial and their purpose is theological.'

But the assumptions highlighted in this quotation are anything but self-evident.

First, F&P repeatedly refer to 'literal' interpretations without any proper definition.[1] *Literal* seems to be contrasted with *literary* and a proper appreciation of differing literary genres. Correctly identifying literary genre is undoubtedly vital for the interpretation of any text, but genre does not limit the type of information that can be communicated by a text; it merely alters the form in which the information is conveyed. Historical and scientific information (even modern technical scientific information) may be conveyed in a poem, a letter or a song.[2] The literary structure of the early chapters of Genesis does not make it incapable of communicating factual historical information, and no such restriction is placed on other literary texts. For example, the literary form of Philippians 2:6–11 is commonly described as a 'hymn', but this does not mean the passage can be read as teaching that Jesus did not exist, or didn't really become a man and didn't really die. Nor does literary structure exclude historical sequence. Commenting on Genesis 1, F&P state that in the light of the literary arrangement of the chapter the arrangement of days is, 'not *chrono*logical but *theo*logical' (p. 45). Even assuming their analysis of the literary structure of the chapter is correct,[3] I do not understand the logic of this conclusion. Why does the literary form of Genesis 1 *necessarily* exclude sequence? Luke–Acts has a sophisticated overarching literary structure,[4] but it still maintains *some* historical sequence, even if this does not extend to every sub-unit of the gospel.

Secondly, to discuss the relationship of the creation stories to science (section 4) requires a definition of what is meant by *science*. Table 1 suggests F&P are arguing that Genesis is not written in the style of a modern scientific paper. Since I have never come across anyone who ever claimed it was, this point seems superfluous, and it also assumes a strangely narrow definition of science. If science is defined in terms of modern research journals, then by definition the Bible makes no scientific statements, but that is as unhelpful as arguing that the Bible says nothing about theology because its literature does not fit the form of modern theological journals. Why should it be impossible for the Bible to communicate data (in non-technical language) relevant to scientific models? Were scientific questions really 'foreign to the minds of the ancient

Israelites' (p. 40)? Statements like, 'I have given every green plant for food', 'Death came through one man', or 'Jesus is alive' are at some level scientific (medical?) statements, as well as being historical and theological. Given that F&P argue that evolution is history (p. 64) and that the Bible is all about history it would follow that the historical claims of the Bible may, on occasion, be providing data relevant to scientific models. F&P quote Douglas (p. 57): 'The purpose of the biblical doctrine, in contrast to that of scientific investigation, is ethical and religious.' The *purpose* of biblical doctrine is just that. But it does not mean the *content* of that doctrine (or the biblical texts from which that doctrine is derived) cannot have scientific or historical implications. I do not understand the dichotomy presupposed in the statement, 'The interest is not *geo*logical and *bio*logical but *theo*logical' (p. 46). Why is it impossible for a biblical writer to be interested in geology and biology (within his own cultural context) *and* theology?[5]

Of course, there are dangers. As I pointed out in my chapter, both sides in this debate can make the mistake of reading modern scientific interpretations into the Bible. F&P do this in their argument linking plant and cell death to human death (p. 60). It is modern science that connects cell death and human death, not the Bible. If F&P want to argue that the existence of cell death requires human death, then Jesus' resurrection body (which digested food) must also be subject to death.

Third, I question the assumption that the presence of *some* figurative language (or other literary form) necessarily makes the whole passage figurative, or a-historical.[6] This is a false all-or-nothing choice that F&P present when they argue (pp. 60–61) that the warning in Genesis 2:17 does not include the consequence of *physical* death. In the following chapter, when God says to the serpent (Gen. 3:15), 'I will put enmity between you and the woman, and between your offspring and hers; he will strike your head, and you will strike his heel', there is a mixture of figurative and non-figurative language. Jesus did not physically tread on the head of the serpent, but he was a physical descendant of Eve and he did in reality ('literally'?) defeat Satan. A similar mixture of metaphor and history is common elsewhere. For example, Ezekiel 16 is a complex passage themed around the extended metaphor of spiritual adultery, yet this does not mean the Israelites were not actually guilty of unfaithfulness to God. Nor does it mean that the passage contains no non-metaphorical historical information. Verse 17 refers to the factual reality that Israel made physical idols out of gold and silver.

Fourth, I doubt that F&P would be happy to apply consistently to other parts of the Bible the hermeneutical assumptions that they bring to Genesis. Genesis 1 does not occupy privileged status when it comes to literary artistry. In fact, crafted literary structure is ubiquitous in the Bible, in all its literary forms. If *literary* is to be pitted against *literal*, why should other stories in Genesis, or the stories of Jonah, or Balaam, which are replete with literary artifice, be understood in a historical way? The same could be said of the gospels.[7] F&P argue that the differences in the creation accounts in Genesis 1 and 2 suggest that a 'literalist' interpretation is not viable (p. 52). Does this mean that the stories of Jesus' temptation in Matthew and Luke should be understood as a-historical because they are presented in differing orders? The desire to find room for Darwinism in Genesis has unfortunate consequences when the same arguments are applied elsewhere in the Bible.

Fifth, identifying the literary structure and genre is only the first step in any interpretative exercise. Despite the space devoted to Genesis 1 I am still unclear about what F&P think this chapter *is* saying, as opposed to what it is *not* saying. For example, what do the 'days', and the creative acts on each day, refer to? What is the significance of the ordering of the days? Their concern is to show that the early chapters are compatible with Darwinism, but in doing so they are making an argument that these chapters are compatible with *any* scientific model of earth history. They imply that the genre of these chapters precludes their relevance to an assessment of any scientific model of origins. As a result they are in danger of reading into the text what they want to find (or not find) – a strategy not unlike the allegorical approach they criticise (p. 38).

In summary, I am not arguing that the early chapters of Genesis must, *a priori*, be read in a wholly 'literal' fashion, only that none of the arguments presented by F&P *require* it to be read in a wholly 'non-literal' fashion. The literary structure of Genesis does not make its early chapters a-historical in the way that would be required to create a reading consistent with Darwinism. Furthermore, this focus on the literary structure of Genesis distracts us from the parts of the biblical storyline that are more fruitful and determinative in assessing the compatibility of Darwinism and the Bible: Adam, the flood, agony and death.[8]

Is Neo-Darwinism the only scientifically viable model of origins?

I have focused on issues of interpretation of the Bible so far in my response, but is this really the 'heart of the matter' (p. 35), as F&P suggest? They make this statement in the context of the need to question interpretations of both scientific data and Scripture, a concern with which I entirely agree. What lacks symmetry in their position is their lack of similar energy and imagination in being ready to question the interpretation of scientific data. Rather than the interpretation of the Bible, I would argue that it is the strength of attachment to a particular scientific model that is crucial in explaining our different conclusions.

F&P's approach is to ask whether it is possible to interpret the Bible in another way in the light of compelling scientific evidence. For them, methodologically science has priority in making us question preconceived interpretations of Scripture. For example, they refer to the idea that death post-dating sin is 'not a tenable interpretation' of Genesis 3 (p. 53). I could understand if they wanted to argue that it was not the *best* understanding of the passage (although I would disagree), but not that is 'untenable'. This is a very strong statement that flies in the face of the mainstream understanding of the church (and Jewish interpretation) down many ages, not to mention Paul's own understanding of the passage.[9] The only basis on which this interpretation could be 'untenable' is if the Darwinian story is taken as given because of an overwhelming weight of scientific evidence. Elsewhere Finlay explicitly states that human evolution is an 'unequivocal fact'.[10] If Darwinism is 'an unequivocal fact' (as well established as, say, the roundness of the earth) this must affect our interpretation of Scripture if we hold to the compatibility of scientific and biblical knowledge. In fact, such a starting point severely curtails the interpretative exercise when it comes to certain passages of Scripture. Particular interpretative options must be excluded *a priori*. For example, if Darwinism is a fact, then Romans 5:12–14 *cannot* include any reference to human physical death as a consequence of sin. It is not sufficient to argue that Paul was not necessarily referring to physical human death. This possibility must be absolutely excluded if Darwinism is true. Paul must be referring to 'spiritual death' *exclusively*. At this point theistic Darwinists are not willing to question their interpretation of Scripture. In fact, they require interpretative certainty here, or else (as F&P acknowledge, p. 53) Darwinism is falsified. A similar limitation of interpretative options applies in other passages that I highlighted in my chapter. If Darwinism is true, a global flood is not an interpretative option in any exegesis of 2 Peter 3.

Their commitment to Darwinism forces F&P to make empty statements like, 'Genesis 1 – 3 nowhere states that there was no death before the fall' and '*Nowhere* does Scripture teach the radical re-creation that a sudden introduction of death might imply' (p. 60). Indeed. But equally, nowhere does the Bible tell us that Jesus was a bachelor, or state that God is one in essence who exists in three distinct co-equal persons, but that does not mean that these statements are not a helpful synthesis of what the Bible does teach. When we work from what the Bible does positively teach, for example that Jesus needed to die physically to pay the penalty of our sin, the case that death did not pre-exist sin becomes compelling.

As a sceptic of Darwinism I have a greater range of interpretative options. I am free to consider the possibility that Paul was talking about physical death, or spiritual death, or some combination of the two in Romans 5:12–21.[11] I am also free to consider the possibility that Noah's flood was a local event and that our relationship with Adam need not include physical descent. I have no *a priori* reason to ensure that my interpretation is either compatible or incompatible with Darwinism. Scepticism towards Darwinism allows me to make full use of the hermeneutical tools that F&P advocate and assess interpretations on their exegetical merit.

A stance of scepticism also facilitates better science. A healthy questioning of consensus scientific models is how science advances. If the big story of Neo-Darwinism is an 'unequivocal fact' then there is no incentive to look for an alternative narrative that could explain the same data, and more, even better. It closes down research avenues. If we find that multiple lines of interpretation point towards an incompatibility between the Bible's story and Darwinism it is our duty to look for an alternative scientific model.[12] To say it can't be done smacks of laziness and a lack of imagination. How can we know whether a better alternative to Darwinism can be found without looking? Given the vast range of data and fields of study involved it is a project that can be tackled only by large teams of scientists involved in long-term research. A valid response to conflicting interpretations of the Bible and scientific models is to do better science. If the Copernican fiasco has any lessons for today's church, it is for Christian supporters of Darwinism. They are in danger of tying their interpretation of Scripture to the prevailing scientific consensus.

In short, I suggest that our most basic disagreement is not over the interpretation of the Bible, but over the invincibility or otherwise of Darwinism. There is little point discussing our interpretation of Scripture unless we are also ready to develop alternative interpretations of earth history that can compete with Darwinism in a 'survival of the fittest' struggle between scientific models.[13]

Which story of origins has the greatest apologetic problems?

But there is, finally, another crucial area of disagreement. It concerns our assessment of the most pressing apologetic problems we face. Whatever our view of Darwinism, questions about origins present apologetic challenges for Christians. A rejection of Darwinism as the best model of origins presents the formidable challenge of coming up with a better model. But this is a challenge that has, at the very least, the possibility of success. In contrast, the apologetic problems of accommodating Darwinism and therefore embracing an 'agony-before-Adam' position are more compelling, and more widely appreciated, and lack any prospect of being resolved. For that reason I am reassured to be in agreement with mainstream Christianity that multiple lines of biblical interpretation point to the incompatibility of the biblical and Darwinian stories.

Notes

1   Confusingly, the only definition offered is on p. 39, where N.T. Wright is quoted to explain what the Reformers meant by a 'literal' interpretation, a definition that I presume is not what F&P mean by *literal* elsewhere in the chapter.

2   For example, the science of the new Large Hadron Collider in Geneva has been communicated in the form of a 'rap' that accurately, though not exhaustively, explains its operation. See http://news. nationalgeographic.com/news/2008/09/080910-odd-particl-AP. html.

3   The oft-noted connections in Genesis 1 between days 1 and 4, 2 and 5, and 3 and 6 are not beyond challenge. For example, the sky is made on day 2, but the lights in the sky on day 4, not day 5. The seas are made on day 3, but the aquatic creatures on day 5, not day 6.

4   C.L. Blomberg, *Jesus and the Gospels* (Nashville: Broadman & Holman, 1997), pp. 142–4.

5   Given the way Christian theology rests on history, downplaying the Bible's history can lessen its theological message. For example, Gen. 1 is a far more compelling polemic against Babylonian creation myths if it is saying that the sun and moon were *in reality* created after the light of day one, rather than merely later in a literary scheme.

6   Nor does the use of idioms necessarily limit the precision of information that can be conveyed. For example, the English idiom 'It's raining cats and dogs' is as precise as 'It's raining heavily'. It does not mean it is only drizzling or that it isn't raining at all.

7   Robert Grundy, for example, argued that the literary structure of Matthew's gospel suggests it is a form of writing in which history was embellished to make theological points. See M.A. Noll, *Between Faith and Criticism* (Leicester: Apollos, 1991), pp. 167–9.

8   It is not only exegesis that should focus on these doctrinal areas. Historical studies should not concentrate on how interpreters through the ages understood the days or genre of Genesis 1, but whether they thought that the Bible spoke of a universal flood, or that Adam was the physical ancestor of all humanity, or that human physical death post-dates the fall.

⁹ F&P (p. 61) acknowledge that it is possible that Paul himself (in keeping with many of his contemporaries) understood the Old Testament to teach that physical death post-dated the fall, but because he did not explicitly *teach* this (in their opinion), it is not a view that we are compelled to accept by apostolic authority. This raises many questions, not least why we should discount Paul's interpretations of the Old Testament as authoritative, as F&P do (p. 59). They also do not explain how the theology of the stories in Gen. 2 can be authoritative if they are not historical (p. 59), a position which would seem to conflict with their belief that the biblical faith is 'based on history' (p. 64).

¹⁰ See *Science & Christian Belief* 15 (2003), pp. 17–40. Denis Alexander is similarly dogmatic in his *Creation or Evolution: Do we have to Choose?* (Oxford: Monarch, 2008). For example, he rejects certain interpretations of Scripture because the presence of physical pain, disease and death from before the fall is a 'reality that will not go away' (p. 274).

¹¹ My own chapter needs clarification at this point. I agree with F&P that spiritual death is also included in the meanings of *death* in Rom. 5:12–21, for the reasons they cite (p. 62). What I dispute is that physical death is *excluded*.

¹² Such a response is exactly what theistic Darwinists would advocate for other areas in which there is a conflict between external evidence and our interpretation of the Bible. Archaeological difficulties with the Exodus story or the existence of David have not compelled us to abandon our interpretation of the Old Testament as history.

¹³ By *fittest* I mean the model that explains the most evidence in the most compelling way.

4

The Story of Redemption:
Contra Lloyd

GRAEME FINLAY and STEPHEN PATTEMORE

Stephen Lloyd has focused the debate on a vital issue: the coherence of the story of the Bible. We agree fully with him regarding the crucial importance of the overarching narrative of salvation, and regarding the bodily resurrection of Jesus Christ as the decisive climax of that history. However, it turns out that the story he describes is not really the biblical story after all.

Sadly, Lloyd's opening statement has made the empirical truth of the resurrection dependent on the empirical falsehood of a scientific theory. This makes the resurrection hostage to unsupportable attempts to explain away the overwhelming weight of empirical evidence for the evolving history of the world. To say that the resurrection is true only if evolution is false is precisely the (il)logic of Richard Dawkins.

Every story, and especially every metanarrative, is an interpretation of data, achieved by assembling, analysing, and ordering the data. This is true equally of science and the Bible. Lloyd has confused a particular *interpretation* of the biblical data with the data itself. So his fundamental commitment to that *interpretation* leads him to reject the currently most plausible and powerful interpretation of the data of science.

We must, firstly, be obedient to the data presented by empirical history. We believe in the resurrection because it is required by the data of Israel's history. We believe in evolution because it is required by the data of natural history. We may, secondly, interpret these facts, based as they are on independent lines of evidence, and see how they may be integrated. And when we do, we find they belong to a larger story that has been written by God – the creation of a people who will bear the likeness of his Son.

This part of the debate focuses on the theological issues, but we must note that Lloyd frequently supports his argument by appealing to supposed alternative interpretations of scientific data. His scientific thinking is framed by 'Creationist' presuppositions, which *assume* a literal reading of the early chapters of Genesis and then attempt to manipulate the data to fit this.[1] Such manipulations do not meet the criteria of science. They represent not a grand new project (p. 25), but a desperate rearguard action. They are simply not necessary or (we believe) legitimate for Bible-believing Christians.

It is disingenuous of Lloyd to imply that his interpretation of Scripture disallows only biological evolution among all the sciences. In fact it rejects *all* the historical (*storied*) sciences: cosmology, geology, evolution, archaeology (with its interlocking time scales of human migrations) and linguistics. The Creationist position is particularly tragic because so many ardent Christian scientists have contributed to the development of the historical sciences. To reject the heritage we have received from them is to revert to medievalism. Further scientific issues are addressed in note 2.

Many of Lloyd's specific points have been addressed at least in outline in our essay, and we would like to focus our response on the issue of *story*. However, we need to preface this with a note of some problems we have with his presentation of the three doctrines.

Three 'Doctrines' Against Evolution?

Adam and the judgement of God on sin

We have no argument with the assumption that the New Testament writers understood Adam to be a unique historical individual. But we reject the elevation of this assumption to a fundamental biblical principle and we reject the suggestion that Paul's doctrine of salvation stands or falls on its validity or on the accuracy of his understanding of various details of history. The truths taught about God and humanity in the parables of Jesus do not depend on the literal truth of the narratives. For Paul, Adam is (as Lloyd states) the representative head of old sinful humanity. Whether all people today are physically descended from him is neither here nor there – any more than all the inheritors of the promise to Abraham are his physical descendants.

In discussing Adam, Lloyd appears to imply that God's judgement is arbitrary. Adam sins … and God makes polar bears into predators. However, the biblical pattern is that we reap what we sow. The idea that God should inflict suffering on innocent children because of one couple's sin is no basis for theodicy. God has granted freedom to his creation, and this entails the possibility of suffering and sin. And God remains answerable for a world in which this suffering and sin exist. Indeed he has bound himself in utter loving faithfulness to his creation in order to redeem it. The Cross is the centre and sum of biblical theodicy. It is our only and sufficient answer to the agony of suffering and sin. The Cross is the means by which God would take irremediably sinful creatures and transform them into new creatures suited for the environment of the new creation. The supreme wonder is that the triune God would have to experience suffering, death and abandonment in order to remove sin from his creatures and clothe them with immortality.

'A flood of biblical proportions'

If the flood is so central to the story of the Bible it is surprising that it features so rarely in the subsequent Bible narrative. After Genesis 11, the only Old Testament reference to Noah and the flood is in Isaiah 54:9. There are more New Testament references, but examination of these shows that the features being drawn on are the suddenness and unexpectedness of the judgement (Mt. 24:37–9; Lk. 26–7), the faith of Noah (Heb. 11:7), the patience and salvation of God (1 Pet. 3:20) and God's judgement on ungodly humanity (2 Pet. 3:5–6). The Bible's own use of this incident simply will not allow it to bear the weight that Lloyd wishes to place on it

– especially to make the significance of the resurrection dependent on his interpretation of the flood narrative (p. 14).

No agony before Adam?

The existence of evil is an extremely troubling question, at whatever stage in the history of life on earth you wish to focus it. But Lloyd's treatment of it is itself highly problematical. He *cannot* define the class of living creatures for which suffering and death before the fall is unacceptable. His insistence that physical death is the immediate ('on the day') result of the fall makes God a liar and the snake the truth-teller. Thus his argument is based entirely on a fallacy.

Lloyd proposes that the fall destroyed the goodness of creation (p. 20). It would follow that we must deny the goodness of the Kew Gardens because there is predation and death in them. It would follow that we must deny the goodness of the interlocking nutrient (carbon, nitrogen, phosphorus) cycles upon which the biosphere depends because of the death that is inherent in their operation: the cycles that sustain the biosphere are manifestations of the curse! It would follow that we must loathe lions and dolphins, yearning for a day when these hideous Monsters of the Curse will revert to herbivory. Surely, any idea of 'goodness' that would lead us to pour scorn on the world that God has created has to be unbiblical (1 Tim. 4:4). Predation is part of that good world: Christ in resurrection glory ate fish.

Gnostics, Manichaeans and Creationists may disdain God's world, but we insist that creation *is* resoundingly good! The physical creation is like a baby: unambiguously, wonderfully, gloriously good – *but we would be horrified if it stayed at that stage of development!* Creation has yet to be made perfect. Lloyd seems to reject all the historical sciences on the basis of a denial of the goodness of creation that we believe has greater affinities with Gnosticism and certain non-biblical religions.

Finally, we agree fully with Lloyd's concern for theology to be useful in both evangelism and pastoral care. However, we greatly fear that for evangelism, a 'head-in-the-sand' attitude to the whole method and substance of the scientific enterprise is counter-productive in the extreme. And pastoral concerns can never be adequately met by approaches to reality that are less than fully rigorous. Other theological issues are addressed in note 3.

Which story?

And so we come to the issue on which Lloyd has based the success or failure of his project: the compatibility of the stories told by evolution and the Bible.

We applaud the emphasis on story (p. 2). And we fully agree that the story of the Bible is incompatible with the story of evolution – *but only if the Bible story is understood as being cyclic, and not linear.* However, we do not interpret the Bible story as ending up more or less where it started. On the contrary, the Bible story emphasises God's ever-unfolding plan for his world; time moves forward; breathtakingly novel realities arise as history unfolds; and there is a denouement, a climax, an eschaton, the culmination of a new heaven and a new earth. *It is this directional pattern of time that is magnificently compatible with the progressively unfolding (evolving) history revealed by science.*

Consider the first great historical act of salvation in the history of Israel, the Exodus, which becomes the paradigmatic narrative of salvation history and prefigures the work of Christ in so many ways. God's redemption of Israel did *not* restore something that Israel had lost. They never had possessed the Promised Land. They never had been a populous nation. They never had blessed the rest of the world. God did infinitely more than simply restore what was lost: he did something qualitatively *new.*

The Creationist version of 'story' disdains the historical sciences, and leaves us with a truncated condensation of cosmic story. The true biblical story describes God's continuous, covenantal and sacrificial relationship to his world. God creates all that exists. But we know that this created history is ambiguous. There is suffering and sin in heartbreaking abundance. How is this? God does not create suffering and sin, but God has created a cosmos upon which he has graciously endowed the gloriously *good* gift of freedom – a gift that necessarily entails the possibility of suffering and sin. History is created – but not all that happens in history is the will of God! Thus Israel's created history is full of suffering and carnage. Our own personal creation-in-progress stories incorporate accident, disease and sin. God works patiently within the chaotic process of his world to bring his purposes to fruition and – o wonder! – to bring the histories of life, of Israel and of each of us to a glorious consummation. Created histories are incomplete, work-in-progress; and en route to perfection. Table 1 illustrates some of the common features of the various narratives which make up the history of life on earth.

Table 1   **Shared elements in the stories of biology, of Israel, of Jesus, and of our own lives**

	class of (hi)story			
	biological	of Israel (OT)	Eschatological 'history of Jesus' (NT)	our own (personal)
new initiatives arise from inconspicuous beginnings	all mammals, primates, apes are ultimately descended from a single individual	new directions arise from the obedience of *individuals*: Abraham, Moses, David	the unique pioneer of the new humanity; ('the scandal of particularity'); the Kingdom of God is like a mustard seed	we develop from a single cell
operation of lawfulness	lawful effects of natural selection as shown by evolutionary convergence	consistent effects of the moral law: Israel reaped what she sowed	moral law: life of obedience. 'It was impossible that death should hold him prisoner.'	consistent effects of the moral law: we reap what we sow
operation of random happen-stance	novelty in evolution from mutations, genetic assortment	Joseph: 'You meant it for evil, but God intended it for good.'	Satan entered Judas, but God intended that Christ should die	there are 8×10^6 ways of randomly assorting chromosomes when human gametes are produced

	class of (hi)story			
	biological	of Israel (OT)	Eschatological 'history of Jesus' (NT)	our own (personal)
shattering setbacks occur	extinctions, devastation from meteorite impacts	slavery in Egypt, destruction of Samaria and of Jerusalem; the Exile	crucifixion, abandonment by the Father	accident, sinful choices, sickness, old age
new initiatives arise from disaster	mammalian radiation from meteorite impacts	nationhood from slavery; purification through exile	resurrection from death	justification from sinfulness; patience from suffering
increasing degree of perfection	non-life to life to sentience to community	from 'not a people' to 'you are now my people'	made perfect, Heb. 2:10	mortality to immortality; new creation
heads to a magnificent climax	humanity as the (provisional) Image of God	advent of the Lord Jesus as the perfect Image of God	glorification of Christ	final union with Christ; conferment of the perfect Image of Christ upon us

Stephen Lloyd's fundamental confusion is obvious in the way he refers to God's mission in the world as *re-creation* (pp. 14, 22) or *new creation* (pp. 22, 24). *But these terms are not synonymous.* Re-creation is a patch-up job, a repair programme that returns an undesirable situation to an idyllic past. New creation is the bringing into being of realities that are fresh, wholly unprecedented, previously unimaginable, and qualitatively more wonderful than anything that has ever existed before.

We again appeal to the Scriptures to illustrate and affirm our point. The picture of the new creation given to us in the final chapters of the book of Revelation is *not* simply, or even primarily, of Eden restored. There is indeed mending of what went wrong – the curse is no more, and the tree of life now provides perpetual healing. But the tree is in a city. The garden/forest is contained within a redeemed city – that ancient symbol of man's hubris and rebellion (Gen. 11)! This is not simply a replay of Eden; it is infinitely more, *including* the redemption of the results of human sinfulness.

The concept of re-creation is not biblical, but rather encapsulates an understanding of 'story' in which the atonement merely *re-instates* what was once present. The Creationist 'story' ends *back* at the Prologue. According to this 'story', we go *back* to immortality, *back* to the absence of suffering, of disease, predation and pain; *back* to the absence of natural evil and of sin, *back* to a world without earthquakes. The sequence of world events is essentially cyclic, and this has more in common with the conception of time entertained by Israel's neighbours. That's no story (Figure 1)!

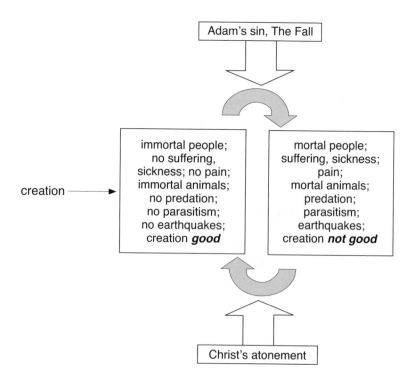

Figure 1   Lloyd's 'story' is cyclic or retrogressive

And Lloyd's cyclic 'story' arises from a simple misreading of the narrative. Lloyd seems to think that paradise was transformed *in time* into a harsh wilderness. But a careful reading of the narrative indicates that Adam and Eve were expelled from the Garden (a circumscribed, particular place) into the surrounding wilderness that *co-existed* with the Garden (Gen. 3:23–4; cf. 3:8). This provides no basis for arguing for a transformation of an idyllic world into a fallen one (or vice versa). We all face two options: the Garden with God – or the desert without him. (Lloyd's cyclic presuppositions are tabulated in note 4.)

If the atonement in fact represents God's eternal plan to take creation far beyond what it had ever been before – to reveal His glory to mortal creatures, to forgive them, to glorify them, to instil his eternal Holy Spirit into them, to give them new birth and

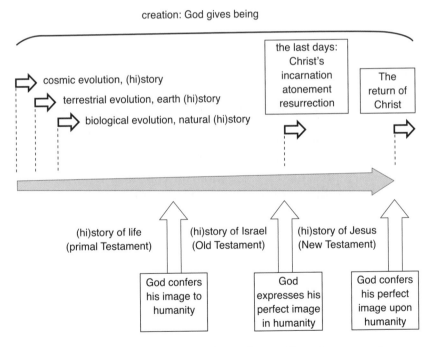

Figure 2   God's dealings with creation are linearly progressive, directed to the eschaton.

No attempt has been made to depict an appropriate time scale.

adopt them as his children, to confer the Image of his Son upon them – then evolution is a story that is pregnant with purpose and part of the vast sweep of created history. That God should create creatures that are free is good; that he should create new creatures that are free *and made righteous* ... that is *amazing*. What no one could ever think or imagine is the very thing God prepared for those who love him!

God has committed himself to remove evil from the world. The triune God has entered into his creation to deal with suffering and our otherwise irremediable sinfulness through the Son's suffering and death. Through this means he will inaugurate the glory of the new creation where righteousness will be at home. This is story in which 'the Lamb was slain before the creation of the world'. God planned from eternity to extirpate our abuse of freedom, our sin, and our rebellion from his creation. Creation and redemption are more closely related than we commonly recognise (Figure 2).

Summary

In our commitment to faith in the God of creation, our reverence for Scripture as his revealed truth, and our understanding of the centrality of the resurrection in the story of God's interaction with this world we have much in common with Stephen Lloyd. However, the differences in our approach to both Scripture and science are vast. We conclude with a table illustrating how the cyclic story presented by Creationism contrasts with what we understand as the unfolding story of God and the world presented in the Bible (Table 2).

Table 2   The basic features of (hi)story as cyclic or as linear

	the cyclic 'story', retrogressive	the linear unfolding story, progressive
understanding Scripture	historical context irrelevant	historical context important
God's creative work	a sequence of past events	a continuous, ongoing relationship with his world, living creatures, humanity, Israel, each of us
the value of the physical creation	no longer 'good'	emphatically good – but incomplete
validity of empirical science	rejected	accepted as integral to the biblical world view
the story of creation	cyclic: the atonement restores what was there before	linear: the atonement goes far beyond what ever existed before
God's judgement	wholly arbitrary: everything gets cursed because of Adam's rebellion	relates to the nature of human sin: humans bring upon themselves the consequences of their wrongdoing (Rom. 1); 'bad stewards' do reap what they sow

Notes

[1] See pages 6–7, 9–10, 13–14, 16, 23, 24 and bibliographical notes on those pages, although at times Lloyd seems ready to concede the mechanisms and time scales of evolution (pp. 1–2, 7– 8, 15, 23).

[2] Some scientific issues raised by the Creationist 'story'.

Creationist 'story'	Page	Our response
'prominent theistic evolutionist like Denis Alexander'	1	In our experience, all Christian biologists in universities and research laboratories who have an opinion on the issue accept the evidence for evolution.
Genetic similarities 'do not imply a common ancestor'	6–7	This statement is false in the light of what we know of tumour monoclonality, founder mutations, hereditary disease, paternity issues, forensic DNA evidence.
'Our "image of God-ness" is not something that emerges gradually'	7	This requires that in our own development our 'image of God-ness' was fully present at conception, and did not change subsequently! Surely it emerged gradually during our development.
A favoured date of a historical Adam is between 8,000 and 6,000 years ago (implied)	7–8	The dates of a suggested historical Adam are evaded – the literal model is silent on its central datum.
The most recent date for Adam is 6,000 years ago	7	The history of Jericho goes back at least 9,000 years.
Neanderthals had the image of God and therefore post-dated Adam.	7	The last Neanderthal remains must be dated at 25,000 years ago.
Aboriginals post-dated Adam (more recently than 10,000 years ago)	7–8	Aborigines have been in Australia for 40,000 years.
global flood involving 'a major change in the topography of the earth's crust'	14	unrestrained speculation
the ages of fossils: 'questions that can be addressed only by scientific investigation'	15	questions that *have been* answered!

Creationist 'story'	Page	Our response
'some pain is not always a bad thing'	15–16	Pain is (unfortunately) *absolutely essential* for our survival.
All human and animal suffering and all animal fossils post-date Adam.	23	A non-realist approach to the historical sciences undermines a realist approach to biblical history. If God created a young earth with an implanted record that makes it *look* old, how do we know that *any* history (including the story of Jesus) is real?

3 Some theological issues raised by the Creationist 'story':

Creationist 'story'		Our response
Assertion	Page	
references to Adam, Lk. 3:38, Jude 14	4	References to Adam reflect the *authority* of the OT literature, but do not address the question of its *genre* (and in any case, how literally true are the words attributed to Enoch, which are not recorded in the OT?).
references to the creation of male and female, Matt. 19:4–6	4	References reflect the *authority* of the OT theology about marriage, but do not address the issue of *genre*.
rejection of Genesis accounts as 'myth'	4	This is a straw man: Gen. 1–11 is not myth but divinely inspired theology-in-narrative
historical Adam indicated by 'one man', Acts 17:26	6	May be translated 'one stock'; emphasises the unity of humanity
requires physical descent from Adam	6	Physical descent from Abraham is not required for us to be his descendants.

Creationist 'story'		Our response
Assertion	Page	
requires a global flood	9	Needs to address the *genre* of the flood story.
Tower of Babel story understood universally	12	The story mocks pagan religion in the form of the temple tower (ziggurat) of Babylon.
Babel describes the origins of all languages	12	Languages evolve: English is less than 1,000 years old!
N.T. Wright's 'drama in several acts'	13	Misrepresents Wright: these acts are based upon Israel's sacred and authoritative scriptures, whether literary story or history.
Noah a parallel to Christians, 2 Pet. 2:5–6	14	The issue is one of the judgement of sinful humanity
physical death, Gen. 3:19	15–16	If physical death is the predicted result of Adam's sin then the snake told the truth.
the necessity of Christ's *physical* death emphasised	17	The mystery of Calvary included, *but surely extended beyond,* physical death.
death a terrible monstrosity, 1 Cor. 15:26; Heb. 2:14–5	17	It is 'death-with-a-sting' that is the monstrosity.
no animal death to start with	17-18	Genesis simply makes no comment on meat-eating before the Fall; we dare not create a doctrine when Scripture makes no statement.
'a point in time when "creation was subjected to futility"', Rom. 8:19–23	19	The creation experiences emptiness and frustration ('futility') as it waits for liberation; the issue is not the sudden appearance of death.

Creationist 'story'		Our response
Assertion	**Page**	
creation with suffering is no longer 'good'	20	Our *created* bodies and lives contain suffering; Lloyd must conclude that humanity as the Image of God (Jas. 3:9) cannot be 'good'.
how can broken relationships make farming more difficult?	21	Biblically, injustice and the fecundity of the land are *inseparable*!
queries that 'the problem with creation is bad stewardship'	21	Another straw man: the problem is bad *stewards*!
'If Darwinism is true, the Bible's story unravels into incoherence.'	24	A Dawkins-like statement that denies any empirical or evidential basis to God's redeeming work.

[4] Terms that reveal how Lloyd presupposes a cyclic 'story':

Creationist cyclic 'story'	Page	Our response
creation-fall-redemption-*restoration*	2	Does not just *restore* what was past but *transcends* it.
Christ the *turning point* of salvation history	5	An unfortunate metaphor that implies a backward direction: rather, Christ is the promised climax to which OT salvation history *progressed*, and from whom NT salvation *progresses* to its conclusion.
reversal of Babel	27, note 28	The NT church does not merely *undo* the effects of Babel.
un-creation and *re-creation* at the flood and parousia	13	The flood is hardly a general metaphor for the parousia: God's plan is not *re*-creation at the parousia but *new* creation.

Creationist cyclic 'story'	Page	Our response
the new creation a *turning point*	14	Not a turning point but the goal, climax, fulfilment, telos, eschaton, consummation.
Christ's physical resurrection contrasted with physical death	13	Christ's resurrection was unprecedented and goes vastly beyond what existed before.
The physical healings of Jesus *undo* the effects of sin.	21	The healings are proleptic *anticipations* of the eschaton.
The *restoration* or *re-creation* of creation is necessary.	21	We look forward to a *new* creation.
The physical resurrection of Christ is the *antidote* of the death introduced by Adam.	24	Christ is not an equal-and-opposite of Adam, but the pioneer of an unprecedented eternal quality of life.

5

A Scientific Critique of the Theory of Evolution

DAVID SWIFT

Evolving thoughts on evolution

I was privileged to grow up in a Christian home, and from childhood had some measure of faith in Jesus. In secondary school I became interested in science, was of course taught about evolution, and completely accepted it. How did I reconcile the two? Mainly, I did not see them as being in conflict and needing to be reconciled.

It was not until studying for a degree in natural sciences that I began to question, and hence doubt, the truth of evolution. Part of my course was biochemistry and I started to learn about DNA and proteins and the elaborate molecular mechanisms, including the genetic code, which link them, as outlined in the Introduction. These mechanisms certainly *look* designed; but through formal education and the popular media we are brought up to believe it is only 'apparent' design – that the daunting odds of life arising spontaneously are overcome by the immense age (billions of years) and size (billions of planets) of the universe.

Fortunately my studies also included statistics, and one day I thought to see how likely it was that a typical protein could have arisen by chance, taking into account the age and size of the universe. And I was shocked to see how utterly hopeless the odds were. For example, the chance of obtaining even a small protein (e.g. one having only 100 amino acids – most have several hundreds) is much less than 1 in the number of atoms in the universe (estimated at 10^{80}) multiplied by the age of the universe in seconds (even 15 billion years is only about 10^{17} seconds).[1] So there is not the slightest hope that even individual molecular components could have arisen by chance, even less the sophisticated interaction of interdependent molecular mechanisms which we now know are essential for the functioning of even the most basic organism.

In the 1980s I wrote a short essay which outlined the bio-chemical challenge to evolution and what I then saw as some of the biblical and theological implications. Most of all, it whetted my appetite to look at the subject more thoroughly, and the opportunity to do so arose about a decade later, culminating in my book *Evolution under the microscope*. Until then, my reasons for doubting the truth of evolution had been based almost entirely on biochemistry – the impossibility of molecular biology arising in an evolutionary way. I had believed what I had been taught: that the evidence from fossils and homology (e.g. the similarities of vertebrate skeletons) completely supported evolution. But when I looked at the evidence for myself, I was shocked (again) to find that it did not. In fact, the evidence of non-homology (which I explain below) is some of the strongest evidence *against* evolution.

Some readers may be wondering if I am trying to fit the science to suit my Christian views. This is not the case, because where science and theology are concerned I am inclined to follow Augustine (354–430). In his work *The Literal Meaning of Genesis* – with remarkable wisdom and forethought, given that he was writing a millennium before the scientific revolution – he cautioned Christians against basing views about the natural world on their interpretation of the Bible. It is regrettable that the official Church in Galileo's day did not heed that advice, and even more regrettable that some Christians still do not do so. The anti-scientific comments of some Christians continue to discredit the gospel – just as Augustine feared.

Do not misunderstand me. As indicated above, I recognise that there are difficulties reconciling evolution with some biblical or theological issues, but I think that we cannot be so sure of our interpretation of the Bible on these issues that they are adequate reason to reject evolution. Evolution is essentially a scientific theory, not a theological or philosophical issue. So my reasons for thinking that the (overall) theory of evolution is wrong are *entirely scientific*, and I endeavour in the following pages to explain why.

Evolution – true *and* false

A common perception is that evolution must be true because of the 'overwhelming' evidence supporting it. But there are a couple of points to note in response to this.

1. *No scientific theory can be proved true, but must always be open to scrutiny.* Yet in saying this, I emphasise that I am not hiding behind the weak creationist argument that evolution is 'only a theory'. I am merely pointing out that we must not be so taken with the evidence that is consistent with evolution that we think we can ignore the evidence that contradicts it. We must give proper weight to the contrary evidence.

And it is important to note that this is not a balancing act – weighing whether there is more evidence for or against the theory: even a small amount of attestable data that clearly contradicts evolution is sufficient to demonstrate that it is false, despite a much larger body of evidence that is consistent with it. This is what is meant by falsifiability – a concept introduced by the philosopher Karl Popper as an essential criterion for a theory to be regarded as scientific.[2] A common complaint from proponents of evolution is that creationism and intelligent design (ID) are not scientific because they are not falsifiable, whereas the theory of evolution is. That may be so, but unfortunately evolutionists themselves often seem unwilling to allow the theory of evolution to be properly exposed to the counter-evidence and risk being falsified! What I seek to show – though in the space available I can only give an indication – is that there are some key facts that clearly contradict evolution. They are not merely trivial 'problems' that are likely to be solved, but fundamental matters that appear to be without prospect of solution.

2. *Some evolution does occur.* Indeed, as mentioned in the Intro- duction, some degree of evolution is inevitable as a consequence of

there being variation and competition in nature. However, it does not follow from this *limited* evolution that the *whole* of the theory of evolution is true. One of my objectives here is to show that there is a fundamental difference between the type of evolution that does occur (microevolution) and the type of evolution that is claimed to occur but does not (macroevolution). Although evolutionists argue that macroevolution is merely the long-term accumulation of microevolution, this extrapolation is not justified, because substantially different processes are involved.

Natural selection and incremental improvement

As already mentioned, there is no doubt that natural selection occurs: individuals with an advantageous variation will, in general, survive better and have more offspring than those lacking the variation; and, provided the variation has a genetic basis, it will tend to be passed on to the individual's offspring and, over time, become more prevalent.

So we need to take natural selection fully into account and accept that, at least in theory, an overall unlikely end result could be arrived at gradually through progressive improvement, via a series of not-too-unlikely steps. Richard Dawkins is right to claim that this is a very elegant concept. It is the crux of several of his books, notably *The Blind Watchmaker*, and is neatly summarised in his *The God Delusion* as follows:

> What is it that makes natural selection succeed as a solution to the problem of improbability, where chance and design both fail at the starting gate? The answer is that natural selection is a cumulative process, which breaks the improbability up into small pieces. *Each of the small pieces is slightly improbable, but not prohibitively so.*[3]

However, it should be noted that the point he makes in the last sentence is merely asserted: it is *never substantiated*; indeed, it is never even *scrutinised*. He rightly extols the power of cumulative natural selection, yet never examines the crucial issue of the likelihood of occurrence of the variations on which natural selection can act. Despite his comments about breaking down immense improbabilities into smaller steps, nowhere is there any attempt to quantify the probability of those steps. And Dawkins is typical of widespread evolutionary thinking which simply *assumes* that appropriate advantageous variations will arise, without any thought to the crucial question of *how*. We must not be so taken with the elegance of the theory that we overlook examining whether it can work in practice. For example, in discussing the possible evolution of the eye, Dawkins *assumes* that it can be broken down into infinitesimally small steps (his rationale being that once they are small enough they are not too improbable).[4] But this is not correct, because of the discrete nature of genes – which I shall consider now.

Molecular biology poses fundamental challenges to evolution

The need for each step in the evolutionary process to (a) have a reasonable chance of happening, and (b) confer an advantage – so that natural selection can act – presents serious difficulties when it comes to the supposed evolution of genes which code for proteins and the like.

Since the 1960s, when we began to understand the structure and functioning of proteins and appreciate that they are highly dependent on their amino acid sequence, it was recognised that their specific amino acid sequences are prohibitively improbable and could not realistically have arisen by chance. For example, as there are 20 different kinds of amino acid, the number of different possibilities for a small protein that is only 100 amino acids long is 20 multiplied by itself 100 times, which equates to approximately 10^{130}. This is an incomprehensibly large number which, as I said earlier, means it is totally out of the question to think that useful proteins could have arisen by chance.

Evolutionary biologists responded to this by saying that we should not expect proteins etc. to have arisen fully-formed in one grossly improbable step. Rather, they propose that proteins would have evolved gradually from early short ones which had a much better chance of arising. This is the widely accepted evolutionary explanation, and is written into textbooks.

It was entirely appropriate for evolutionists to propose this sort of scenario; but it seems to have been accepted uncritically, without considering what would actually be involved. When it is examined properly, however, we find there are some formidable obstacles. Unfortunately I do not have space here to explain the difficulties fully; but to illustrate the key issues I shall look at some of the criteria that need to be met for a protein to function. Note that we are not even considering here having improved activity, but merely having any biological activity at all – the minimum first step in the putative evolution of a protein.

1. Protein folding

First of all, although a protein is a linear sequence of connected amino acids (usually a few hundred long), somewhat like the wagons of a train, in order to have biological activity it is essential for the polypeptide (the unfolded protein) to fold up into a specific three-dimensional shape which depends critically on the actual sequence of amino acids. Protein folding is illustrated in Figure 1.[5]

Broadly speaking, amino acids can be categorised as either hydrophilic (water-loving) or hydrophobic (water-hating, or 'oily'), depending on their particular chemical composition. In order for a polypeptide to fold successfully, it must have an appropriate mix and distribution along its length of hydrophobic and hydrophilic amino acids. The sequence needs to be such that it is possible to pack the hydrophobic amino acids on the inside (away from the aqueous environment of the cell) and with the hydrophilic ones on the outside where they can readily associate with water.

In order to form a stable structure, all of the amino acids must be able to pack together very closely – especially the hydrophobic ones on the inside – rather like a three-dimensional jigsaw or Chinese puzzle with an assortment of pieces selected from 20 different shapes. And this is with the added constraint that all of the pieces are connected in a linear sequence, the connection between them resembling a universal joint that can swivel but cannot be strained, rather than a spring that can stretch.

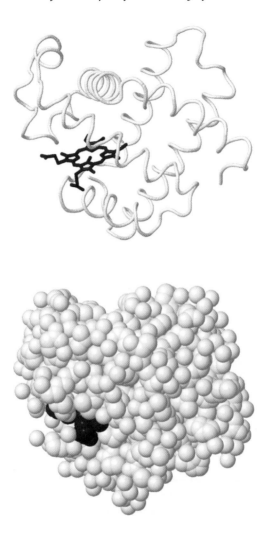

Figure 1   Protein folding

Protein folding is illustrated here using the protein myoglobin which transports oxygen in muscle. The upper graphic shows how the linear polypeptide backbone of the protein is tortuously coiled and twisted on itself to form the folded protein. Most proteins fold spontaneously, and they are held in their folded state by the very weak forces between their constituent atoms – made possible only because the amino acids are packed together so compactly. The compactness of the folded protein is illustrated in the lower graphic. In both graphics the dark-coloured component is the haem group which binds the oxygen. (The graphics were produced using Jmol: an open-source Java viewer for chemical structures in 3D. http://www.jmol.org.)

It is hard to stress enough how good the fit must be (the hydro-phobic amino acids are packed together even more closely than in crystals of the respective amino acids), and consequently how unlikely it is that a sequence of amino acids that can fold will arise by chance. Perhaps an indication is that it is only recently, by harnessing the power of modern computers, that it has become possible for us to predict how a polypeptide chain will fold (when we know that it will fold). We are still unable to design an amino acid sequence from scratch that we know will fold – so how much less could mindless nature 'know' of a foldable sequence?

The ability to fold is so dependent on the specific amino acid sequence that it is easily lost (in most cases, changing just one amino acid for another will mean it no longer folds), and has been described as 'all or nothing'.[6] So any foldable sequence can be found only by chance, not by a 'learning curve', e.g. by starting off with a sequence that will fold poorly, and then gradually improving through natural selection favouring beneficial changes. And this is accentuated by the indirect connection between mutations and the protein sequence: what actually changes by mutation is the nucleotide sequence in the DNA that codes for the amino acid sequence, not the amino acid sequence itself.

2. Active site

Although being able to fold is an essential prerequisite for a protein to have biological activity, by itself it is clearly insufficient to confer an advantage which natural selection can use: it must also have a useful function. For that it is also necessary that at least some parts of the folded protein's exposed surface should be of appropriate shape and chemical character to bind other chemical compounds (substrates) with which it will interact. For example, enzymes are astonishingly good catalysts (facilitate chemical reactions), and they achieve this function by having appropriate chemical groups positioned in such a way as to interact with the substrates to facilitate the desired reaction. These 'active sites' require specific amino acids (those having the right kind of chemical groups) to be present at precise locations to enable the required interaction with the substrates. It should be noted that the amino acids that contribute to the active site, although in close proximity in the folded protein, are usually widely separated in the linear sequence. So not only must the amino acid sequence be able to fold, it must also include in its sequence the right amino acids which *when folded* will form the active site.

This is the absolute minimum requirement for even a rudimentary biologically active protein; and an evolutionary origin would require that a protein meeting these criteria could arise only by chance. It is all very well for evolutionists such as Dawkins to extol the power of natural selection (and in this they are right); but for natural selection to operate there has to be at least some biological activity. Similarly, they are right that evolution does not necessarily need to find a specific amino acid sequence, because some variation is permissible. But these variations must be within the constraints of a sequence that will fold and have a functioning active site. It is these constraints that make it prohibitively improbable to find a useful protein by chance.[7]

3. Control sequence(s)

And that is not all, because even a nucleotide sequence in DNA that codes for a useful protein is of no use at all unless it is associated with another sequence of nucleotides (called a control or regulatory sequence) which directs that the protein-coding sequence is used. (At its simplest, this control sequence acts as a binding site for the enzyme that makes a copy of RNA from the DNA, as the first step of protein synthesis.) Without a suitable control sequence, no matter how potentially useful the protein-coding sequence is, it will not be used, so it is of no value, natural selection cannot operate on it, and the chances are that it will degrade through mutation. Similarly, if a control sequence arises so that the adjacent length of DNA is used to produce a polypeptide, but it has no biological use, then the control sequence is also likely to degrade (because there is no advantage in keeping it – indeed there is a disadvantage in the waste of producing a useless polypeptide). Hence, for a new protein to arise requires the extraordinary coincidence of an extremely improbable protein-coding sequence arising in conjunction with a fairly unlikely control sequence. And I stress that this is at its simplest; in most cases there are several control sequences associated with a gene, providing the means for quite sophisticated regulation which ensures that the protein is produced only where and when required (example later).

Unfortunately, these sorts of considerations are not even glossed over in evolutionary textbooks – usually they are totally ignored – it is simply *assumed* that useful proteins can arise readily.

4. *Interdependent macromolecules*

As if that were not enough, the problem is actually much more severe because almost all proteins do not act in isolation, but necessarily in conjunction with other macromolecules (proteins and/or nucleic acids such as DNA).

A simple example would be the replication of DNA. As many readers will know, DNA consists of two matching strands of nucleotides, wrapped into a 'double helix'. DNA is replicated by unwinding a section of the DNA, separating the strands, and then using each strand as a template on which to construct a new matching strand – resulting in two double helices, each comprising one 'old' and one 'new' strand.

This may sound straightforward but, in fact, necessarily involves several different proteins (see Figure 2): some to get the process started, at least one to unwind the DNA, some just to sit on the exposed strands so that they do not rejoin before being copied, and some to do the actual building of the new strand (and this takes as given the many enzymes required to synthesise the nucleotide building blocks).

In addition to this, because of the helical structure of DNA, the replication process would result in the DNA still to be replicated becoming progressively more tightly coiled until it stopped the process. Fortunately, there is an enzyme called a Type I topoisomerase which identifies over-coiled DNA, snips one of the strands, allows the DNA to unwind, and then rejoins the strand. Even more remarkable is that in 'simple' organisms such as bacteria (which are assumed to have evolved first) the DNA is in the form of a ring, and the replication process results in two interlinked rings of DNA. Fortunately, there is also a Type II

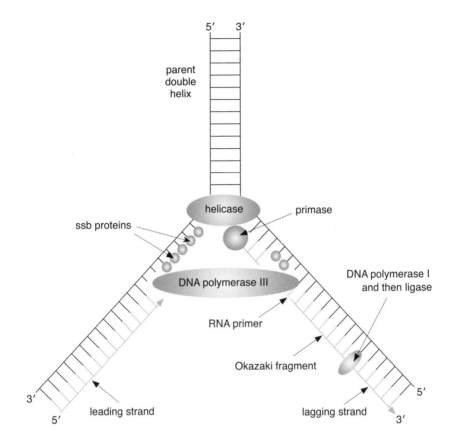

Figure 2   Replication of DNA: the major components at a typical replication fork

Replication begins by a protein dnaA (not shown) binding to specific DNA 'starting' sequences; the DNA:dnaA complex is then recognised (with the help of a further protein dnaC, also not shown) by helicase which attaches to the DNA and progressively uncoils and separates it. As soon as the strands separate, small single strand binding (ssb) proteins attach to the exposed bases to prevent rejoining of the strands while they await duplication. Duplication is carried out by the enzyme DNA polymerase III which has two active sites and extends both strands simultaneously. However, DNA can be synthesised in only one direction, but the complementary strands of DNA are oriented in opposite directions. So, although the leading strand can be synthesised continuously, the 'lagging' strand must be synthesised in short lengths (Okazaki fragments) by the repeated operation of primase (which starts the process by making a short RNA primer), DNA polymerase III, and then DNA polymerase I and ligase to join up the fragments.

topoisomerase which can cut the DNA of one ring right through (both its strands), pass DNA from the other ring through the gap, and then rejoin the first ring (correctly rejoining both strands), thus freeing the two rings. (How likely is it that even rudimentary topoisomerases, but with their elaborate function, could arise by chance?)

The point of all this is to illustrate that for any biological process that necessarily requires multiple proteins, all of them must arise together by chance (each being able to fold, into the right shape, have the required active site(s), and have appropriate associated control regions) before there is any activity that could provide an advantage which natural selection can work on. That is, natural selection will not act to retain any one of them until all are available. (For example, there is no advantage in having an enzyme that will unwind DNA without the enzyme(s) for synthesising a new strand, and vice versa.) It is this compounding of improbabilities that totally defies any realistic possibility of an evolutionary origin of molecular biology – but which is scarcely even mentioned in evolutionary textbooks. This interdependence is what is meant by 'irreducible complexity'. And the strength of the argument about irreducible complexity is not so much that many molecular biological systems require multiple interdependent components, but that each of the individual components is so unlikely to arise by chance.

In terms of the well-known example of irreducible complexity used by Michael Behe in his book *Darwin's Black Box*,[8] it is not just that even a mousetrap requires a minimum number of interacting components, but that each component also needs to be fabricated. Importantly, the fabrication is not done intentionally (because natural selection is only opportunistic – it has no prior knowledge of potential usefulness), but by, for example, aimless bending of bits of wire. And for the same reason, no component is retained until all are available, as it is only then that their use can be realised. Even this is an inadequate analogy, because there is no molecular-scale inventor who can see how the pieces might work together and assemble them appropriately: they must all fall into the right places in relation to each other *by themselves*. (In fact, another remarkable feature of molecular biology is self-assembly, which unfortunately I cannot elaborate on here.)

Suggested solutions

Proponents of evolution point to a number of possibilities to try to overcome the above-mentioned difficulties.

1. Short proteins

As already indicated, perhaps the most common strategy to try to circumvent the prohibitive improbability of obtaining real proteins is to propose that they evolved from shorter ones which would have had a better chance of arising. There are two major objections to this proposal:

(a) First is the question of folding. The forces (between the packed amino acids) holding a folded protein in place are so weak that there need to be many amino acids involved to give overall stability, generally at least 70.[9] So it is utter nonsense to suggest, as some textbooks do,[10] that early proteins could have started off with just a handful of amino acids.

(b) Second is that key amino acids, notably those which contribute to an enzyme's active site, are generally scattered throughout the linear sequence of the polypeptide, and are brought together only once the enzyme has folded. If proteins had evolved from short polypeptides, one might have thought that at least these critical amino acids (which must have been close together in a short protein) would still be grouped together; because to disperse them during the course of subsequent evolution would require restructuring of the protein, which would incur the same sort of improbability that the postulated small proteins are intended to overcome. In fact, to progress from short polypeptides, where the critical amino acids are necessarily close together, to longer ones, where they are dispersed, requiring some measure of activity at all of the intervening stages (indeed, *improved* activity, so that natural selection would favour the change) seems to be overall even less probable than getting the required polypeptide in one go.

2. Gene duplication

A favourite response is to point to gene duplication. Because of the similarity of sequence between some proteins it is confidently assumed that they have arisen from a common source – that one has diverged from the other. That is, it is proposed that if a useful gene happens to be duplicated, then while one copy retains its original function, the other is free to mutate without causing the host organism any harm and to 'experiment' to find another function. However, as Kimura (who proposed the neutral theory of protein evolution) commented:

> This process that facilitates the production of new genes will, at the same time, cause degeneration of one of the duplicated copies. In fact, the probability of gene duplication leading to degeneration must be very much higher than that leading to production of a new gene having some useful function.[11]

In addition, what is always overlooked is that the change in amino acid sequence, to give the protein its new function, must – by an extraordinary coincidence – be accompanied by changes in the regulatory sequences that ensure that the new protein is produced in the right place and / or at the right time. Let me illustrate what I mean by reference to the supposed evolution of the globins, which is easily the most commonly cited example of gene duplication in evolutionary textbooks.

It is proposed that at some point an early haemoglobin was duplicated: one copy retained its function for carrying oxygen in the blood, and the other evolved into myoglobin, which is a somewhat similar protein (although there are substantial differences) used in muscle to help extract oxygen from the blood for use by the muscle. What is completely ignored is that the substantial changes in amino acid sequence to change a haemoglobin into a myoglobin (which has a greater affinity for oxygen), in order to present an advantage that natural selection could favour, would need to have been accompanied (at more or less the same time) with changes in its regulatory sequence(s) such that the modified protein was produced in muscle rather than bone marrow (where red blood cells are produced). For example, a myoglobin present in red blood cells would be harmful because it would bind oxygen too tightly and not release it to the tissues.

At best gene duplication only shifts the problem back a stage; and it is applicable to only some genes. At some point the problem has to be faced of how the original genes arose.

3. Gene 'recruitment'

An issue related to gene duplication is that of 'recruitment'. Trying to come to terms with the problem of multiple interdependent proteins, where a biological structure requires several proteins, if some of them can be seen to be similar to other proteins (albeit with very different functions) then it is suggested that evolution has recruited or commandeered the original proteins into another function. For instance, a commonly cited example of irreducible complexity is the bacterial flagellum which operates like a small motor and propeller. Evolutionists have pointed out that the type III secretion system uses some similar proteins to the flagellum, and have suggested that the flagellum could have evolved from it.[12,13] However, as with the simpler case of gene duplication:

(a) Sequence homologies are exaggerated – with proteins being grouped into the same 'family' and assumed to be derived from a common source even if there is as little as 30 per cent similarity of sequence.[14] Whereas it is realistic to obtain one useful sequence from another only if it requires less than a handful of mutations (see later), or there is a series of biologically useful intermediates with only a few mutations required from one to the other.

(b) The changes in control sequences that are necessary to ensure that the modified proteins are produced when and where required in order to fulfil their new roles, are usually overlooked.

Natural selection in action

I have little doubt that the points I have just made are likely to seem rather theoretical to some readers, especially those for whom the biochemistry is new and rather unfamiliar territory. Perhaps some are thinking of various clear examples of evolution taking place and wondering – despite the apparent strength of the biochemical argument – whether these do not show that nature has, in fact, found a way around the difficulties, even if we do not yet know how. To answer this, I shall look at a couple of quite well-known examples of evolution.

Peppered moth

Before the middle of the nineteenth century the peppered moth was known only in a light-coloured (pale) form, but thereafter, as industrialisation spread, a dark (melanic) variety was found, and over the succeeding 50 years or so the species became predominantly dark-coloured, at least in industrial areas.

This was a clear case of natural selection taking place. The explanation was attributed to selective feeding by birds: in industrial areas, where tree trunks were dark, birds preferentially captured the pale variety, whereas in non-industrial areas they tended to select the melanic ones. The differential predation by birds accounted for the relative survival of the two forms, which in turn accounted for the shift in population from light to dark. And although the peppered moth is the best-known, similar changes in population were observed in well over 100 other species of moths and butterflies in industrial areas of the Northern Hemisphere. Interestingly, following improvements in air quality since the 1950s, there has been a gradual return of the pale variety. (In recent years, some doubt has been cast on whether bird predation is the main reason for the difference in survival of the different forms; but whether or not we know the correct explanation, there seems little doubt that natural selection was taking place.)

So what can we conclude from these observations? Undoubtedly the change in relative abundance of the pale and melanic forms is a clear demonstration of natural selection (whether due to differential bird predation or for other reasons). And the outcome – the change of predominant coloration depending on the environment – can certainly be seen as an adaptation. Also, in so far as the theory of evolution includes changes in gene frequencies as a result of natural selection, it is appropriate to use the term *evolution* to describe those changes.

However, we need to be quite clear about what we mean by *evolution* in cases such as these. So far as the moths are concerned, all that occurred was a change of the frequencies in the relevant populations of the gene(s) responsible for coloration. *Extrapolation beyond that is not justified.* For example, in a well-known textbook on evolution it is stated that, 'If the process that operated in the nineteenth century in a single species of moth had been continued for the thousands of millions of years since life originated, much larger evolutionary changes could be accomplished.'[15] This is a wholly unjustified statement. The 'process that operated in the nineteenth century' was natural selection operating on an existing pool of genes. The development of complex organisms from simple life forms would have required the *production of new genes* – an entirely different process from that demonstrated in the moths.

So the evidence regarding the moths provides *no insight at all* into the origin of genes, *no evidence whatever* of a way around the prohibitive improbability of useful macromolecules. Changes in gene frequencies are part of the evolutionary process, but only one part; it requires other completely different processes too in order to produce the genes in the first place.

Galapagos finches

The finches which Darwin observed on the Galapagos Islands illustrate a different kind of evolution. They are all quite similar – sparrow-like and dark brown or black – but have distinctive beaks which are associated with different foods and habitats. There are six ground finches which feed mainly on seeds, three tree finches which are insectivorous and one which is vegetarian, another two with habits like woodpeckers, and a warbler. It seemed incredible to Darwin that any creator would have individually made these similar species and far more likely that they had all descended from a common ancestor. He wrote of them: 'one might really fancy that from an original paucity of birds on this archipelago, one species had been taken and modified for different ends'.[16]

What appears to have happened is that the limited interbreeding between the different groups of birds on the various islands allowed distinctly different variations to arise, resulting in the original finch species diversifying and occupying different ecological niches. Eventually the various groups were sufficiently different to be regarded as distinct species, each adapted to a particular food and way of life. So here we have evolution in the sense of diversification, even to the point of one species splitting into several.

However, as with the moths, whilst it is appropriate to call these changes *evolution*, we need to be clear about what it has involved. And it seems that all that happened was that from an original finch population which had high genetic variability (a large gene pool), different species arose solely through the selection and segregation of different gene combinations from the original gene pool. Genetic studies have confirmed their close relationship. It is analogous to conventional domestic breeding (i.e. not including genetic modification): variations arise naturally through the mixing of genes in different ways in the course of reproduction, and breeders choose which of these to breed from; through repetition of this procedure, very different breeds can eventually be derived from a common stock. An excellent example of this is how all of the breeds of domestic dog have been derived by selection from the common wolf.[17] There is no doubt that many of the different dog breeds, if they had arisen in the wild, would have been regarded as different species. Yet all that has happened is that the genes in the original wolf stock have been segregated in different ways. Consequently, as with the moths, *none of this evolution of the finches has required the production of new genes.*

The limits of evolution

The foregoing examples clearly show that some evolution does occur – involving adaptation and/or diversification which may even lead to speciation. But, as I have already indicated, all of this evolution that actually occurs is entirely due to changing the frequency of, or segregating, existing genes in different ways.

What we do not see is evolution that requires the production of new genes, and hence there is no evidence that the problem posed by the improbability of obtaining new genes has been overcome.

Microevolution and macroevolution

Further, it also means that we are now in a position to clarify what we mean by *microevolution* and *macroevolution*. Traditionally, species were regarded as fixed and not capable of evolving at all. As evidence such as that mentioned above emerged, it became clear that some evolution does occur; and even those who reject the overall theory of evolution came to accept that some microevolution, though of limited extent, is possible, sometimes describing it as being 'within the natural range of variation' of the species concerned. It is not surprising that evolutionists see this as simply the thin end of the wedge and argue that macroevolution is no more than accumulated microevolution. However, it has become clear that a dividing line can – and should – be drawn: microevolution involves the mixing and/or segregation of genes which are already available, whereas macroevolution would require the origination of new genes. In other words, *the crucial distinction is not so much in the degree of morphological change* (consider the very wide range of sizes and shapes of different dog breeds), *but in the genetic basis for the change.*

The edge of evolution

What I have just written presents a fairly clear demarcation between evolution that is and is not possible; but the situation is not quite that clear-cut. In particular, it is important to note that I am not saying that no advantageous mutation whatever is possible.

The problem posed by molecular biology is that the origin of genes requires so many mutually compatible mutations (in order to get a useful sequence) that the chance of its happening is totally out of the question.

However, where an advantage can be attained by just one or two mutations, and provided the population is large enough (e.g.

of the order of billions, as is the case for insects and bacteria) then it is reasonable for an advantageous change in a gene to arise by mutation. This is the case for some instances of acquiring resistance to insecticides or antibiotics; although it should be noted that in many cases acquiring resistance involves only selection from the appropriate gene pool, not the modification of genes.[18]

Perhaps the most important point to note here is that this sort of advantageous mutation cannot be extrapolated to the production of new genes, or to change the function of a gene, unless only a few nucleotides need to be changed. For instance, even just to change a haemoglobin to a myoglobin would be realistic only if it could be achieved through a series of intermediates (with each conferring some advantage) where the step from one to the next is no more than two or perhaps three nucleotide changes. Once the step requires four or more, then it is beyond the bounds of reasonable possibility, no matter how large the population or years available.[19] Unfortunately, this sort of consideration is usually completely overlooked, with phylogenies (molecular family trees) freely showing jumps of tens of amino acid changes. And all of this has not taken into account the simultaneous changes in control sequence at the crucial change from a haemoglobin-like function to a myoglobin-like function, which in itself is probably too large a jump to occur at random.

Michael Behe explored this issue of what degree of evolution is possible in his book *The Edge of Evolution*, clearly demonstrating that any evolution achieved by mutation is very limited; and I direct readers who are interested in pursuing this issue further to that book. I will give just one short quote which sums up Behe's conclusion:

> The structural elegance of systems such as the cilium, the func-
> tional sophistication of the pathways that construct them, and the
> total lack of serious Darwinian explanation all point consistently
> to the same conclusion: They are far past the edge of evolution.
> Such coherent, complex, cellular systems did not arise by
> random mutations and natural selection any more than the Hoover
> Dam was built by the random accumulation of twigs, leaves, and
> mud.[20]

The essential genetic basis of variations

This leads me to point out a fundamental flaw in proposed scenarios for how new structures – such as an eye or feather – may have evolved. I shall illustrate it by reference to a well-publicised account of the supposed evolution of the eye which has been used widely to try to show that it would, after all, be quite easy for an eye to evolve.[21]

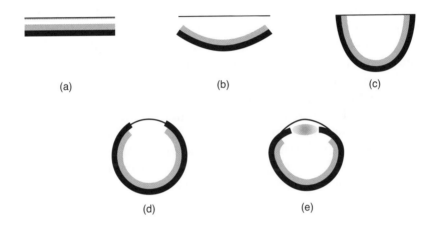

(a)   (b)   (c)

(d)   (e)

Figure 3   Key stages in a proposed evolution of the vertebrate eye (based on Nilsson and Pelger, 1994[21])

(a) Initial stage comprising a transparent cell layer, a light-sensitive cell layer (grey) and a dark-pigmented bottom cell layer (black). The first change is for the initially flat light-sensitive and pigmented layers to form a depression (b), which gradually deepens until it is as deep as it is wide (c), after which the neck contracts to resemble a pin-hole camera (d). After this a lens forms and gradually develops until it is able to focus an image on the pigmented layer (e).

The scenario illustrated in Figure 3 starts off from a patch of light-sensitive cells – which is a huge presumption in itself. It is then envisaged that an eye evolves first by a flat patch of cells becoming a depression, which gradually deepens into a small pit, the neck of which then narrows. Each of these stages, taking place over several generations, is driven by the advantage of increased optical acuity. When this stage has been reached, further improvement can be achieved only by addition of a lens, and the authors boldly assert that 'Even the weakest lens is better than no lens at all, so we can be confident that selection for increased resolution [i.e. improved optical acuity] will favour such a development all the way from no lens at all to a lens powerful enough to focus a sharp image on the retina.'

The totally unjustified assumption in this scenario is that if a variation will offer some advantage, then we can be sure that it will arise. No thought whatsoever is given to the crucial question of *how* those variations will arise. I think this blind spot (if you will excuse the pun) has arisen for two reasons.

First, before we knew about genetic and molecular mechanisms, it was thought that biological tissues were innately plastic in the sense that variations would arise spontaneously. Favourable ones could then be passed on, rather like the inheritance of acquired characteristics mentioned in the Introduction. However, we now know that the formation of morphological structures – whether it be an eye, feather or leaf – is not by some sort of vague plasticity, but through the closely orchestrated action of many genes. In other words, *new structures need appropriate new genes.*

The second reason arises from the fact that much variation is possible through the mixing of genes that are already available, which also seems to have lulled some biologists into overlooking that substantially new structures require new genes. This is illustrated by the fact that the above-mentioned authors' calculation of the rate of eye evolution is based on intentional domestic breeding (not even opportunistic natural selection!) *from an existing gene pool.* Whereas there can be no doubt at all that the evolution of an eye would require very many *new* genes – for several proteins used exclusively in the eye, and for the molecular mechanisms that construct the eye in the course of embryological development.

Fossils

Bearing in mind the above distinction between microevolution and macroevolution, we can now take a (necessarily brief) look at the fossil record. And I shall focus on what is probably the best-known example – the evolution of the horse.

Horse evolution

A simplified diagram of the various genera of horses, as they appear in the fossil record over the last 55 million years, is shown in Figure 4. The first to appear was *Hyracotherium*, which was about the size of a fox. It had three and four toes respectively on its hind- and forelimbs. Its teeth were relatively small, but clearly those of a herbivore, and it is thought to have fed primarily on leaves (browsing). Over the succeeding years various horse-like species appeared, generally becoming more like the modern horse, being larger, and having single toes and modifications of the teeth so that they were more suited to eating grass (grazing). This progression of horse species is widely seen as one of the best examples of evolution in the fossil record.

However, I suggest there are good reasons to think that this evolution was entirely due to the segregation into different combinations of genes that were available in *Hyracotherium*, and not through the production of new genes.

First, the changes in morphology are of limited degree – indicated by the fact that all of these horse species are classified within a single family, Equidea. And although evolutionary texts generally emphasise the gradual increase in size, some lines became even larger than modern horses, while others became very small. Similarly, although the general trend was for feet bones to become longer, some became shorter.

Second, all of the morphological changes were relatively minor modifications of characteristics already present in *Hyracotherium*. Even changes of the skull were only quantitative rather than qualitative, i.e. can be accounted for in terms of differential growth of various parts of the skull (termed allometry), rather than requiring novel features.

Third, and probably the strongest indication, is that the features used to distinguish the various horse species, such as the changes in toes, teeth and skull, 'evolved time and again in very different lineages of horses'.[22] And this included the genera (collectively

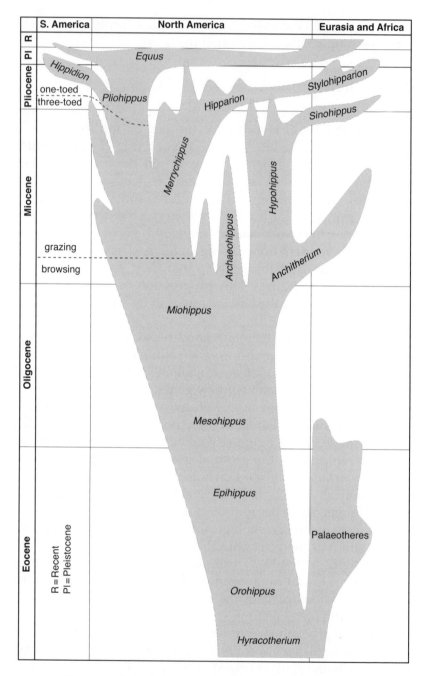

Figure 4   Principal genera in the ancestry of the horse

known as the Palaeotheres) that emerged in Europe during the Eocene, quite independently of those which arose much later in North America.

Now we could choose to believe that the same mutations arose independently in diverse lineages, perhaps persuading ourselves that the horse-like mammals had some sort of propensity for these particular mutations. But surely a much more credible explanation is that the genetic bases for these features were already available within *Hyracotherium*. Then, through a combination of random fluctuations and selection, in various lines appropriate gene combinations arose and the various traits emerged. That is, the evolution of the horse is analogous to the diversification of different species of Galapagos finches, or the derivation of different dog breeds from the wolf. In other words, *the evolution of the modern horse from Hyracotherium is an example of microevolution, not macroevolution.*

Abrupt appearance of new groups

However, this conclusion – that the evolution of the various horse species from a common ancestor which had considerable genetic variability – raises the question: Where did *Hyracotherium* come from? The answer is that it appears on the scene abruptly, not in a gradual evolutionary manner.

And, importantly, this is the pattern we see throughout the fossil record, although lack of space here prevents me from elaborating further examples. It is true of the founding species of all of the mammalian groups (orders), notably of the bats and whales, which are specialised for flight and marine life respectively; and of all the vertebrate classes (e.g. fish, amphibians, reptiles, birds, mammals). Indeed *all phyla* – such as the chordates (which includes the vertebrates), arthropods (which includes insects), molluscs, sponges and plant phyla – appear abruptly, and most of them in the relatively short period known as the Cambrian explosion.

It is commonly argued that, because we can see some evolution within the fossil record from a founding group, this justifies assuming that the founding group itself arose in a gradual evolutionary manner. But this is not so. Importantly, this pattern which we see in the fossil record of some evolution from a founding group which has extensive genetic variability, but of the sudden appearance of that founding group, is entirely consistent with the prohibitive improbability of new genes arising in an evolutionary way.

Homology

Morphological homology

One of the lines of evidence put forward in support of evolution is homology, by which is meant the similarities of structure between different groups of organisms. A prime example is the tetrapod limb. It is believed that the tetrapod leg, from its first appearance with the early amphibians, has been progressively modified to produce structures as diverse and specialised as a bird's wing, seal's flipper and human arm, all based on a common bone arrangement which is clearly discernible despite the very different overall shapes and functions. So the essence of homology is that the same structure in a common ancestor has, through the evolutionary process, been modified in different ways, to adapt it to different uses.

With this in mind, embryology acquired an important role in identifying and interpreting homologies; the point being that even if adult structures look rather different, if they are homologous then they may be traced to a common embryological source. Conversely, even if adult structures from two different species look similar, if they have developed from different embryological tissues then they would not normally be regarded as homologous but due to convergent evolution.

Although most evolutionary texts convey a consistent and hence persuasive picture of homology there are, in fact, many substantial anomalies. In particular, as we discover more of how tissues are formed embryologically, increasing doubt is being cast on much of the homology that has been perceived for so long at the morphological level.

Notably, in view of the importance attached to the apparent homology of the vertebrate skeleton, and the weight given to embryology for interpreting homology, it is especially relevant that vertebrae – major components of the vertebrate skeleton – form embryologically in significantly different ways for different classes of vertebrate (such as mammals, birds, amphibians and fish), and even from different groups of early embryonic cells.[23] This clearly implies that the vertebrae of these different vertebrate classes are not, in fact, homologous. Taking this further, in the course of embryological development the members of different classes of vertebrate pass through a similar-looking stage (called the phylotypic stage), which is seen as clear evidence of their common ancestry. However, what is confounding (from an evolutionary perspective) is that even though the phylotypic stage looks similar, and we would have expected it to be formed from a fertilised egg in substantially the same way, there is, in fact, remarkable diversity, including some fundamental anomalies. And there are similar anomalies in other phyla, not only the vertebrates. Raff, commenting on these anomalies, says:

> The process of early development from the egg to the phylotypic stage should be at least as conserved as the pattern of the phylotypic stage. One might reasonably expect mechanisms of early development to be especially resistant to modification because all subsequent development derives from early processes.[24]

So the fact that the phylotypic stages are formed in different ways *prima facie* at least undermines, if not completely negates, the notion that they are derived from a common ancestor. Indeed, non-homologies present an even clearer case *against* macroevolution than those based on the complexity of molecular biology or the abrupt appearance of major groups in the fossil record which might be regarded as based on gaps – the absence of a viable mechanism for generating new genes, or the absence of intermediates leading to founding groups.

Biochemical homology

As well as there being similarities on the large (morphological) scale – although, as we have seen, some of these are not actually homologous – we also see similarities at the biochemical level.

Notably, across most groups of organisms there is considerable similarity in their metabolic and genetic mechanisms, and this is widely seen as evidence of their common ancestry. In recent years we have also discovered marked similarities in the genes used to carry out various functions, notably many of those used in the course of embryological development. And this, too, is seen as further evidence in support of evolution.

However, we must recognise that there is also *significant contrary evidence*. Most readers will have heard of the human genome project. The first step was to sequence all of the DNA in our chromosomes, and we are now trying to figure out how it all works. In a major scientific paper which reported progress to date, the authors concluded that 'perhaps the biggest surprise' was that 'we have also encountered a remarkable excess of experimentally identified functional elements lacking evolutionary constraint, and these cannot be dismissed for technical reasons'.[25] In other words, whilst evolutionary rationale is that DNA sequences with a clear function should be resistant to change (be evolutionarily constrained) and hence be similar (homologous) within a group of species (such as the mammals), they found many cases where this is not the case, i.e. where the sequences are non-homologous.

In addition to these non-homologies, which challenge an evolutionary explanation, we are also discovering examples of where the similarities are *too close* for an evolutionary explanation! A particularly clear example of this is the embryological development of the eye. In the 1970s some biologists categorised the eyes of different groups of organisms according to embryonic origin and final structure, and thus determined where it was reasonable to infer that an eye had been inherited from one group to another, and where it had not.[26] They concluded that eyes must have evolved independently at least 40 different times, possibly up to 65. This result was used in part to try to convince us that it must not be so difficult to evolve an eye after all.

However, we have now discovered that even in species as different as insects and mammals, with very different kinds of eyes (compound and camera respectively), and whose evolution is thought have diverged so far back that their common ancestor did not have eyes, the embryological formation of the eyes uses remarkably similar genes (notably those called *eyeless* and *Pax6* respectively).

Even evolutionists accept that this is too good to be a coincidence. So their response, despite the morphological evidence that points to the eyes having independent origins, is to advocate that in fact their common ancestor must have had some sort of rudimentary eye which used the common gene in its formation, the use of which has persisted through the evolution of the different types of eyes. Unfortunately, this explanation is becoming increasingly difficult to sustain for the use of similar genes (such as *sine oculus* and *Six*) which have a role in the *later* stages of eye development in both types of species.

I agree that it is too much of a coincidence that the similar genes could have arisen independently and there must be a common source. But in the light of these facts, it at least raises the question whether the common source is not an ancestor, but a designer. That is, although my main reason for advocating that life must have had a designer is based on the specificity and complexity of molecular biology, the use of similar genes in embryological development provides further support for this view.

Common descent?

The most important issue is whether or not life could have evolved through exclusively natural processes – and it certainly seems to me that it could not. However, there is the secondary question of common descent which – if one accepts that natural processes are insufficient, and taking a Christian perspective – transmutes into the question of whether God created each new group of organisms *de novo* or by modification of a previously existing form. I mention this only because some writers see evidence of common descent as evidence that the theory of evolution as a whole is true. But this does not necessarily follow.

Evidence cited in support of common descent generally focuses on DNA sequences which apparently have no function, yet appear in different groups of organisms as if they had been inherited in the course of evolution. (The argument carries weight only if the features have no function, because if they have a use then this would be sufficient reason for their existence.) However, we need to be cautious about concluding that a particular feature is without a use. For example, because much of DNA consists of multiple repetitions of short sequences, for a long time we have thought it was of no use, and labelled it 'junk' DNA. But recently we realised that even these repeating sequences may have an important role in gene regulation.[27]

And on the opposite side of the coin are the non-homologies, especially of embryological development, which *prima facie* strongly contradict common descent. If I were to take falsifiability seriously on this issue, then I would need to give more weight to the non-homologies than the circumstantial evidence based on DNA sequences that may have no function. But probably, for me, the jury is still out on the question of common descent.

Design – some related issues

We like to put people in 'boxes'; but as with any other issue there is a broad spectrum of views, even among Christians, on the subject of evolution. So with this in mind, I emphasise that the views here are my own: I do not claim to be speaking for or representing any particular group; indeed, I know that some of my views regarding design are not shared by many who advocate ID. But I have the opportunity here of saying how I see it – so I'm taking it!

Design and science

1. To begin with I want to make it clear that I see 'design' essentially as a conclusion, or the most reasonable inference, from applying the scientific method to nature, not as an *alternative* to the scientific method.

In the absence of any natural processes by which life could realistically have arisen (and I do not mean just the origin of life, but also the origin of all of the major groups of life), at the very least we need to be open to the possibility that life appeared through non-natural or supernatural causes. (Unfortunately, this chapter must focus on the science of evolution, and there is no opportunity to unpack this, to expand on the distinction between what we mean by 'natural' and other processes.)

My own conclusion is stronger: it seems to me that the combined specificity and complexity of biology at the molecular level completely defies any realistic possibility of life arising 'naturally'. And it is not through lack of knowledge: what is so striking is that the more we learn about how biology works, the stronger the case becomes. Because on one hand our increased knowledge of molecular biology illustrates that perhaps biological life is completely reducible to physics and chemistry; but on the other, it is revealing how astonishingly complex the biology of life is – even some of its apparently 'simple' features – and hence how utterly inconceivable it is that it could have arisen naturally. (Please note the important distinction: accepting that the *functioning* of biology could be entirely accounted for in terms of the operation of natural processes, but rejecting the notion that those same biological systems could have *originated* through exclusively natural processes.)

Lest some interpret this as me falling into the trap of what Dawkins calls the Argument from Personal Incredulity,[28] I stress that this conclusion is not subjective, but largely objective, based on what we now know of molecular biology and the inability of natural processes to generate anything like the specificity and complexity that are required.

So, to repeat: I see 'design' essentially as a result of applying the scientific method to nature. I do not see it as a rival or alternative approach to carrying out science and, indeed, have doubts about the rationale of an 'ID research programme'.

Although I do not see ID as equivalent to a scientific theory, I think it is on an equivalent footing, especially in terms of being subject to revision or even complete falsification in the light of new scientific discoveries. I recognise that there is some tension here: on one hand holding to a design viewpoint because I think the evidence is overwhelming against any realistic possibility of there being a natural explanation for biology; yet on the other hand being open to the possibility that, despite my convictions, new discoveries could prove me wrong. However, if nothing else, it underlines that I hold my position on exclusively scientific grounds: I do not have a prior commitment or ulterior motive to reject evolution for non-scientific reasons.

2. Second, I think scientists are right to be concerned that being open to the possibility of 'design' as an explanation is in danger of being lazy and may inhibit scientific enquiry.

Nature appears designed. Although many are happy to accept this superficial conclusion, it is entirely appropriate to scrutinise it to see if natural processes could account for biological organisms. And even though the evidence is now clearly against it, I am not suggesting for a moment that scientists stop looking.

However, the objective of science is to explain how the universe operates (and came into being), and we should try not to have prejudices about what we find. So, for example, when we see homologies – whether morphological or biochemical – it is quite right to infer a common origin and at first presume this was a common natural origin. However, if the complexity of molecular biology cannot be accounted for by natural processes (whether or not there are homologies), it becomes reasonable to deduce that the source of the homology may be a common designer rather than a common ancestor. (It seems paradoxical that biologists are willing to accept the statistical argument that it is too unlikely for two proteins to arise by chance with similar sequences, but unwilling to give weight to the statistical argument that they are too unlikely to arise at all by chance.) Further, as already mentioned, some 'homologous' features are actually too similar for an evolutionary explanation, which again points to a common designer, rather than a common ancestor.

Scientists cannot legitimately rule out a designer *a priori*. As the philosopher Bertrand Russell wrote:

> This [design] argument has no formal logical defect; its premises are empirical and its conclusion professes to be reached in accordance with the usual canons of empirical inference. The question whether it is to be accepted or not turns, therefore, not on general metaphysical questions, but on comparatively detailed considerations.[29]

Indeed it is scientists who are best equipped to examine those 'detailed considerations'.

So, although scientists are right to be concerned that being open to the possibility of design may blunt scientific enquiry, we cannot turn this on its head and conclude that biology is not the result of design.

Naturalism

'When I use a word, it means just what I choose it to mean', said Humpty Dumpty. And one of the problems with naturalism is that it means different things to different people – even when we try to distinguish between 'ideological' and 'methodological' naturalism. (The fact that I prefer the term *ideological naturalism* to the more commonly used *ontological naturalism*, at least in this context, is further indication of this minefield which I cannot explore here.)

Perhaps the main point I want to make is that it seems to me unavoidable for the practising scientist to presume 'methodological naturalism'. Science is about finding out how the universe works; and without the presumption of a consistent cause and effect, I do not see how a scientist can even begin to design an experiment. Some have argued that methodological naturalism implies ontological naturalism,[30] and this is perhaps the reason why many ID proponents reject methodological naturalism; but I think that is unfortunate, for the reason I have just given.

However, whilst accepting that in order to pursue scientific enquiry it is necessary to presume methodological naturalism, I think that presumption must be open to review in the light of what is discovered. Whether or not naturalism holds true is an empirical question. (The problem of induction illustrates that we cannot prove naturalism philosophically.[31])

Another way of looking at this is to see naturalism itself as a scientific theory. Perhaps it is the earliest – we generally credit the classical Greeks with being the first to propose that the world operates in conformity with natural laws, rather than at the whim of the gods, and thus began the scientific study of nature. And it seems to be the most fundamental: as I have just noted, without the presumption of methodological naturalism we cannot do science. If so, then, like any scientific theory, naturalism cannot be assumed to be true, but must be open to falsification in the light of observation and experience.

So, whilst it is reasonable, if not essential, that scientists adopt methodological naturalism in their approach, there must also be this tension that perhaps their discoveries will reveal exceptions. And it seems to me that the origin of biology poses such counter-evidence.

Design and theology

Finally – although this should more properly be in a chapter dealing with theological rather than scientific issues – I shall comment briefly on the theology of ID.

It is unfortunate that some writers have denounced ID as implying a poor theology, specifically of the relationship between God and the cosmos. I disagree strongly, and it seems to me that such a criticism can be made only by misrepresenting the ID position. The objection seems to be that ID proponents, whilst accepting that natural processes can account for the vast majority of natural phenomena but identifying instances where they cannot, are in some way saying that God is only involved in the latter but not the former.

This is certainly *not* my view, nor of other Christian ID proponents I know. On the contrary, our view is that God is immanently involved with the entirety of nature; and that even 'natural laws' operate consistently only by His will (and so ultimately there is no distinction between the natural and the supernatural). And it is inappropriate to think of God 'intervening' in nature at specific points, because He is involved in *all* places *all* of the time.

Nevertheless, there are times when God acts in an unusual or non-normal way; and, by their very nature, such instances reveal God's hand more readily than in the normal. The miracles performed by Jesus are such examples – and it is clearly biblical to regard them as signs of God at work in a special way (notably in John's gospel) – especially the resurrection. The Bible also clearly portrays the creation itself as evidence of God's handiwork. So it seems entirely biblical to say that God's hand is also especially evident in the creation of life.

Notes

1. Scientific notation: $10^n = 10$ multiplied by itself 'n' times; so $100 = 10^2$, $1000 = 10^3$, etc.; and 10^{80} multiplied by $10^{17} = 10^{97}$.
2. K. Popper, *The Logic of Scientific Discovery* (New York: Basic Books, 1959).
3. R. Dawkins, *The God Delusion* (London: Bantam Press, 2006), p. 121. My emphasis.
4. R. Dawkins, *The Blind Watchmaker* (London: Penguin Books, 1991), ch. 4.
5. For a not too technical description of protein folding – its dependence on the correct amino acid sequence, and its importance for the protein to have biological activity – see the Wikipedia article at http://en.wikipedia.org/wiki/Protein_folding.
6. J.M. Berg, J.L. Tymoczko and L. Stryer, *Biochemistry* (New York: W.H. Freeman, 6th edn, 2007), p. 55.
7. D.A. Axe, 'Estimating the Prevalence of Protein Sequences Adopting Functional Enzyme Folds', *Journal of Molecular Biology* 341 (2004): pp. 1295–315.
8. M.J. Behe, *Darwin's Black Box* (New York: The Free Press, 1996).
9. J. Kyte, *Structure in Protein Chemistry* (New York: Garland Publishing, 1995), p. 243.
10. M. Strickberger, *Evolution* (Boston: Jones & Bartlett Publishers, 2nd edn, 1990).
11. M. Kimura, *The neutral theory of molecular evolution* (Cambridge: Cambridge University Press, 1983), p. 316.
12. M.J. Pallen, 'Evolutionary links between FliH/YscL-like proteins from bacterial type III secretion systems and second-stalk components of the F_oF_1 and vacuolar ATPases', *Protein Science* 15 (2006), pp. 935–41.
13. N.J. Matzke, 'Evolution in (Brownian) space: a model for the origin of the bacterial flagellum' (2006) www.talkdesign.org/faqs/flagellum.html#update.
14. H. Lodish et al., *Molecular Cell Biology* (New York: W.H. Freeman, 6th edn, 2007), p. 55.
15. M. Ridley, *Evolution* (Cambridge, MA: Blackwell Science, 2nd edn, 1996), p. 73.

[16] C. Darwin, *The Voyage of the Beagle: Journal of Researches Into the Natural History and Geology of the Countries Visited During the Voyage of HMS Beagle Round the World* (New York: Modern Library, 2001).

[17] Some variations, such as extremely short legs, may arise through mutation – but only by corrupting a viable gene, not through producing a new one – similar to achondroplasia in humans.

[18] D.W. Swift, *Evolution under the microscope* (Stirling: Leighton Academic Press, 2002), ch. 9.

[19] Swift, *Evolution*, ch. 9.

[20] M.J. Behe, *The Edge of Evolution* (New York: The Free Press, 2007), p. 102.

[21] Dan-Erik Nilsson and S. Pelger, 'A pessimistic estimate of the time required for an eye to evolve', *Proceedings of the Royal Society of London Series B – Biological Sciences* 256 (1994), pp. 53–8.

[22] A. Forsten, 'Horse diversity through the ages', *Biological Reviews of the Cambridge Philosophical Society* 64 (1989), pp. 279–304.

[23] K.V. Kardong, *Vertebrates: Comparative anatomy, function, evolution* (Boston: McGraw-Hill Publishing Co., 3rd edn, 2005).

[24] R. Raff, 'Larval homologies and radical evolutionary changes in early development', in *Homology*, Proceedings of Novartis Foundation Symposium 222, 21–23 July 1998 (eds B.K. Hall, G. Bock and G. Cardew; Chichester: John Wiley & Sons, 1999), p. 111.

[25] The ENCODE Project Consortium, 'Identification and analysis of functional elements in 1% of the human genome by the ENCODE pilot project', *Nature* 447 (2007), pp. 799–816.

[26] L.V. Salvini-Plawen and E. Mayr, 'On the evolution of photoreceptors and eyes', *Evolutionary Biology* 10 (1976), pp. 207–76.

[27] ENCODE, 'Identification', pp. 799–816.

[28] Dawkins, *Watchmaker*, ch. 2.

[29] B. Russell, *A History of Western Philosophy* (London: Routledge, 2000), p. 570.

[30] B. Forrest, 'Methodological Naturalism and Philosophical Naturalism: Clarifying the Connection', *Philo* 3(2) (2000), pp. 7–29.

[31] No matter how many times a scientific 'law' seems to hold, and even if we know of no exceptions, we cannot prove that it always will.

6

A Scientific Case for Neo-Darwinism

GRAEME FINLAY

The last tsar and tsarina of Russia were murdered in 1918 during the Bolshevik Revolution. The fate of their bodies remained unknown until 1989, when the location of a possible burial site in Yekaterinburg (Siberia) came to light. In 1991, human remains were exhumed from a mass grave, and DNA was extracted from bone samples. DNA analysis showed that the bones belonged to a couple and three females who were their daughters, and that the parents were the tsar and tsarina. And DNA from the tsarina's remains matched that of her living grandnephew, the Duke of Edinburgh.[1]

This type of story is now commonplace. DNA analysis is routinely used in criminal trials to identify criminals and exonerate people unjustly charged with crimes. DNA evidence brings closure to otherwise irresolvable forensic mysteries. If only a similar revolution could bring resolution to the seemingly endless controversy over evolution. In this chapter I will describe how such a revolution has come. And it involves the study of DNA markers. Just as DNA evidence establishes paternity in the courts, so it establishes that different species of organisms share common ancestry.

1. An overview

Biologists list several strands of evidence for evolution.[2] Some of these, considered separately, may be susceptible to other explanations. Taken together, however, they converge to provide a mutually supporting evidential framework. For example, the large-scale movement of the earth's continents was once controversial. But it has been established through multiple intersecting lines of evidence: the similarity of rocks found in South America and Africa; the distribution of volcanoes; and direct measurements of continental movement (five to ten centimetres per year). We take cumulative evidence seriously.

Evidence for evolution comes from two basic approaches. We can study the fossilised remains of organisms that once lived on earth, and observe how their shapes changed over time (the historical approach). And we can compare features of living organisms in order to infer how they came to possess similarities and differences (the comparative approach).

1.1 The historical approach

The progressive development of living forms as recorded in the fossil record is compatible with the concept of biological evolution. For example, a fossil fish with lungs and bony fins (complete with elbow and wrist joints) called *Tiktaalik* was discovered in 2004. *Tiktaalik* may be similar to creatures that made the transition from sea to land.[2]

---

chromosome   A single DNA molecule and its associated proteins; it is visible as a compact structure when cells divide. We have twenty-three pairs of chromosomes and each has a characteristic appearance.

Eocene   An era 55–34 million years ago when many modern forms of mammal appeared.

genera   Families of similar species.

Mesozoic   An era that ended 65 million years ago, that spans the age of dinosaurs (including the Triassic, Jurassic and Cretaceous eras) when the earliest mammals lived.

Oligocene   An era 34–24 million years ago.

species   Populations of organisms that can freely interbreed.

The fossil record is notoriously incomplete. Fossilisation occurs haphazardly and only under particular conditions. Even so, the transition from pre-mammalian forms into mammalian forms has been 'richly documented' and our understanding of it 'has been rapidly re-written by recent discoveries of very informative fossils'. The *number* of identified mammalian fossil genera has increased explosively in the past few years. In 1979, only 116 genera were known from the Mesozoic (dinosaur) era. By 2007, the number had increased to 310 genera.[3]

The *quality* of available fossils has also greatly increased. Eighteen Mesozoic mammals are known from nearly complete skeletons, and twice that number from well-preserved skulls. Mesozoic mammals came in an extensive diversity of specialised forms. They operated as diggers and ant- or termite-eaters, predators and scavengers, tree-climbers, gliders and fliers.[3] Indeed, the Mesozoic mammal *Maelestes* was described only in 2007.[4]

The Eocene fossil *Indohyus* links terrestrial mammals with whales, and was described in 2007. The primitive bat fossil *Onychonycteris* was described in 2008. The Oligocene fossil *Aetiocetus* represents a step in the development of filter feeding in baleen whales, because it possessed both baleen and teeth, and was analysed in 2008. Palaeontology, as they say, rocks![5]

1.2 The comparative approach

When we compare living organisms, we note that certain plants and animals are endemic to a restricted geographical range. Australia is known for its marsupials, for example. This distribution is compatible with the hypothesis that ancestral species lived within regional boundaries (continents, islands, lakes) and subsequently diversified into many species that fulfil all kinds of ecological roles.

Different species may possess anatomical features in common. The bones of a bat's wing, a cow's leg and the human arm share an underlying pattern that is evidence that such species are related, and that they have evolved from a common (now extinct) ancestor in which the basic anatomical pattern was already present.

Certain species of organisms possess chromosome sets that look very similar to those of other species. The chromosome set of one mammal species can be rearranged into that of another by cutting-and-pasting parts of chromosomes. Such rearranging of chromosomes reflects natural events. The appearance of the chromosome sets of extinct ancestors can be inferred with some confidence.[6]

Species of organisms vary in the degree of similarity of their DNA sequences. For example, it might be expected that the DNA sequences of different species of bears are more closely related to each other than they are to the DNA sequences of ruminant herbivores. Comparisons of aligned DNA sequences from different organisms thus indicate evolutionary relatedness. These statistical approaches are very useful in constructing family trees of species, but can (and at times do) mislead. Nevertheless, as more extensive databases of DNA sequences become available, such analyses become more reliable, as demonstrated by recent impressive animal and mammal family trees.[7]

Christians should be very comfortable with this type of comparative analysis. Thousands of old biblical manuscripts exist. Manuscripts are just like DNA sequences, because they accumulate variations ('mutate' due to copyists' errors) each time they are copied. They evolve into different families. By lining them up against one another, textual critics have derived the wording of the original text (the unique 'common ancestor') from which all existing manuscripts are derived. We are very confident that we can get close to the original text of the New Testament. We should be equally confident about the ability to infer relatedness of species from their genetic 'texts'.

2. Evidence for common descent

In what follows, I will describe an emerging field that strikingly illuminates our evolutionary past. Darwin knew no genetics, and yet it is genetics – especially the study of *particular features* of the genome – that has amply vindicated the Darwinian revolution. I will discuss human genetics because I work in a medical school, and because we are most interested in our own species. If we

DNA Deoxyribonucleic acid, the thread-like genetic material of all organisms apart from some viruses, which contains genetic information embodied in the order of four chemical letters (A, C, G, T).

gene a segment (or series of segments) of DNA that can be copied into an RNA molecule that in turn directs the production of proteins, or regulates cell functions.

genome the sum total of genetic information, embodied in DNA, that specifies the form and function of an organism.

leukaemia a cancer of blood cells.

retrovirus a type of virus that copies its genetic material from RNA 'backwards' into DNA when it invades cells; it uses a virally encoded enzyme called reverse transcriptase.

reverse transcriptase an enzyme of retroviruses and jumping genes that copies RNA into DNA (the reverse of what cells do).

reverse transcription the copying of an RNA molecule into DNA.

RNA ribonucleic acid, a thread-like molecule that is related to DNA and that is copied from DNA in cells.

target site duplication a duplication of a short segment of DNA (typically up to 20 bases long) that defines the point at which a unit of retroviral or jumping gene DNA has integrated into cellular DNA.

can satisfy ourselves that we have evolved from extinct ancestral species, then we will be less inclined to argue about moths. My discussion of medical genetics may seem like a diversion, but please be patient: it will lead back inexorably to the study of our evolutionary history.

When I started out as a cell biologist engaged in cancer research in the early 1980s I had little interest in controversies over evolution. Evolutionary biology seemed to be a morass of irresolvable conflict. I was fascinated rather by the power of molecular biology to throw light on the mechanisms of life. My attention was focused on the molecular biological revolution in our understanding of cancer. Almost every week radically new insights were being reported. We were learning how cancer developed when important genes were deranged by mutations. Genes that normally activate cell multiplication were transformed into disruptive *oncogenes*. Genes that normally restrain cell multiplication (*tumour suppressor genes*) were disabled.

Many such mutations are rare or unique. It has been shown repeatedly that all the cancer cells that populate a particular tumour possess common mutations. It follows that those millions of cancer cells are descended from the *single* cell in which each of those very particular mutations occurred. Such mutations establish that cancers arise from one deviant cell. Several analogies illustrate this:

- Any teacher recognises the value of mistakes when marking essays. If two students submit essays that contain the same set of highly original spelling or grammatical mistakes, then one suspects plagiarism. There is an infinite number of ways of abusing language, and it is very unlikely that the same set of abuses occurred independently in the work of two (or more) students. Conclusion: one student has copied from the other.

- If two computer programs contain the same sequence of computer instructions, it may be impossible to assert whether one is a copy of the other, because there may be only one way of achieving the intended goal. But if the two programs contain the same comment lines (perhaps with shared spelling mistakes) it is almost certain that one is a copy of the other, because the comment lines are for the convenience of the (human) programmers and have no effect on the function of the program.

- A few years ago a scientist called Charles Dinarello accused the staff of a biotech company (Immunex) of stealing the genetic sequence of a gene he had discovered, cloned and sequenced. The company claimed that it had isolated the gene, and was attempting to patent it. The issue was settled when Dinarello found that his original sequence contained seven errors and all the errors were present in the sequence Immunex claimed as their own! Immunex had been caught out and paid US$21 million out of court.[8]

Analogously, the DNA we have inherited is full of novel 'errors' in the form of rare mutations. Many of these are shared with other species. Each genomic 'error' that is shared by multiple species has been copied from the one ancestor in which that 'error' arose.

2.1 Retroviruses in cancer

When I was a student I heard a famous virologist argue that viruses would never be shown to cause human cancers. But from about 1980 I read with fascination how several types of viruses drove cancer development. The most extraordinary of these were the retroviruses. A retrovirus of special interest was the human T-cell leukaemia virus (HTLV-1) that induced aggressive leukaemias in humans. Up to twenty million people worldwide may be infected with this virus, and one per cent of them may develop leukaemia.

Retroviruses are cunning parasites. The infective virus particle contains genetic material in the form of RNA. When a cell is

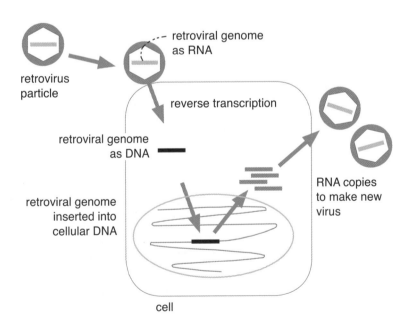

Figure 1 Retroviral infection

infected, this genetic material is copied 'backwards' from RNA into DNA by a viral enzyme called a *reverse transcriptase*. Another viral enzyme selects a short sequence of bases in the chromosomal DNA of the infected (host) cell, and cuts the DNA. This creates a gap into which the viral DNA is inserted. The resulting viral DNA insert becomes part of the chromosome and is passed on to all future generations of cells. Retroviral inserts are recognisable by their organisation and characteristic set of genes. Directly flanking the retroviral insert is a short duplication of host cell DNA (the tell-tale *target site duplication*) (Figures 1 and 2).

When retroviruses such as HTLV-1 infect an individual, each infected cell acquires its own unique pattern of retroviral DNA inserts. This pattern arises because insertion events occur largely at random into myriad sites scattered throughout the genome.[10]

But (years later) if a leukaemia arises as a result of the infection, *every* leukaemic cell will have the *same* retroviral DNA insert located at *precisely* the same site in its genome (although no two tumours will have the same insert). This pattern arises because

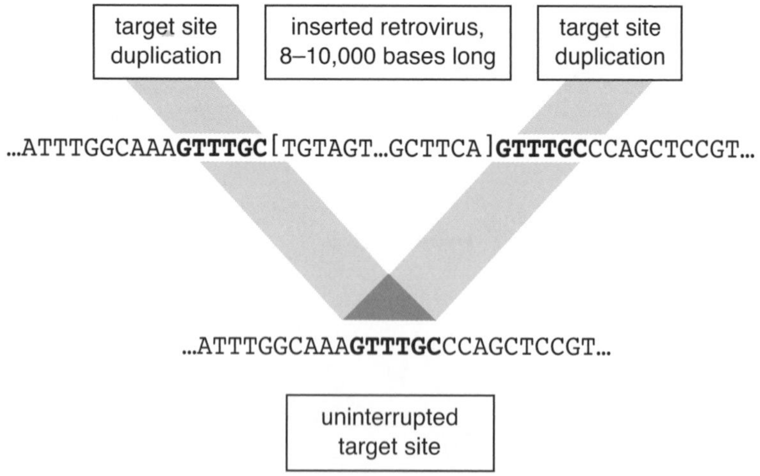

Figure 2   An example of a retroviral insertion
Lower sequence: part of the DNA of a normal cell.
Upper sequence: the product of a retroviral insertion in a tumour cell.
The target site and its duplications are in bold.[9]

one cell harbouring *one particular retroviral insert* became the progenitor of *every* cell that comprised the cancer. The inserted retrovirus directed this cell and its offspring into a programme of uncontrolled multiplication, producing an expanding population of descendants, all of which *inherited* the original inserted retrovirus (Figure 3).[11]

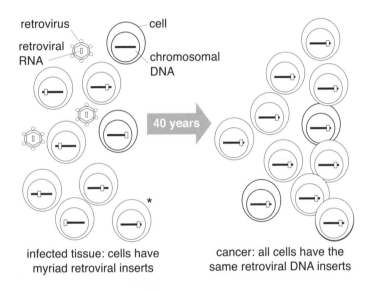

infected tissue: cells have myriad retroviral inserts

cancer: all cells have the same retroviral DNA inserts

Figure 3   Unique insertion sites show how cancers arise from a single progenitor cell

Small boxes represent the retroviral DNA insert. The cell marked by an asterisk is the progenitor of the cancer.

2.2   *Inherited retroviruses*

Big surprises were ahead. As the study of retroviruses gained momentum, scientists discovered that many creatures, including humans, possess segments of retroviral DNA as an integral part of their genomes. Retroviral DNA inserts are widely distributed through our chromosomal DNA. We did not acquire them by infection with virus particles. We inherited them from our parents

ape a class of higher primate including the great apes (humans, chimps and bonobos, gorillas and orang-utans) and lesser apes (gibbons and siamangs).

bases the chemical 'letters' that spell out our genetic information, and that are abbreviated as A, C, G and T.

endogenous retrovirus the genetic material of a retrovirus (typically 8–10,000 bases long) that has been inserted into chromosomal DNA and transmitted as part of the genome of a species.

ERV endogenous retrovirus

germ-line the cells that are dedicated to producing eggs and sperm, and that pass their genetic material to future generations.

New World Monkeys monkeys that live in the Americas, including the marmoset, spider monkey, squirrel monkey and owl monkey.

Old World Monkeys monkeys that live in the Eurasian-African land mass, including macaques and baboons.

in the same way that we inherited our genes. These segments of resident retroviral DNA are called *endogenous retroviruses* (ERVs). These ERVs have accumulated mutations and are inactive genetic fossils.

The Human Genome Project revealed the extent to which ERVs have colonised our genome. This big science project set out to determine the order (or *sequence*) of the four chemical letters (*bases*) in the human genome. When the sequence of the 3,000,000,000 bases that comprise our genome had been determined, scientists performed computer searches for ERVs and their relatives. They found at least 400,000 individual ERV inserts. These are classifiable into four broad classes, and at least 200 families, and they constitute eight per cent of our DNA.[12] Regardless of our ethnicity, we are one-twelfth virus!

The ERV inserts were added to the DNA of our forbears when retroviruses invaded germ-line cells that contain the DNA that is transmitted to future generations. Strikingly, all of us have inherited essentially the *same* set of ERVs as part of our genetic

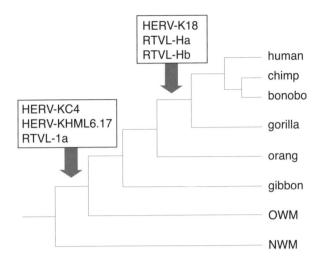

Figure 4   Primate relationships ascertained from the distribution of six ERVs in the genomes of apes and monkeys[14]

endowment. Each one of this multitude of ERVs occurs at precisely the *same* place in the genomes of all human beings. This indicates that the germ-line cells that suffered the original invasion of retroviral DNA were ancestral to all of us. When did the common ancestor(s) live?

In the 1980s some reports suggested that humans and chimpanzees possessed ERVs at the same locations in their respective genomes.[13] At that time it was not established that the ERVs were precisely the same in the two species, but it looked like it. The implications of these reports were huge. If humans and chimps did, in fact, possess the same ERV inserts, then both *species* must be co-inheritors of a collection of ERVs, each of which entered the primate germ-line in one unique insertion event. The presence of a shared (but uniquely arising) ERV would establish that humans and chimps are the descendants of a common ancestor.

The fact that humans and chimps share particular ERVs was confirmed by a study of six human ERVs, all of which are present in the DNA of humans and chimps, and indeed of other primates. Three of the ERVs are present only in humans, chimps, bonobos and gorillas, and therefore entered primate germ-line DNA in an ancestor of the African great apes. The other three are present in the apes and Old World Monkeys, but not New World Monkeys. They entered primate germ-line DNA in an ape-Old World Monkey ancestor (Figure 4).[14]

The insertion site of one particular ERV is given as an example (Figure 5).[14,15] It is hugely improbable that an ERV of one particular type would insert independently into the same DNA site of individual ancestors of all four African great ape species (and of no other species). In *precisely* the same way as all the cells comprising an HTLV-1-induced leukaemia are known to arise from one progenitor cell, the presence of the unique ERV flanked by the unique target site duplication establishes that the African great apes are descended from a single ancestral reproductive cell of a single individual of a single species.

Confirmatory studies defined the distribution of particular ERVs in multiple primate species (Figure 6). I confess to feelings of sheer wonderment when viewing such genetic data. Figure 6 confronts us with seven blocks of DNA sequence, each aligned from multiple species. Each DNA sequence alignment can be seen unambiguously to share the ERV insert, complete with its defining target site duplication (providing confirmation that the ERV arose by the standard retroviral mechanism (Figure 1)). Inscribed in

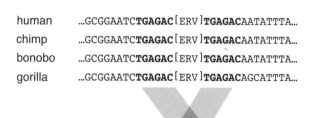

human   ...GCGGAATC**TGAGAC**[ERV]**TGAGAC**AATATTTA...

chimp   ...GCGGAATC**TGAGAC**[ERV]**TGAGAC**AATATTTA...

bonobo   ...GCGGAATC**TGAGAC**[ERV]**TGAGAC**AATATTTA...

gorilla   ...GCGGAATC**TGAGAC**[ERV]**TGAGAC**AGCATTTA...

orang   ...GCGGAATC**TGAGAC**AATATTTA...

Figure 5   The insertion site of an ERV

Short segments of DNA sequence are shown for five primate species. The sequence for the orang-utan includes the undisturbed target site (bold). The sequences for the African great apes show the presence of an ERV (called K18 or K110), flanked by duplications of the target site (bold).[14,15]

ERV	species	insertion site with target site duplication, **bold**
K105	human	...TCTG**GAATTC**[ERV]**GAATTC**TATG...
	chimp	...TCTG**GAATTC**[ERV]**GAATTC**TATG...
	bonobo	...TCTG**GAATTC**[ERV]**GAATTC**TATG...
H/env59	human	...AAC**AATATT**[ERV]**ATATT**ATGTT...
	chimp	...AAC**AATATT**[ERV]**ATATT**ATGTT...
	gorilla	...AAC**AATATT**[ERV]**ATAT**- --GTT...
	orang-utan	...AAC**AATATT**[ERV]**ATATT**ATGTT...
	gibbon	...AAGC**AATATT** ATGTT...
H/env60	human	...TCTCC**AAATA**[ERV]**AAATA**TACTA...
	chimp	...TCTCC**AAATA**[ERV]**AAATA**TACTA...
	gorilla	...TCTCC**AAATA**[ERV]**AAATA**TACTA...
	orang-utan	...TCTCC**AAATA**[ERV]**AAATA**TACTA...
	gibbon	...TCTCC**AAATA** TACTA...
H/env62	human	...GTTAT**CCAAC**[ERV]**CAAAC**TAAAT...
	chimp	...GTTAT**CCAAC**[ERV]**CAAAC**TAAAT...
	gorilla	...GTTAT**CCAAC**[ERV]**CCAAC**TAAAT...
	orang-utan	...GTTAT**CCAAC** TAAAT...
β-globin gene	human	...ATTA**GTAT**[ERV]**GTAT**GTCA...
	chimp	...ATTA**GTAT**[ERV]**GTAT**GTCA...
	gorilla	...ATTA**GTAT**[ERV]**GTAT**GTCA...
	orang-utan	...ATTA**GTAT**[ERV]**GTAT**GTCA...
	gibbon	...ATTA**GTAT** GTCA...
	OWM species	...ATTA**GTAT** GTCA...
axin gene	human	...CACC**CCGG**[ERV]**CCGG**GACG...
	chimp	...CACC**CCGG**[ERV]**CCGG**GACG...
	gorilla	...CACC**CCGG**[ERV]**CCGG**GACG...
	orang-utan	...CACC**CCGG**[ERV]**CCGG**GACG...
	gibbon	...CACC**CCGG** GACG...
	OWM species	...CACC**CCGG** GACG...
RNU2 gene	human	...AGCTG**AGATAA**[ERV]**AGATAA**GATAT...
	chimp	...AGCCG**AGATAA**[ERV]**AGATAA**GATAT...
	gorilla	...AGCCG**AGATAA**[ERV]**AGATAA**GATAT...
	orang-utan	...AGCCG**AGATAA**[ERV]**AGATAA**GATAT...
	baboon	...AATCG**AGATAA**[ERV]**AGGTAA**GATAT...

Figure 6   **Insertion sites of seven ERVs**

Target sites and their duplications are in **bold**. *Sequences from species lacking inserts show gaps to allow alignment of sequence.*[15,16] *OWM, Old World Monkey; –, deleted bases* the DNA we carry – present in a hair or a drop of saliva – is the evidence that removes all uncertainty about our evolutionary origins. All humans, chimps, bonobos and gorillas are descended from one individual of a long-extinct species of ape that busied itself on the plains of Africa a few million years ago. Patterns of ERV insertion conform overwhelmingly to the established primate family tree.[15,16]

The definitive 'experiments' were done by sequencing the genomes of other primates. The chimpanzee genome study[17] was published in 2005 and that of the rhesus macaque[18] in 2007. Researchers could now compare the insertion site of *every* ERV in the human, chimp and macaque genomes. The results were amazing. At least 99.9 per cent of all the ERVs found in our genome are shared with chimps, and the 'great majority' with macaques (Table 1). The few ERVs that are peculiar to our genome are very recent additions. They inserted into the genomes of ancestors that lived after our lineage separated from the chimp lineage.

Let's take stock. One of Darwin's fundamental proposals was that multiple species share common ancestry. The further one peers back in time, the more species are linked. The study of ERVs has established that this is true in the case of a species of particular

Table 1   ERVs in the human genome[12,17,18]

Class of ERV	Number of ERVs in human genome			
	Total	Unique to human	Shared with chimp	Shared with macaque
Class I	112,000	5	Essentially all	'great majority'
Class II	8,000	100	99%	
Class III	83,000	None	All	
Class IV	240,000	None	All	

interest to us: *Homo sapiens*. Eight per cent of our DNA has arisen from the insertion of 400,000 segments of retroviral DNA. At least 99 per cent of these inserts are shared with our closest relative, the chimp. Most of them are shared with Old World Monkeys. Each instance of an ERV arises from a unique event. We and other species share particular ERVs only because we have inherited them from the unique common ancestor in which each arose. This establishes the truth of speciation and of macroevolution. Human descent from (now extinct) ape and monkey progenitors is an unassailable finding of genome research. This DNA evidence has vastly more weight than that which would induce a judge to lock a man up for life!

2.3 *Jumping genes*

The study of our genome has provided more big surprises. ERVs and their ilk are not the only unruly segments of DNA that reside in our genome. Many other defined segments of DNA (or *elements*) with the capacity to replicate themselves are present as part of the human genome. They are collectively called *jumping genes* or *transposable elements*, and are classifiable into nearly 1,000 different types. Some of their features are indicated below:

Alu element a class of jumping gene, 300 bases long and found only in primates, that replicates though an RNA intermediate.

element a length of DNA sequence that is identifiable as a functional unit, such as a jumping gene, or a regulatory element (a defined segment of DNA that controls the activity of genes).

jumping gene a defined length of DNA with the capacity to copy-and-paste itself into new sites in the genome, without any regard for the integrity of the genome.

LINE-1 element a class of jumping gene, up to 6,000 bases long and found in all mammals, that replicates though an RNA intermediate.

simian primates of the ape and monkey groups.

- They are recognisable as defined lengths of DNA sequence.
- They exist only within cells, and are transmitted from generation to generation as an integral part of an organism's genome.
- They contain the genetic information that allows them to reproduce themselves by a copy-and-paste mechanism, for which they co-opt cellular enzymes. They act as miniature genomes-within-a-genome.
- They act haphazardly and may cause damage when they insert themselves into new sites.
- They have propagated to very high numbers in primate genomes. The DNA that we have inherited contains 2,700,000 segments of inserted jumping gene DNA in addition to ERVs and their relations. ERVs and jumping genes comprise half of our genome.

Some classes of these jumping genes have 'inhabited' genomes since deep primeval history. Other classes are restricted to (and presumably arose within) particular groups of organisms. We know that different classes have proliferated at different times during the formation of the human genome, because of the way examples of younger classes have inserted into examples of older classes.[19] This hierarchical pattern of the activities of jumping gene families provides a vast panorama of our genomic history.

The analogy below illustrates how these inserts accumulate.

Jumping genes are found in the genomes of most species and new copies insert randomly into the DNA.

⇩ copy-and-paste '*insert*'

Jump*insert*ing genes are found in the genomes of m*insert*ost species and n*insert*ew copies insert randomly into the D*insert*NA

⇩ add new inserts (bold)

Jum*insert*ping **ginsert**enes are**insert** found in the genomes of m*insert***insert***t*ost species and n*insert*ew copies insert randomly into the D*ins***insert***ert*NA

I will concentrate on those classes of jumping gene that copy-and-paste themselves by a two-step process involving an RNA intermediate (Figure 7). In the first step, a parent element that is resident in chromosomal DNA is copied into a free-floating RNA copy. This RNA directs the production of proteins needed for the element's propagation. One of these proteins is a reverse transcriptase (the enzyme that copies RNA 'backwards' into DNA). In the second step, the RNA molecule is reverse-transcribed into a new DNA copy, which is inserted elsewhere in the genome as a daughter element.

2.4 Jumping genes in medical genetics

The two most abundant classes of jumping gene in our genome are known as LINE-1 and Alu elements. Most classes of jumping gene are comprised entirely of inactive fossils, but LINE-1 and Alu elements are currently proliferating in the human genome. Ten per cent of the human population may possess a new LINE-1 or Alu element inserted somewhere in their germ-line DNA.[20]

When a new element is spliced into chromosomal DNA, the choice of the insertion site is largely random. New elements may insert into essential genes. When this happens, they may disable those genes and cause devastating genetic diseases, such as cancer, haemophilia, and muscular dystrophy.[21] At least 0.1 per cent of all cases of human genetic diseases have arisen from a recent insertion event.[20]

There are a vast number of potential insertion sites in animal genomes. If any two people have a jumping gene inserted in precisely the same site of their genomes, they are recognised as being descendants of the one person in whom that insert arose. This has been described for inserts that cause breast cancer in Portuguese populations, and muscular dystrophy, abnormal brain development, and altered immunity in others.[22] The concept of the unique *founder mutation* which surreptitiously spreads in human populations is well established in medical genetics. It follows that if two or more *species* of animal share a particular LINE-1 or Alu insert, they must be descendants of the one unique individual in which that insertion event occurred.

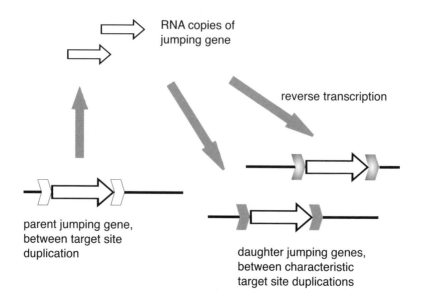

RNA copies of
jumping gene

reverse transcription

parent jumping gene,
between target site
duplication

daughter jumping genes,
between characteristic
target site duplications

Figure 7   Jumping gene action

Jumping genes are lengths of DNA (open arrows) that are copied into RNA. Their reverse transcriptase enzyme copies this RNA back into DNA, which is inserted haphazardly into the cell's DNA. Horizontal lines, chromosomal DNA surrounding an inserted jumping gene

2.5 Jumping genes in primate genetics

Over 500,000 LINE-1 elements, classified into dozens of families, are scattered through our genome.[23] Experimental work has established that independent insertions into the same DNA site of different species are too infrequent to be observed. One can be confident that any insertions that are shared by individuals or species are inherited from the one ancestor in which that unique insertion arose.[24]

Humans share many relatively young LINE-1 inserts with chimps, others with chimps and gorillas, and others with chimps, gorillas and orang-utans (Figure 8).[25] The presence of particular LINE-1 elements in different primate species establishes that the great apes are derived from common ancestors.

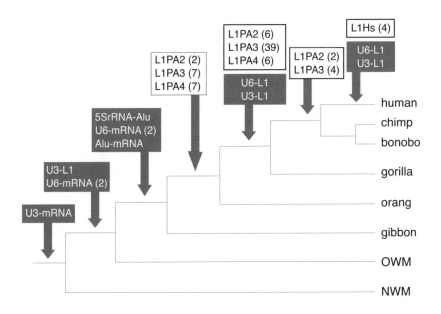

Figure 8 **Primate relationships ascertained from the distribution of LINE-1 elements in primate genomes**

Open boxes: LINE-1 elements found only in humans (L1Hs) and primates (L1P) respectively; numbers in brackets indicate the number of individual inserts mapped.[25] Grey boxes: times when singular hybrid inserts appeared in primate genomes.[26]

Sometimes, during the copying of the LINE-1 RNA molecule into the DNA daughter element, a LINE-1 element's reverse transcriptase abruptly starts copying an innocent bystander RNA. The result is a hybrid DNA element that is composed of sequences derived from the LINE-1 element and the bystander RNA molecule, joined at a particular point. Such hybrid daughter elements are generated by compounded random events. They are highly specific markers of evolutionary relationships. Dozens have been identified and mapped in our DNA. Most are shared with other primate species (Figure 8). The U3-mRNA hybrid insert demonstrates that humans and New World Monkeys share a common ancestor.[26]

Over 1,100,000 Alu elements, classified into more than 200 subfamilies, are present in our genome.[27] Careful studies of Alu

Alu	species	insertion site with target site duplication, **bold**
ACE gene	human	...AAAA**GTGACTGTAT**[Alu]**GTGACTGTAT**AGGC...
	human	...AAAA**GTGACTGTAT** AGGC...
	chimp	...AAAA**GTGACTGTAT** AGGC...
	gorilla	...AAAA**GTGACTGTAT** AGGC...
HPRT gene (a)	human	...A--**GAATGTTGTGA**[Alu]**GAATGTTGTGA**TAA...
	chimp	...A--**GAATGTTGTGA**[Alu]**GAATGTTGTGA**TAA...
	gorilla	...A--**GAATGTTGTGA**[Alu]**GAATGTTGTGA**TAA...
	orang	...AGA**GAATGTTGTGA** TGA...
	baboon	...AGA**GAATGTTGTGA** TGA...
	macaque	...AGA**GAATGTTGTGA** TGA...
HPRT gene (b)	human	...TAAGA**CAAGAAACA**[Alu]**CAAGAAACA**AATTA...
	chimp	...TAAGA**CAAGAAACA**[Alu]**CAAGAAACA**AATTA...
	gorilla	...TAAGA**CAAGAAACA**[Alu]**CAAGAAACA**AATTA...
	orang	...TAAGA**CAAGAAACA**[Alu]**CAAGAAACA**AATTA...
	baboon	...TAAGA**CAAGAAACA** AATTA...
	macaque	...TAAGA**CAAGAAACA** AATTA...
MLH1 gene	human	...TATAAAC**TCCCTG**[Alu]**TCCCTG**AAGTACGT...
	chimp	...TATAAAC**TCCCTG**[Alu]**TCCCTG**AAGTACAT...
	gorilla	...TATAAAC**TCCCTG**[Alu]**TCCCTG**AAGTACGT...
	orang	...TATAAAC**TCCCTG**[Alu]**TCCCTG**AAGTACGT...
	baboon	...TATAAAC**TCCCTG**[Alu]**TCCCTG**AAGTATGT...
	macaque	...TATAAAC**TCCCTG**[Alu]**TCCCTG**AAGTACGT...
	target site	...TATAAAC**TCCCTG** AAGTACGT...
MOG gene	human	...**TAAAGATATGAGTTTT**[Alu]**TAATAATACAAGTTTT**...
	chimp	...**TAACGATACGAGTTTT**[Alu]**TAATAATACAAGTTTT**...
	gorilla	...**TAACGATACGAGTTTT**[Alu]**TAATAATACAAGTTTT**...
	orang	...**TAACGATACGAGTTTT**[Alu]**TAATAAT--GAGTTTT**...
	gibbon	...**TAACGATACGAGTTTT**[Alu]**T-ATAATACAAGTTTT**...
	macaque	...**TAACGATACGAGTTTT**[Alu]**---TAATACGAGTTTT**...
	baboon	...**TAATGATAAGAGTTTT**[Alu]**TAATAATACAAGTTTT**...
	marmoset	...**TAATAATACAAGTTTT**[Alu]**TA-TAACACAAATTTC**...
	target site	...**TAATAATACAAGTTTT**

Figure 9 Insertion sites of five Alu elements

Target sites and their duplications are in bold.[29] *−, deleted bases* elements recently inserted into human DNA have failed to observe independent insertions of Alu elements into the same site of the DNA of other primate species. Thus if a particular Alu element is present in multiple species, those species must all be descendants of the one reproductive cell in which the unique insertion event occurred.[28]

Five Alu inserts and their flanking host cell DNA are shown in Figure 9. The most recently arising Alu elements (exemplified by that near the ACE gene) are present in only some of us. They were added to the human genome after the human species formed. On the other hand, we share the Alu element near the MOG gene with all other ape and monkey species. We have inherited this Alu element along with Old World Monkeys (macaques, baboons) and New World Monkeys (marmosets). The insertion event occurred in an ancestor of all simian primates.[29]

Systematic studies have strikingly revealed our primate roots, have elucidated primate relationships, and have resolved important controversies.[30]

Ape relationships have been elucidated by mapping the distribution of a panel of Alu elements (Figure 10). Sixty-five individual

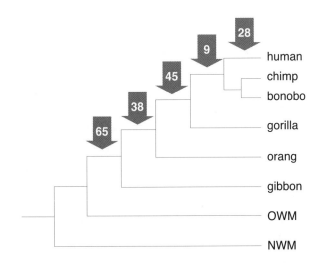

Figure 10   Primate relationships ascertained from the distribution of Alu elements in the genomes of apes and monkeys

Numerals indicate the number of individual elements studied.[31]

Alu elements were shown to be shared by all ape species, establishing that all apes are derived from common ancestors.[31]

There has long been debate over the early branching of the primate family tree. There are three recognised groups: the lorises and lemurs, the tarsiers, and the simians (apes including humans and monkeys). Which group branched out earliest? Arguments have been proposed in support of each of the three possibilities. The issue was resolved when four Alu elements were shown to be shared by tarsiers and simians, but absent from the genomes of lorises and lemurs (Figure 11). So humans and tarsiers are derived from a common ancestor that lived after the time when the lineage of lorises and lemurs branched off the primate family tree.[32]

Two issues present themselves at the base of the primate order: Are all the primates descended from one progenitor? And should creatures called flying lemurs (colugos) be included in the primates? The presence of particular jumping genes including a primitive Alu element in all primates established the fact that all

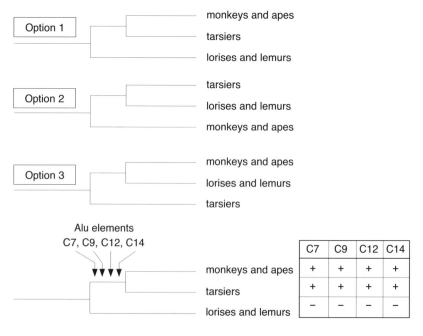

Figure 11   The three-way fork at the base of the primate family tree[32]

Table 2   **Major classes of jumping gene in the human genome**[12,17,18,34,35]

Class of jumping gene	Number of jumping gene inserts in the human genome			
	Total present	*Unique to human*	*Shared with chimp*	*Shared with macaque*
LINE-1*	570,000	2,000	570,000	>500,000
LINE-2	360,000	Few if any	Essentially all	Essentially all
MIR	580,000	Few if any	Essentially all	Essentially all
Alu*	1,100,000	7,000	1,100,000	1,000,000
SVA*	3,400	970	1,800	100
DNA transposon	360,000	Few if any	Essentially all	Essentially all

* Elements still actively replicating in our genome.

primates are derived from a common ancestor. And colugos lacked these markers, excluding them from the primate order.[33]

The weight of evidence becomes evident when we resort to the results of the completed genome projects (Table 2). Of 500,000 LINE-1 elements strewn through our DNA, all but 2,000 are shared with chimps, and the large majority are shared with macaques. Of 1,100,000 Alu elements, all but 7,000 are shared with chimps, and the large majority are shared with macaques. The jumping genes that are unique to our DNA are new additions. Our DNA contains important classes of jumping genes that have not been discussed. Some of these have arisen recently, such as the SVA elements that are found in apes, and that currently cause human disease.[34] Others are very ancient, such as the DNA transposons, all of which were already in place in the genomes of common ancestors of the apes and Old World Monkeys.[35]

It is time to take stock again. Jumping genes have been added to primate genomes in such as way as to provide a definitive map of primate relationships. Primate species can be classified purely on the basis of a panel of Alu elements. This strategy makes sense only if Alu elements accumulated in primate genomes even as species and groups of species formed. The distribution of particular LINE-1 and Alu elements has established that the ape, simian (ape plus monkey), and primate groups are all descended from a single ancestor.

2.6 Jumping genes in mammalian genetics

Statistical approaches based on the comparison of DNA sequences from many mammals have suggested that the Eutherian (placental) mammals are classifiable into four main groupings (Table 3).[7] We primates, together with flying lemurs, tree shrews, rodents and rabbits, are placed in a category called Euarchontoglires. We belong with a sister group (Laurasiatheria) in a larger grouping called Boreoeutheria. More distantly related groups are Afrotheria and Xenarthra. One might wonder whether such hypothetical groupings relate to the real world. And it is easy to be suspicious of statistical approaches.

As genome science gathered momentum, ancient jumping genes were identified that dramatically confirmed Euarchontoglires as a real category of mammals. The relationships of the five orders that constitute Euarchontoglires were established. The primates, flying lemurs and tree shrews are derived from a common ancestor and form one branch. The rodents and rabbits form another.[36]

Table 3   Subdivisions of Eutherian (placental) mammals

Two major subdivisions	*Four major subdivisions*	*Examples*
Boreoeutheria	Euarchontoglires	Primates (including humans), flying lemurs, tree shrews, rodents, rabbits
	Laurasiatheria	Whales and cattle, carnivores, bats
Atlantogenata	Afrotheria	Elephants, aardvarks, manatees, tenrecs
	Xenarthra	Anteaters, armadillos, sloths

Elements arising in primate-rodent (Euarchontoglires) ancestors

human	...CCTATAA**ATCAT**[MLT1A0]**GTCAC**CTTAGAGG...	
baboon	...CTTGTAA**ATAAT**[MLT1A0]**GTCAC**CTTAGAGG...	
mouse	...CCTG--------[MLT1A0]**GTTGT**CTCAG---...	
rat	...CCTGCAA**GCCAC**[MLT1A0]**CTTGT**TGCAGAAG...	
cat	...C-TAAAA**GCCAT**	CTTAGAAT...
dog	...C-TAAAA**GTCAT**	CTTAGAGT...
cow	...CTTATAC**ATCAT**	CTTAGAGG...
pig	...CCTGTAC**ATCAT**	CTTAGAGG...

human	...C**AAAAAGCAATCTTTT**[LINE-1]**AAAAGCAATCTTT**CTG...	
baboon	...CG**AAAAGCAATCTTTT**[LINE-1]**AAAAGCAATCTTT**CTG...	
mouse	...C**A**----------**TTTC**[LINE-1]**AAGGGGAGCCTTT**CTG...	
rat	...C**A**----------**TTTC**[LINE-1]**AAGGAGAA-CTTT**CTG...	
cat	...-**AAGAAGC**----**TTTA**	TG...
dog	...----**AAGCAATCTTTC**	TG...
pig	...T**AAAAAGCAXCCTTTC**	TG...

An element arising in a Boreoeutherian ancestor

human	...**AAAAATGATTTAATGCA**[LINE-1]**AAAAATTATTTAATACA**...
mouse	...A**GAAATTACTT-TTAAA**[LINE-1]**ATA--CTCCTTAATACA**...
cow	...A**GAAATTCTTTAATACA**[LINE-1]**AAAAATTCTTTAATAAA**...
dog	...**AAAAATTCCTAAGACAA**[LINE-1]**AAAAAATACTTA**-----...
pangolin	...**AAAAATCCTTTAATACA**[LINE-1]-----**TTACCTAATAAA**...
mole	...**AAAAATTACTTACTAAA**[LINE-1]**AAAATGTCCTGGATAAA**...
tenrec	...**TGTCA-TTGCTAACACG**
elephant	...**TTACATTCTTTAATGTA**
manatee	...**TTACATTTTTTAACTTA**
sloth	...**AA-AATTCTTTAATACT**
armadillo	...**AAAAATTCTTTAATATA**

An element arising in a Eutherian ancestor

human	...AA-----**ATTTAGTGT**[LINE-1]**TGTTAATTTTT**CTAC-...	
mouse	...CCACG--**TATTAATCT**[LINE-1]**TGCTAATTTTT**----...	
dog	...AAATACT**AAGTAGTGC**[LINE-1]**GGTTCATTTTT**GTAC-...	
tenrec	...CAATGTC**AGCCAACCC**[LINE-1]**TATGAACTC**CGTTTGT...	
armadillo	...A------**TGTTAATCT**[LINE-1]**TGTTAATCA**CATGTAC...	
opossum	...AAA----**TGCTAATCA**	GATTTTT...

Figure 12   Insertion sites of ancient jumping genes in mammals
Target site duplications are in bold.[37,38] *–, deleted bases*

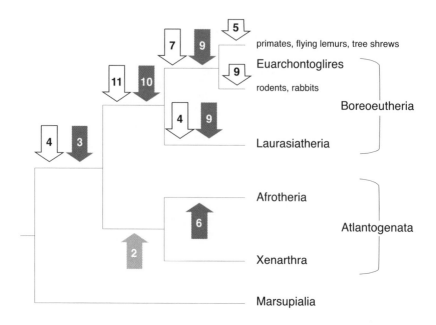

Figure 13 Mammalian relationships ascertained by the distribution of jumping genes

Numerals indicate the number of shared jumping genes documented in each study. Different arrows represent different studies.[36,38,39]

Other inserts are shared by primates (human, baboon) and rodents (mouse, rat). The target site duplications are still recognisable, although somewhat tattered at these great evolutionary distances. Each of these jumping genes is situated in a larger genetic environment that confirms it to be the same inserted element in each species. However, these inserts are not shared by Laurasiatherian mammals (cattle, cat, dog, pig), which retain the uninterrupted target site (Figure 12).[37] Systematic studies have identified multiple inserts, each of which demonstrates that the species comprising Euarchontoglires are derived from a common ancestor (Figure 13).[38,39] Indeed the human and mouse genomes contain myriad jumping genes at the same relative positions of our genomes.[40] We and the mice that scurry around under the floorboards have common ancestors.

More ancient inserts have been found. These demonstrate that Euarchontoglires (exemplified by humans and mice) and Laurasiatheria (cows, dogs, pangolins, moles) are derived from common ancestors (Figures 12, 13).[38,39] Thousands of shared jumping gene markers in the DNA of humans, rats, mice and dogs have been catalogued.[41] Scientists have designed computer programmes that align DNA sequences from multiple species and reconstruct the ancestral sequence (textual criticism again!) Such studies in multiple Boreoeutherian species have revealed that 2.7 per cent of the DNA consists of jumping genes, shared by all the species subjected to the analysis, that had become unrecognisable in any one species analysed individually.[42]

This research has established that all Eutherian mammals are derived from a common ancestor (Figures 12, 13).[38,39] Indeed, shared jumping genes have established that Eutherians are derived from the same ancestors as marsupials and egg-laying monotremes. The latter creatures are so remote from us that non-essential DNA has been shuffled beyond recognition. One must assume that surviving jumping gene sequences have acquired vital roles in the genome and so have resisted mutational change.[43] One class was identified only when the opossum genome was sequenced. Some inserts of this class are present in the same genomic locations in chickens.[44]

Jumping gene research has established that humans and all other living mammals are descended from common ancestors. The genomics revolution of this century has confirmed Darwin's proposal of modification with descent. Many old controversies can be laid to rest – just think of the old arguments over horses, bats and the giraffe's neck.[45] There has not been space to detail the many jumping genes studies that have added to this understanding.

3. Evidence for natural selection

Establishing common ancestry is one thing. Establishing the truth of natural selection is another. But the genomics revolution of this century has powerfully addressed the Darwinian postulate of natural selection: naturally occurring variations can confer reproductive success on the creatures in which those variations arise. And random mutations have been selected to provide new functions.

We are faced with challenging questions here. Genetic sequences provide brilliant markers of evolutionary relatedness. Postgraduate students routinely clone genes and determine the sequence of their bases. But the question of what a gene does (the function of its encoded protein) is an open-ended one that could occupy an experienced research team indefinitely. Nevertheless, comparative genomics research has established that random mutational events have created genetic functionality that has made us what we are.

3.1 How ERVs have contributed to our survival

ERVs invaded our DNA as disruptive agents that may cause disease. With the passage of time they accumulated mutations and degenerated into fossilised relics. This is because ERVs provide no advantage to the host organism and natural selection does not support the maintenance of their genes. However, against all odds, a few ERVs in our DNA have retained one of their genes in a functional state. Most of these ERVs are shared with other primates, two having been added to the primate germ-line in distant ancestors of all simian primates.

One ERV gene sometimes retained in an active form is called the *envelope* gene. This gene encodes a protein that is displayed on the surface of the infectious virus particle and that enables it to stick to cells as a first step in invading them. Retroviral envelope proteins also have the harmful effect of suppressing the immune system of the infected organism. It is tempting to hypothesise that some ERV envelope genes remain intact because they have been co-opted to perform new functions that benefit the host organism. Survival of the genes in a functional form would be linked to the survival of the host organism. The genes would have been maintained by natural selection. Examples of genetic function that is now integral to our biology, and that became part of our genome when retroviral DNA was inserted into it, are given below.

- The ERV-WE1 insert has resided in the primate germ-line since an ape-Old World Monkey ancestor (Figure 14). In cell culture experiments its envelope protein causes cells to stick to one another and fuse into giant cells. During foetal development the envelope protein is made in the placenta. As the placenta develops, cells fuse to form a cell layer called the syncytiotrophoblast. The ERV-WE1 envelope protein (renamed syncytin-1) may contribute to this fusion process.[46]

  There is evidence for this hypothesis. Abnormal human pregnancies are associated with reduced expression of syncytin-1 in placental tissue.[47] And sheep have an ERV of their own which makes an envelope protein in the placenta. When production of this ERV envelope protein is blocked experimentally, the placenta becomes abnormal and the lamb aborts.[48] It seems that a randomly inserted ERV has provided new functions on which our very lives now depend.

- The unique ERV-FRD insert has been present in primate DNA since a simian ancestor. Its envelope protein is also made in the placenta, makes cells fuse, and is expressed abnormally during abnormal pregnancies. In addition, the immunity-suppressing effect of this envelope protein may contribute to one of the wonders of Eutherian reproduction:

Apes

human	...CAATTATCTTG**CAAC**[ERVWE1]**CAAC**CATGAGGGTG...
chimpanzee	...CAATTATCTTG**CAAC**[ERVWE1]**CAAC**CATGAGGGTG...
gorilla	...CAATTATCTTG**CAAC**[ERVWE1]**CAAC**CATGAGGGTG...
orang	...CAATTATCTTG**CAGC**[ERVWE1]**CAAT**CATGAGGGTG...
gibbon	...CAATTATCTTG**CAAC**[ERVWE1]**CAAC**CATGAGGGTG...

New World Monkeys

marmoset	...CAATTATCTTG**CAAC**CATGAGGGTG...
spider monkey	...CAATTATCTTG**CAAC**CATGAGGGTG...
prosimian, lemur	...CCACCATCTTG**CAAA**TATGAGGGTG...
non-primate, dog	...CAACCATCTTG**CAAA**TGTGAGAGTG...

Figure 14   The insertion site of ERV-WE1

the lack of an immune response of the mother against her foetus.[49]

- The placenta appeared in ancestors of Marsupial and Eutherian mammals. Ancient ERV-like inserts, shared by all these mammals, have donated other genes that are essential for placental formation. Placental mammals clearly owe much to these co-operative parasites.[50]

- Some ERVs that inserted themselves *into* pre-existing genes have donated lengths of genetic sequence that have modified the protein-coding information of those genes. Hundreds of genes may have undergone alterations in protein-coding information as a result of ERV insertions.[51] Other ERVs that inserted themselves *between* genes have provided sequence information that regulates gene function. Wholly natural genetic processes have moulded our genome and added novel and essential functions over the course of evolution.[52]

3.2 How jumping genes have contributed to our survival

Jumping genes propagate by defined biochemical mechanisms. Geneticists are finding out how they colonise genomes. In the short term, jumping genes disrupt genomes and cause genetic disease. They are potentially pathogenic. But in the long term some of them have been recruited to provide novel functions and to drive genetic diversification.

Some of our genes have been formed out of the genetic material of jumping genes that were spliced into the chromosomal DNA of primate or mammalian ancestors. For example, the *SETMAR* gene was formed when a jumping gene of the *Hsmar1* type inserted itself into a pre-existing primate gene named *SET*. This event occurred in the DNA of a simian ancestor (Figure 15).[53] The hybrid *SETMAR* gene specifies the production of a hybrid protein in which the 'head' is derived from the *SET* gene and the 'tail' from the *Hsmar1* insert. The Hsmar1-derived part of this protein retains most of the enzymatic activities of the original Hsmar1 protein. The protein encoded by the *SETMAR* gene may currently regulate gene activity.[54]

side-by-side jumping gene inserts

human	...TAAAAGATGG[Alu][Hsmar1]TATCT	TCATA...
chimpanzee	...TAAAAGATGG[Alu][Hsmar1]TATCT	TCATA...
gorilla	...TAAAAGATGG[Alu][Hsmar1]TATCT	TCATA...
orang	...TTAAAGATGG[Alu][Hsmar1]TATCT	TCATA...
siamang	...TAAAAGATGG[Alu][Hsmar1]TATCT	TCATA...
vervet	...TAAAAGATGG[Alu][Hsmar1]TATCT	TCATA...
macaque	...TAAAAGATGG[Alu][Hsmar1]TATCT	TCATA...
owl monkey	...TAAAAGATGG[Alu][Hsmar1]TATCT	TCATA...

tarsier	...TTTAGAGTGGCATGTATCTAGCTCATG...	
dog	...TAAAAGGTGGCATATATCT	TCATG...

Figure 15   Insertion site of the *Hsmar1* jumping gene

An Alu element inserted beside the Hsmar1 element did not contribute to gene content. The hatched triangle indicates a four-base deletion in the simian primates; the gap in the sequence on the right represent an insertion of the bases AGC in the tarsier.[53]

Alu elements have helped to form genes. Thousands of Alu elements contain short runs of DNA bases that allow hormones to communicate with the genome and regulate its activity.[55] Many ancient jumping genes (including some shared by humans and mice) have been turned into genes that now act as master regulators of the genome.[56] It seems inevitable that they have contributed in profound ways to the biological basis of our humanness. It will be a colossal challenge to elucidate their effects on our biology.

DNA is the repository of the genetic information in the cell. It is carefully stored in the nucleus. Its stable maintenance is essential. Genes exert their functions by being copied into RNA molecules, which are highly disposable. They perform the functions entrusted to them and are then degraded. However, jumping genes can undo this tidy arrangement. When their reverse transcriptase is let loose in cells, it may latch on to RNA molecules, reverse-transcribe them into DNA, and splice them back into the chromosome. Our genome is a graveyard of randomly inserted units of DNA sequence representing RNA molecules that have been directed back into DNA. In most cases, they are unable to specify the production of proteins.

Rarely, a reverse-transcribed gene is inserted into chromosomal DNA in an environment that allows it to be copied into RNA. Such mutational events thus generate new genes. These redundant genes are free to mutate into forms that can make novel proteins. An example of a novel gene generated by the chancy process of reverse transcription is the *GLUD2* gene, generated in an ancestor of the apes (Figure 16). The undisturbed target site is apparent in Old World Monkeys, and the perfectly preserved target site duplications are present in all the apes.[57] Following its insertion, the *GLUD2* gene acquired mutations that resulted in the production of a novel protein. The protein is made in the brain and shows different enzymatic properties from those of the parent *GLUD1* gene from which it was derived.[58]

Dozens of new genes have appeared in our genome through the unscheduled activities of jumping genes. Reverse-transcribed genes have accumulated in the primate germ-line at the steady rate of about one new gene per million years. The distribution of particular genes in different species allows one to derive primate and mammalian evolutionary trees fully compatible with those generated by other means.[59] The study of such reverse-transcribed genes provides independent proof of common descent and of the origin of new genetic function from mutational events.

In summary: ERVs and jumping genes have helped to form and modify primate genes. The number of genes we possess is not

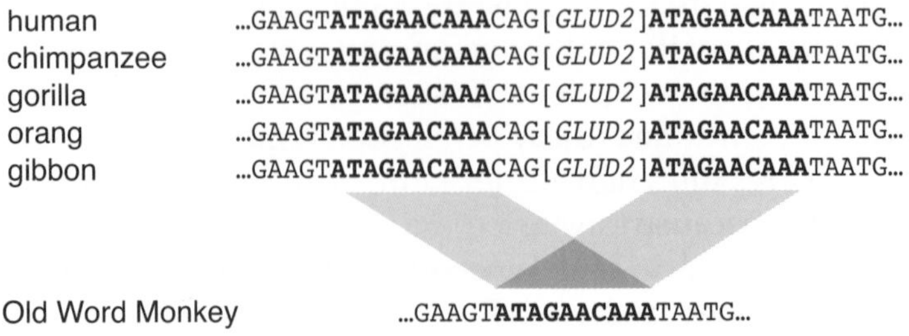

human	...GAAGT**ATAGAACAAA**CAG[*GLUD2*]**ATAGAACAAA**TAATG...
chimpanzee	...GAAGT**ATAGAACAAA**CAG[*GLUD2*]**ATAGAACAAA**TAATG...
gorilla	...GAAGT**ATAGAACAAA**CAG[*GLUD2*]**ATAGAACAAA**TAATG...
orang	...GAAGT**ATAGAACAAA**CAG[*GLUD2*]**ATAGAACAAA**TAATG...
gibbon	...GAAGT**ATAGAACAAA**CAG[*GLUD2*]**ATAGAACAAA**TAATG...

Old Word Monkey   ...GAAGT**ATAGAACAAA**TAATG...

Figure 16   The insertion site of the *GLUD2* gene[57]

greatly different from that of fruit flies or worms. A new awareness is arising that alterations to gene sequences alone have not given us the capacities that we possess. Rather it is *regulation* of those genes that has made us so immeasurably more complex than fruit flies. The increase in regulatory complexity may reside at least in part in the vast accumulation of haphazardly inserted DNA that surrounds our genes. The randomly acquired inserts that clutter our genome may have been recruited to perform functions that are currently unknown. We are at least partially what our randomly operating jumping genes have made us. We would not be *Homo sapiens* without them.

4. Conclusions

The use of genetic markers such as jumping gene insertions has established the truth of speciation and macroevolution. Mammalian genomes are inter-convertible through familiar molecular mechanisms. Natural and random processes have led to the development of complexity in ways that must be as profound as they are currently indefinable. But a vast resource of other genetic markers exists in our DNA. Each genetic marker arises from a highly singular mutation that falls into one of several well-studied classes. These classes of DNA mutation include other types of insertions, deletions of DNA, large duplications, and various types of cut-and-paste events. Each would require an extensive chapter if it were to be adequately described.

One further example must suffice. Five percent of the human genome is composed of large duplicated segments of DNA. They have been copied from one site and spliced haphazardly into other sites. Two-thirds of these duplications are shared by humans and chimps. When large segments of DNA are duplicated, any genes contained within them are also duplicated. Inevitably, these genes will accumulate mutations. If the mutations inactivate them, no harm is done, because they are spare copies. But if the mutations lead to novel and useful functions, the genes will become established as new members of gene families.

Colour vision requires proteins called opsins that act as receptors for light. Apes and Old World Monkeys acquired three-colour vision when an opsin gene on the X chromosome, together with part of an adjacent gene called *TEX28*, was duplicated. One of the junctions between the original DNA and the duplicated segment has been sequenced in multiple species and is identical in humans, chimps and Old World Monkeys. The duplication event was thus a unique happening, and it generated a gene copy that subsequently mutated to become a new gene with altered spectral properties. The acquisition of three-colour vision probably conferred a survival advantage in that it allowed its possessors to find food and mates more effectively (Figure 17).[60]

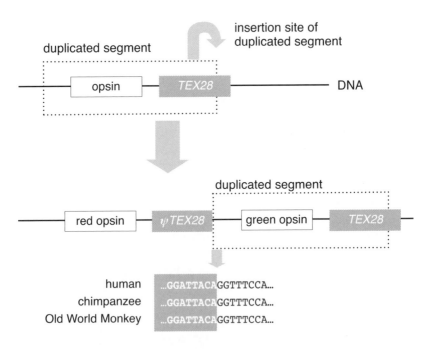

Figure 17   Duplication of an opsin gene

Upper diagram: The original opsin and TEX28 gene arrangement preserved in New World Monkeys. The dotted box indicates the segment that became duplicated. The curved arrow indicates the point at which the duplicated segment was inserted into the original chromosomal DNA. Lower diagram: The derived arrangement showing the duplicated segment (dotted box) and a short length of genetic sequence that defines the unique junction point.[60] ψ TEX28: the truncated gene copy produced by the duplication event.

There is a vast amount of information on the growth of gene families by duplication events. The gene complex that controls our immune system was generated by multiple rounds of DNA duplications (and also contains large numbers of gene relics that did not successfully acquire gene function following duplication episodes). Gene families encoding oxygen-carrying proteins, sensory proteins needed for our sense of smell, regulatory proteins that specify our body shape, and many others, were generated by this mechanism.

In this brief overview I have limited myself to a consideration of our closest (mammalian) evolutionary relationships. But basic genetic mechanisms are common to all organisms. The patterns of jumping gene inserts have successfully elucidated the evolutionary development of groupings within birds, reptiles and fish. It would be perverse to deny that major phyla (sponges, molluscs, worms) arose by natural evolutionary means simply because the events occurred so long ago that unambiguous genetic markers of evolutionary relationship have been obliterated. Other genetic markers may yet be exploited to establish the relationships of major categories of organisms. Our DNA contains, for example, the remnants of three vitellogenin (egg yolk protein) genes, confirming that we are descended from ancestors that laid eggs.[61]

It is sometimes asserted that evolution is not falsifiable, and therefore does not qualify as science. However, the availability of increasing numbers of genome sequences and large numbers of genetic markers constitutes a vast resource in which discordant results would demand reconsideration. It is sometimes asserted that evolution is a religion. But every demonstration of evolutionary relatedness and mechanism described in this chapter would be familiar to a geneticist toiling in the starkly clinical environment of a hospital genetics lab.

All human knowledge is provisional. But some things are less provisional than others. We must allow that science has the capacity to discover truth. We must not be bound by any presumption that problems encountered by evolutionary science are intractable. The revolution of the earth around the sun, the action of the heart as a blood pump, and the evolution of the mammals from a common ancestor are findings of science about which we can be confident. To reject the findings described in this chapter would be to reject the developments in medical genetics over the past few decades. And it would be to reject the legitimacy of using DNA markers in the courts.

Notes

[1] P.L. Ivanov, M.J. Wadhams, R.K. Roby et al., 'Mitochondrial DNA sequence heteroplasmy in the Grand Duke of Russia Georgij Romanov establishes the authenticity of the remains of the Tsar Nicholas II', *Nature Genetics* 12 (1996), p. 417.

[2] F. Ayala, B. Alberts, M.R. Berenbaum et al., *Science, Evolution, and Creationism* (Washington: National Academy of Sciences, 2008).

[3] Z.-X. Luo, 'Transformation and diversification in early mammal evolution', *Nature* 450 (2007), p. 1011.

[4] J.R. Wible, J.W. Rougier, M.J. Novacek and R.J. Asher, 'Cretaceous Eutherians and Laurasian origin for placental mammals near the K/T boundary', *Nature* 447 (2007), p. 1003.

[5] J.G.M. Thewissen, L.N. Cooper, M.T. Clementz et al., 'Whales originated from aquatic artiodactyls in the Eocene epoch of India', *Nature* 450 (2007), p. 1190; N.B. Simmons, K.L. Seymour, J. Habersetzer and G.F. Gunnell, 'Primitive early Eocene bat from Wyoming and the evolution of flight and echolocation', *Nature* 451 (2008), p. 818; T.A. Demere, M.R. McGowan, A. Berta and J. Gatesy, 'Morphological and molecular evidence for a stepwise evolutionary transition from teeth to baleen in Mysticete whales', *Systematic Biology* 57 (2008), p. 15.

[6] R. Stanyon, M. Rocci, O. Capozzi et al., 'Primate chromosome evolution: ancestral karyotypes, marker order and neocentromeres', *Chromosome Research* 16 (2008), p. 17; M.A. Ferguson-Smith and V. Trifonov, 'Mammalian karyotype evolution', *Nature Reviews Genetics* 8 (2007), p. 950.

[7] C.W. Dunn, A. Hejnol, D.Q. Matus et al., 'Broad phylogenetic sampling improves resolution of the animal tree of life', *Nature* 452 (2008), p. 745; O.R.P. Binina-Emonds, M. Cardillo, K.E. Jones et al. 'The delayed rise of present-day mammals', *Nature* 446 (2007), p. 507.

[8] Interview, 'Dr Charles Dinarello elected to the US National Academy of Sciences', *International Cytokine Society Newsletter* 6 (1) (1998), p. 1. The gene is that of interleukin-1β.

[9] D. Westaway, G. Payne and H.E. Varmus, 'Proviral deletions and oncogene base-substitutions in insertionally mutagenized c-*myc*

alleles may contribute to the progression of avian bursal tumours', *Proceedings of the National Academy of Sciences of the USA* 81 (1984), p. 843.

[10] D. Derse, B. Crise, Y. Yi et al., 'Human T-cell leukaemia virus type 1 integration target sites in the human genome: comparison with those of other retroviruses', *Journal of Virology* 81 (2007), p. 6731.

[11] F. Mortreux, A.-S. Gabet and E. Wattel, 'Molecular and cellular aspects of HTLV-1 associated leukemogenesis in vivo', *Leukemia* 17 (2003), p. 26.

[12] International Human Genome Sequencing Consortium, 'Initial sequencing and analysis of the human genome', *Nature* 409 (2001), p. 860. For simplicity, I am describing LTR elements and true endogenous retroviruses as ERVs.

[13] T.I. Bonner, C. O'Connell C and M. Cohen, 'Cloned endogenous retroviral sequences from human DNA', *Proceedings of the National Academy of Sciences of the USA* 79 (1982), p. 4709; R. Mariani-Constantini, T.M Horn and R. Callahan, 'Ancestry of a human endogenous retrovirus family', *Journal of Virology* 63 (1989), p. 4982.

[14] W.E. Johnson and J.M. Coffin, 'Constructing primate phylogenies from ancient retrovirus sequences', *Proceedings of the National Academy of Sciences of the USA* 96 (1999), p. 10254.

[15] M. Barbulescu, G. Turner, M.I. Seaman et al., 'Many human endogenous retrovirus K (HERV-K) proviruses are unique to humans', *Current Biology* 9 (1999), p. 861.

[16] N. de Parseval, J.-F. Casella, L. Gressin and T. Heidmann, 'Characterization of the three HERV-H proviruses with an open envelope reading frame encompassing the immunosuppressive domain and evolutionary history in primates', *Virology* 279 (2001), p. 558; J. Ling, W. Pi, R. Bollag et al., 'The solitary long terminal repeats of ERV-9 endogenous retrovirus are conserved during primate evolution and possess enhancer activities in embryonic and hematopoietic cells', *Journal of Virology* 76 (2002), p. 2410; D. Liao, T. Pavelitz and A.M. Weiner, 'Characterisation of a novel class of interspersed LTR elements in primate genomes: structure, genomic distribution, and evolution', *Journal of Molecular Evolution* 46 (1998), p. 649.

[17] The Chimpanzee Sequencing and Analysis Consortium, 'Initial sequence of the chimpanzee genome and comparison with the human genome', *Nature* 437 (2005), p. 69.

[18] Rhesus Macaque Genome Sequencing and Analysis Consortium, 'Evolutionary and biomedical insights from the rhesus macaque genome', *Science* 316 (2007), p. 222; K. Han, M.K. Konkel, J. Xing et al.,

'Mobile DNA in Old World Monkeys: A glimpse through the rhesus macaque genome', *Science* 316 (2007), p. 238.

[19] J. Giordano, Y. Ge, Y. Galfand et al., 'Evolutionary history of mammalian transposons determined by genome-wide defragmentation', *PLoS Computational Biology* 3 (2007), p. e137.

[20] R. Cordaux, D.J. Hedges, S.W. Herke and M. Batzer, 'Estimating the retrotransposition rate of human Alu elements', *Gene* 373 (2006), p. 134.

[21] D.J. Hedges and P. Deininger, 'Mammalian non-LTR retrotransposons: for better or worse, in sickness and in health', *Genome Research* 18 (2008), p. 343.

[22] P.M. Machado, R.D Brandao, B.M. Cavaco et al., 'Screening for a *BRCA2* rearrangement in high-risk breast/ovarian cancer families: evidence for a founder effect and analysis of the associated phenotypes', *Journal of Clinical Oncology* 25 (2007), p. 2027.

[23] H. Khan, A. Smit and S. Boissinot, 'Molecular evolution and tempo of amplification of human retrotransposons since the origin of primates', *Genome Research* 16 (2006), p. 78.

[24] Some families of LINE-1 elements are found only in humans. When the insertion sites of these human-only LINE-1 elements are investigated in other primates they are always found to be unoccupied by LINE-1 elements characteristic of those other species. H.J. Ho, D.A. Ray, A.-H. Salem et al., 'Straightening out the LINEs: LINE-1 orthologous loci', *Genomics* 85 (2005), p. 201.

[25] L. Mathews, S.Y. Chi, N. Greenberg et al., 'Large differences between LINE-1 amplification rates in the human and chimpanzee lineages', *American Journal of Human Genetics* 72 (2003), p. 739.

[26] A. Buzdin, E. Gogvadze, E. Kovalskaya et al., 'The human genome contains many types of chimeric retrogenes generated through *in vivo* RNA recombination', *Nucleic Acids Research* 31 (2003), p. 4385.

[27] A.L. Price, E. Eskin and P.A. Pevzner, 'Whole-genome analysis of *Alu* elements reveals complex evolutionary history', *Genome Research* 14 (2004), p. 2245.

[28] D.A. Ray, J. Xing, A.-H. Salem and M.A. Batzer, 'SINEs of a *nearly* perfect character', *Systematic Biology* 55 (2006), p. 928.

[29] H. Hamdi, H. Nishio, R. Zielinski and A. Dugaiczyk, 'Origin and phylogenetic distribution of *Alu* DNA repeats: irreversible events in the evolution of primates', *Journal of Molecular Biology* 289 (1999), p. 861; J. Martinez, L.J. Dugaicyk, R. Zielinski and A. Dugaicyk, 'Human genetic disorders: a phylogenetic perspective', *Journal of Molecular Biology* 308 (2001), p. 587; R. Gibbons and A. Dugaiczyk, 'Phylogenetic

roots of Alu-mediated rearrangements leading to cancer', *Genome* 48 (2005), p. 160; B. Crouau-Roy and I. Clisson, 'Evolution of an Alu DNA element of type Sx in the lineage of primates and the origin of an associated tetranucleotide microsatellite', *Genome* 43 (2000), p. 642.

[30] J. Xing, D.J. Witherspoon, D.A. Ray et al., 'Mobile DNA in primate and human evolution', *Yearbook of Physical Anthropology* 50 (2007), p. 2.

[31] A.-H. Salem, D.A. Ray, J. Xing et al., 'Alu elements and hominid phylogenetics', *Proceedings of the National Academy of Sciences of the USA* 100 (2003), p. 12787; J. Xing, A.-H. Salem, D.J. Hedges et al., 'Comprehensive analysis of two Alu Yd subfamilies', *Journal of Molecular Evolution* 57 (2003), p. S76.

[32] J. Schmitz, M. Ohme and H. Zischler, 'SINE insertions in cladistic analyses and the phylogenetic affiliations of *Tarsius bancanus* to other primates', *Genetics* 157 (2001), p. 777.

[33] J. Schmitz and H. Zischler, 'A novel family of tRNA-related SINEs in the colugo and two new retrotransposable markers separating dermopterans from primates', *Molecular Phylogenetics and Evolution* 28 (2003), p. 341.

[34] H. Wang, J. Xing, D. Grover et al., 'SVA elements: a hominid-specific retroposon family', *Journal of Molecular Biology* 354 (2005), p. 994.

[35] J.K. Pace II and C. Feschotte, 'The evolutionary history of DNA transposons: evidence for intense activity in the primate lineage', *Genome Research* 17 (2007), p. 422.

[36] J.O. Kriegs, G. Churakov, J. Jurka et al., 'Evolutionary history of 7SL RNA-derived SINEs in Supraprimates', *Trends in Genetics* 23 (2007), p. 158.

[37] J.W. Thomas, J.W. Touchman, R.W. Blakesley et al., 'Comparative analyses of multi-species sequences from targeted genomic regions', *Nature* 424 (2003), p. 788. Sequences were obtained from 'Supplementary Information' on the journal website, www.nature.com. (Also at http://www.nature.com.ezproxy.auckland.ac.nz/nature/journal/v424/n6950/extref/nature01858-s5.pdf by special subscription to the journal through the University of Auckland server.)

[38] J.O. Kriegs, G. Churakov, M. Kiefmann et al., 'Retroposed elements as archives for the evolutionary history of placental mammals', *PLoS Biology* 4 (2006), p. 537. An update is provided by W.J. Murphy, T.H. Pringle, T.A. Crider et al., 'Using genomic data to unravel the root of the placental mammal tree', *Genome Research* 17 (2007), p. 413.

[39] H. Nishihara, M. Hasegawa and N. Okada, 'Pegasoferae, an unexpected mammalian clade revealed by tracking ancient

retroposon insertions', *Proceedings of the National Academy of Sciences of the USA* 103 (2006), p. 9929. Sequences are available as 'Supporting Information' on the journal website, http://www.pubmedcentral. nih.gov.ezproxy.auckland.ac.nz/picrender.fcgi?artid=1479866& blobname=pnas_0603797103_index.html or at www.pubmedcentral. nih.gov

40 J.C. Silva, S.A. Shabalina, D.G. Harris et al., 'Conserved fragments of transposable elements in intergenic regions: evidence for widespread recruitment of MIR- and L2-derived sequences within the mouse and human genomes', *Genetic Research Cambridge* 82 (2003), p. 1; L. Zhu, G.D. Swergold and M.F. Seldin, 'Examination of sequence homology between human chromosome 20 and the mouse genome: intense conservation of many genomic elements', *Human Genetics* 113 (2003), p. 60.

41 T.S. Mikkelsen, M.J. Wakefield, B. Aken et al., 'Genome of the marsupial *Monodelphis domestica* reveals innovation in non-coding sequences', *Nature* 447 (2007), p. 167; C.B. Lowe, G. Bejerano and D. Haussler, 'Thousands of human mobile element fragments undergo strong purifying selection near developmental genes', *Proceedings of the National Academy of Sciences of the USA* 104 (2007), p. 8005.

42 M. Blanchette, E.D. Green, W. Miller and D. Haussler, 'Reconstructing large regions of an ancestral mammalian genome in silico', *Genome Research* 14 (2004), p. 2412.

43 M. Krull, M. Petrusma, W. Makalowski et al., 'Functional persistence of exonised mammalian-wide interspersed repeat elements (MIRs)', *Genome Research* 17 (2007), p. 1139; A.M. Santangelo, F.S.J. de Souza, L.F. Franchini et al., 'Ancient exaptation of a CORE-SINE retroposon into a highly conserved mammalian neuronal enhancer of the proopiomelanocortin gene', *PLoS Genetics* 3 (2007), p. e166; T. Sasaki, H. Nishihara, M. Hirakawa et al., 'Possible involvement of SINEs in mammalian-specific brain formation', *Proceedings of the National Academy of Sciences of the USA* 105 (2008), p. 4220.

44 A.J. Gentles, M.J. Wakefield, O. Kohany et al., 'Evolutionary dynamics of transposable elements in the short-tailed opossum *Monodelphis domestica*', *Genome Research* 17 (2007), p. 992.

45 Horses share an ancestor with dogs, cows (and whales) and bats; endnote 39.

dog	...ATCTAT**CAAAAGAA**[LINE-1]**TAAAAAAA**GTACAA...	
horse	...ACCTTT**CGAAACAA**[LINE-1]**CAAAAGAA**GAA---...	
cow	...ACCTAT**CAATACAA**	ACATGG...
bat	...ACCTAT**CAAAACAA**	ATA---...
hedgehog	...ACCTAG**C-AAACAA**	ATA-AA...

```
dog        ...TACTTTTAATCTAG[LINE-1]AGTC--ATCTTTT...
horse      ...TACTTCTAATCTAG[LINE-1]AATCTAGTTTTTT...
cow        ...TAC-TTTAATACAA[LINE-1]ACTCTAGTTTTTT...
bat        ...TGCTTTTAATCTAG              AAGCTT...
mole       ...TACTTTTAATCTAG              ACTT--...

dog        ...-------------[LINE-1]TATTGTTTTCAGT...
horse      ...ATTACTGTGTTGTT[LINE-1]TGTTGTTTTTATT...
cow        ...ATTACTGTTCTTTT[LINE-1]TGTTGTTTTCCCT...
bat        ...ATTACTGTGTTGTT[LINE-1]TGTCATTTTC---...
hedgehog   ...ATTGCTATGTTATT             TTCATT...
```

[46] F. Mallet, O. Bouton, S. Prudhomme et al., 'The endogenous locus ERVWE1 is a bona fide gene involved in hominoid placental physiology', *Proceedings of the National Academy of Sciences of the USA* 101 (2004), p. 1731; B. Bonnaud, J. Beliaeff, O. Bouton et al., 'Natural history of the ERVWE1 endogenous retroviral locus', *Retrovirology* 2 (2005), p. 57.

[47] M. Langbein, R. Strick, P.L. Strissel et al., 'Impaired cytotrophoblast cell-cell fusion is associated with reduced syncytin and increased apoptosis in patients with placental dysfunction', *Molecular Reproduction and Development* 75 (2008), p. 175; W. Kudaka, T. Oda, Y. Jinno et al., 'Cellular localization of placenta-specific human endogenous retrovirus (HERV) transcripts and their possible implication in pregnancy-induced hypertension', *Placenta* 29 (2008), p. 282.

[48] K.A. Dunlap, M. Palmarini, M. Varela et al., 'Endogenous retroviruses regulate periimplantation placental growth and differentiation', *Proceedings of the National Academy of Sciences of the USA* 103 (2006), p. 14390.

[49] M. Manganey, M. Renard, G. Schlecht-Louf et al., 'Placental syncytins: genetic disjunction between the fusogenic and immunosuppressive activity of retroviral envelope proteins', *Proceedings of the National Academy of Sciences of the USA* 104 (2007), p. 20534; A. Mallasine, J.L. Frendo, S. Blaise et al., 'Human endogenous retrovirus-RFD envelope protein (syncytin 2) expression in normal and trisomy 21-affected placenta', *Retrovirology* 5 (2008), p. 6.

[50] S. Suzuki, R. Ono, T. Narita et al., 'Retrotransposon silencing by DNA methylation can drive mammalian genomic imprinting', *PLoS Genetics* 3 (2007), p. 531; Y. Sekita, H. Wagatsuma, K. Nakamura et al., 'Role of transposon-derived imprinted gene, *Rtl1*, in the feto-maternal interface of mouse placenta', *Nature Genetics* 40 (2008), p. 243.

[51] J. Piriyapongsa, N. Polavarapu, M. Borodovsky and J. McDonald, 'Exonisation of the LTR transposable elements in human genome', *BMC Genomics* 8 (2007), p. 291.

[52] T. Wang, Z. Zeng, C.B. Lowe et al., 'Species-specific endogenous retroviruses shape the transcriptional network of the human tumour suppressor protein p53', *Proceedings of the National Academy of Sciences of the USA* 104 (2007), p. 18613.

[53] R. Cordaux, S. Udit, M.A. Batzer and C. Feschotte, 'Birth of a chimeric primate gene by capture of the transposase gene from a mobile element', *Proceedings of the National Academy of Sciences of the USA* 103 (2006), p. 8101.

[54] D. Liu, J. Bischerour, A. Siddique et al., 'The human SETMAR protein preserves most of the activities of the ancestral Hsmar1 transposase', *Molecular and Cellular Biology* 27 (2007), p. 1125.

[55] D. Laperriere, T.-T. Wang, J.H. White and S. Mader, 'Widespread Alu repeat-driven expansion of consensus DR2 retinoic acid response elements during primate evolution', *BMC Genomics* 8 (2007), p. 23.

[56] J. Piriyapongsa, L. Marino-Ramirez and I.K. Jordan, 'Origin and evolution of human microRNAs from transposable elements', *Genetics* 176 (2007), p. 1323.

[57] F. Burki and H. Kaessmann, 'Birth and adaptive evolution of a hominoid gene that supports high neurotransmitter flux', *Nature Genetics* 36 (2004), p. 1061.

[58] K. Kanavouras, V. Mastorodemos, M. Borompokas et al., 'Properties and molecular evolution of human *GLUD2* (neural and testicular tissue-specific) glutamate dehydrogenase', *Journal of Neuroscience Research* 85 (2007), p. 3398.

[59] A.C. Marques, I. Dupanloup, N. Vinckenbosch et al., 'Emergence of young human genes after a burst of retroposition in primates', *PLoS Biology* 3 (2005), p. 1970; L. Potrzebowski, N. Vinckenbosch, A.C. Marques et al., 'Chromosomal gene movements reflect the recent origin and biology of Therian sex chromosomes', *PLoS Biology* 6 (2008), p. e80.

[60] K.S. Dulai, M. von Dornum, J.D. Mollon and D.M. Hunt, 'The evolution of trichromatic colour vision by opsin gene duplication in New World and Old World primates', *Genome Research* 9 (1999), p. 629.

[61] D. Brawand, W. Wahli and H. Kaessmann, 'Loss of egg yolk genes in mammals and the origin of lactation and placentation', *PLoS Biology* 6 (2008), p. 507.

7

On Considering *all* the Evidence: a Response to Graeme

DAVID SWIFT

Falsifiability

Early in his chapter Graeme says that we take cumulative evidence seriously, meaning that when different lines of evidence agree then we are inclined to see it as confirmatory. He is right, it is a typically human approach, and Darwin followed it in relation to evolution:

> The present action of natural selection may seem more or less probable; but I believe in the truth of the theory, because it collects, under one point of view, and gives a rational explanation of, many apparently independent classes of facts.[1]

However, we also know from common experience that even a small amount of clearly contradictory evidence outweighs a large body of consistent evidence. For instance, in a court of law, no matter how much evidence appears to incriminate someone, it would be entirely outweighed by, for example, a reliable alibi that the accused was in a totally different place at the time of the crime. And the same is true in science. It does not matter how much cumulative evidence is consistent with a theory, it is outweighed by reliable evidence that clearly contradicts the theory. Towards the end of his chapter Graeme recognises this:

> It is sometimes asserted that evolution is not falsifiable, and therefore does not qualify as science. However, the availability of increasing numbers of genome sequences and large numbers of genetic markers

constitutes a vast resource in which discordant results would demand reconsideration.

As mentioned in my own chapter (5), not only do I agree with the principle of falsification, but it seems to me that we have now become aware of substantial evidence contrary to evolution, including from the human genome project which Graeme alludes to. Indeed, contrary to Graeme's view, the more we learn, the more inconsistencies emerge; and one example of this is homology.

Homologous?

One of the lines of evidence that superficially supports evolution is homology, and Graeme cites the frequently used example of the vertebrate limb. However, although this is still commonly mentioned, it has been known for many years that, despite the superficial similarities, in fact the bones of the manus (hand and equivalent) do not appear to be derived from a common underlying pattern by which they might be considered homologous.[2]

Not only this, but especially notable is that the digits (fingers) of urodeles (one group of amphibians, including salamanders) are not homologous with those of other tetrapods or even of anurans (another group of amphibians, including frogs).[3] And in chapter 5 I explained that even the vertebrae of different groups of vertebrates are not homologous. This non-homology of a central part of the vertebrate skeleton clearly undermines any apparent homology of the skeleton as a whole.

This illustrates how important it is that we should look at the evidence from both sides. All too often evolutionary texts give only the evidence consistent with evolution. However, there is also substantial evidence that is inconsistent with it, but this tends to be brushed under the carpet. Homology is especially important in this respect because, as I explained in chapter 5, examples of non-homology not only fail to support evolution, they are strong evidence *against* common ancestry, clearly falsifying evolution.

Fossil record

There are a number of points I would like to make in response to Graeme's comments about the fossil record.

Incomplete?

First, I must take issue with Graeme's comment that 'the fossil record is notoriously incomplete', thereby implying that we should not be surprised at the absence of transitional forms between major groups.

To begin with, he comments that there has been an explosive increase in both the number of fossil genera and the quality of available fossils. That being so, it is a bit hollow to say at the same time that we shouldn't be surprised that the intermediate ones are missing – you can't have your cake and eat it!

In fact, a few years ago some scientists assessed quantitatively how complete the fossil record is and concluded, '[W]e find that completeness is rather high for many animal groups',[4] *which means that the gaps between known fossil species are likely to be real, and unlikely to be filled in by new finds.* The failure of the fossil record to demonstrate evolution is indeed well known, especially among palaeontologists. Notably, it was Niles Eldridge who famously wrote, 'Evolution cannot always be going on someplace else', leading him and Stephen Gould to propose the theory of punctuated equilibrium to try to explain the gaps in the fossil record.[5] And just a few years ago the staunch evolutionist Ernst Mayr agreed that 'Wherever we look at the living biota ... discontinuities are overwhelmingly frequent ... The discontinuities are even more striking in the fossil record. New species usually appear in the fossil record suddenly, not connected with their ancestors by a series of intermediates.'[6]

Transitional fossils?

Graeme mentions a few fossils that have been proposed to try to bridge some of the notable gaps in the fossil record.

Amphibians

One of the key stages in the supposed evolution of vertebrates was the emergence of the first land animals, amphibians, from fish. The most likely candidates for the amphibian predecessors are thought to be lobe-finned fish (crossopterygians) which had fleshy, bony fins. There are similarities in the bone structure of some of these lobe-finned fish fins and that of the tetrapod limb: they are considered to be equivalent (homologous) to, for example, the human arm and possibly wrist. But there is no suggestion whatever of any bones equivalent to the manus – even though some of these fish had fin rays, they were not equivalent to digits (fingers).

A major part of the supposed transformation (although there are others too) was clearly the conversion of fins used for swimming into limbs for walking. Graeme refers to the recently discovered *Tiktaalik* (a lobe-finned fish) as having had elbow and wrist joints, as if this were a useful step in the right direction.

However, this is somewhat of an overstatement, as a careful reading of the scientific papers written by the discoverers reveals that the fin bones of *Tiktaalik* resembled those of early lobe-finned fish and were not particularly similar to those of the amphibians.[7,8] It is true that, owing to the well-preserved nature of the fossils, the authors could estimate the degree of movement of the fin joints. They were able to confirm that, as well as adopting a fin-like posture suitable for swimming, the fins could adopt a limb-like posture perhaps suitable for, say, crawling along the bed of the watercourse. But they recognise that this was probably true of the early lobe-finned fish too. The editorial accompanying the scientific papers sums up the position as follows:

> Although these small distal bones bear some resemblance to tetrapod digits in terms of their *function and range of movement*, they are still very much components of a fin. There remains a large morphological gap between them and digits as seen in, for example, *Acanthostega* [an early amphibian]: if the digits evolved from these distal bones, the process must have involved considerable developmental repatterning. *The implication is that function changed in advance of morphology.*[9]

Of course, there are still major gaps in the fossil record. In particular we have almost no information about the step between *Tiktaalik* and the earliest tetrapods, when the anatomy underwent the most drastic changes.[10]

Note that the similarity is in terms of *function and range of movement*, but not *structure* which is surely of prime importance. Further, their comment, 'The implication is that function changed in advance of morphology' is quite revealing of misguided evolutionary thinking. So many evolutionary textbooks suggest that using fins for 'walking' (along a river bed, for example) would be a useful precursor to evolving legs suitable for locomotion on land.[11]

However, first, mutations occur at random: even if a fish did move in this way, it would not somehow encourage the right mutations to take place to give rise to legs. Not recognising this is another example of anachronistic thinking along the lines of the inheritance of acquired characteristics, mentioned in my chapter 5.

Second, using the fin bone structure in this way would, in fact, make it *less likely* that a new leg-like structure would arise. This is because the more specialised or adapted the early bone structure became for leg-like locomotion – for example, having greater flexibility – the greater the advantage a new structure would need to offer in order to be favoured by natural selection. It is unlikely that a rudimentary new structure would provide this. Rather, to give the sort of advantage that natural selection could favour, the structure would need to be well-formed *and* function well – which means it would be even *less* likely that all of the mutations necessary for the *new* structure with its *better function* would arise. (I explained in chapter 5 why there is no realistic hope of such mutations arising anyway.) That is, because natural selection has no foresight, improving the function of an old structure is more likely to lead evolution up a blind alley than to a new structure. Natural selection cannot 'see' that a different structure could perform the function even better and make the substantial leap from one to the other; the leap can be made only blindly/by chance, and the leap required becomes greater as the old structure specialises.

Whales

Graeme says that the fossil *Indohyus* 'links terrestrial mammals with whales'. However, *Indohyus* was a land animal resembling a racoon or deer; so one might wonder why it is thought to be an ancestor of whales. The reason is that part of its ear resembled that of whales! So here we have another example of blinkered evolutionary thinking.

If one *assumes* that whales evolved from land animals, then it makes sense to look for similarities to try to identify possible ancestors. The specific ear feature is distinctive among cetaceans (whales, dolphins, porpoises); so, at least from an evolutionary perspective, it seems reasonable that they may have evolved from land animals with a similar feature. But when such similarities are as remote as this, it is hardly evidence for the supposed evolution; and it is certainly stretching the facts to assert that *Indohyus* 'bridges the morphological divide that separated early cetaceans from artiodactyls [a group of land animals which includes *Indohyus*]'.[12]

Bats

As Graeme says, *Onychonycteris* was indeed a primitive bat. But it was primitive only in the sense of being one of the two oldest known species of bat. It was a fully-fledged bat, not in any way a transitional form from, say, tree shrews or any other supposed ancestor of the bats.

Common descent

Much of Graeme's chapter presents evidence in support of common descent. I commented briefly on this aspect in chapter 5, and expand on it here.

Common descent does not prove evolution

Perhaps for many Christians it is not at all important how God created the various forms of life. It does not matter to them whether (a) God designed the universe so that life could emerge and evolve 'naturally'; or (b) the process needed a 'helping hand' at various stages along the way; or (c) God created each major form of life independently. But the purpose of this book is to discuss Neo-Darwinism – whether life could have emerged and evolved solely through the operation of natural processes. And certainly this is the important issue so far as atheists such as Richard Dawkins are concerned. In chapter 5 I explained why I think option (a) is totally out of the question, and that as yet I am undecided between (b) and (c). Sufficient here to say that whilst (b) rejects the theory of evolution as a whole, it would be consistent with common descent, so demonstrating common descent does not prove naturalistic evolution.

Functionality of DNA elements

In chapter 5 I alluded to genomic evidence such as that mentioned by Graeme and make the point that it is evidence of common descent only if the DNA sequences in question have no function. If the sequences have a function then that is sufficient reason for their existence; it is only if they do not have a function that they can act as independent markers of descent – i.e. they are there only because they have been inherited.

So it is relevant that a variety of functions have been identified for many ERVs (one of the types of DNA elements mentioned by Graeme).[13] For example, at the start of pregnancy in mammals ERVs are activated and produced in high quantities during the implantation of the embryo; the ERVs help to protect the embryo from its mother's immune system. These functions substantially reduce, if not completely remove, any significance these ERVs may have as evidence of common descent.

Similarly, Graeme mentions functions of some transposable elements (jumping genes). So, for example, whilst it is true that the occurrence of some transposons corresponds with supposed evolution, their occurrence also corresponds with increased complexity of the organisms concerned, and they may well have a role in gene regulation.

Evidence for natural selection and molecular evolution

It will be apparent from my chapter 5 that I fully accept that natural selection occurs. My argument is not with the action of natural selection, but that at the molecular level the advantageous steps on which natural selection can act are much too unlikely to occur (with very limited exceptions). Interestingly, an evolutionary biologist commented recently that 'The modern synthesis is remarkably good at modelling the survival of the fittest, but not good at modelling the arrival of the fittest'[14] – which is somewhat how I see it. It is all too easy for evolutionists to propose possible evolutionary scenarios, but many do not stand up to careful scrutiny. And this is true of some of the examples cited by Graeme, though the limited space available means I must restrict my comments to just one of those.

SETMAR

Graeme refers to the supposed evolution of the gene *SETMAR* by the amalgamation of a transposon with a previously existing gene, and my following comments are based on the reference he cites (his endnote 53).[15]

In many 'lower' vertebrates (all those the authors examined) there is a *SET* gene which codes for the enzyme histone methyltransferase which has a role in regulating gene expression. In higher primates (anthropoids – monkeys, apes and humans), instead of the *SET* gene there is a *SETMAR* gene in an equivalent location. Part of this gene resembles *SET* and the other part (*MAR*) resembles a transposon. (It would appear that the resulting protein has typical SET activity, but restricts this to DNA associated with a specific sequence; and that it has a role in DNA repair.) Because of the similarities to *SET* and *MAR* it is supposed that the *SETMAR* gene arose from a fortuitous combination of these two components. However, we should note the following:

1. Fewer than half (45 per cent) of the 300 amino acids of the *SET* gene sequence in zebrafish are the same as those in the *SET* part of *SETMAR* (which is a good example of how

molecular homology is exaggerated – see my comments in chapter 5).

2. The proposed formation of the *SETMAR* gene requires all of the following to occur (see Figure 1):

- Occurrence of a transposon (part of *MAR*) on the *down-stream* side, but not too far, of the *SET* gene.

- Removal of 12 base pairs of the TIR (called the target site duplication in Graeme's chapter) of the *MAR* sequence, on the *same* side as the *SET* gene, and of 4 adjacent base pairs; and insertion of a retrotransposon sequence (*AluSx*) in their place.

- Removal of 27 base pairs, including the 'stop' codon at the downstream end of the *SET* gene.

- Modification of the following 77 base pairs of DNA sequence to (a) give the right sequence of amino acids to become the middle part of the *SETMAR* gene, and (b) ending with the right sequence to mark as a splice site, but leave the rest of the sequence before the downstream *MAR* section as an intron (see endnote 16 for an explanation of these terms).

Even the authors of that article comment:

> Equally remarkable [having just mentioned another fortuitous feature] is the fact that all of the mutational events and mechanisms leading to the assembly of the novel *SETMAR* gene took place within a very narrow evolutionary time window of <18 million years, after the emergence of the tarsier lineage and before the diversification of anthropoid primates. (p. 8103)

And I would emphasise that *all of these* must occur before there is any advantage that natural selection could favour. (So, for example, if the 'Stop' codon were lost prematurely it would be a definite disadvantage, and natural selection would act *against* any individual with this mutation.) Indeed, I would add that even a SETMAR protein may have been of no value in itself, but may have required the genetic mechanisms that make use of its selective activity also to be in place.

If you are convinced that we have evolved, then I suppose you are driven to trying to find any hint of possible 'easier' ways of producing genes, for example by modification of pre-existing ones, rather than from scratch. But without that prior conviction, and looking at it objectively, just how credible is it that such a fortuitous combination of events actually took place?

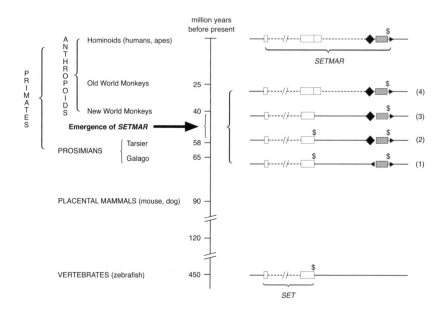

Figure 1   Proposed origin of *SETMAR* from a preceding *SET* gene and a transposon (based on Cordaux et al.[16])

The original SET gene comprised two exons (open rectangles) separated by an intron (broken line), and ending with a 'stop' codon ($). Conversion to the SETMAR gene then involved the following events. (1) Occurrence of a transposon (grey rectangle) downstream of the SET gene, which included another stop codon, along with its flanking TIRs (black triangles). (2) Insertion of a retrotransposon (AluSx, represented by a black diamond), with simultaneous loss of the upstream TIR. (3) Removal of 27 base pairs, including the 'stop' codon at the downstream end of the original SET gene. (4) Modification of the following 77 base pairs of DNA sequence to give the right sequence of amino acids for the middle part of the SETMAR gene (additional open rectangle), and introduce a second intron (broken line).

Summary

My response to Graeme, and to many other proponents of evolution, can be summed up as follows:

1. Most importantly, there is no point in presenting only the evidence consistent with evolution as if it somehow proves evolution is true – it does not. Any serious assessment of evolution must also take full account of the substantial contrary evidence.
2. Many proposed evolutionary scenarios – whether at the morphological or molecular level – just do not stand up to careful scrutiny.

I expanded on both of these in chapter 5.

Notes

[1] C. Darwin, *Variation in Animals and Plants under Domestication* (London: John Murray, 1868). Introduction (p. 16 in 1905 edition).
[2] J.R. Hinchcliffe and P.J. Griffiths, 'The prechondrogenic patterns in tetrapod limb development and their phylogenetic significance', in *Development and evolution* (6th Symposium of the British Society for Developmental Biology) (ed. B.C. Goodwin, N. Holder and C.C. Wylie; Cambridge: Cambridge University Press, 1983).
[3] G.P. Wagner, 'A research programme for testing the biological homology concept', in *Homology* (Proceedings of Novartis Foundation Symposium 222, 21–23 July 1998) (ed. B.K. Hall, G. Bock and G. Cardew; Chichester: John Wiley & Sons, 1999).
[4] M. Foote, J.P. Hunter, C.M. Janis and J.J. Sepkoski Jnr, 'Evolutionary and preservational constraints on origins of biologic groups: Divergence times of eutherian mammals', *Science* 283 (1999), pp. 1310–14.
[5] N. Eldredge. *Reinventing Darwin* (London: Weidenfeld & Nicolson, 1995), p. 95.
[6] E. Mayr. *What Evolution Is* (New York: Basic Books, 2001), p. 189.
[7] E.B. Daeschler, N.H. Shubin and F.A. Jenkins Jnr, 'A Devonian tetrapod-like fish and the evolution of the tetrapod body plan', *Nature* 440 (2006), pp. 757–63.

[8] N.H. Shubin, E.B. Daeschler and F.A. Jenkins Jnr, 'The pectoral fin of *Tiktaalik roseae* and the origin of the tetrapod limb', *Nature* 440 (2006), pp. 764–71.

[9] P.E. Ahlberg and J.A. Clack, 'A firm step from water to land', *Nature* 440 (2006), pp. 747–9. Emphasis added.

[10] Ahlberg and Clack, 'Firm step', pp. 747–9.

[11] See, for example, M. Ridley's comments regarding preadaptation in *Evolution* (Oxford: Blackwell Science, 3rd edn, 1996), p. 346.

[12] J.G.M. Thewissen, L.N. Cooper, M.T. Clementz, S. Bajpai and B.N. Tiwari, 'Whales originated from aquatic artiodactyls in the Eocene epoch of India', *Nature* 450 (2007), pp. 1190–195.

[13] P.N. Nelson, P.R. Carnegie, J. Martin, H.D. Ejtehadi, P. Hooley, D. Roden, S. Rowland-Jones, P. Warren, J. Astley and P.G. Murray', 'Demystified ... Human endogenous retroviruses', *J Clin Pathol: Mol Pathol* 56 (2003), pp. 11–18.

[14] Comment by Scott Gilbert in J. Whitfield, 'Postmodern evolution?', *Nature* 455 (2008), pp. 281–4.

[15] R. Cordaux, S. Udit, M.A. Batzer and F. Cedric, 'Birth of a chimeric primate gene by capture of the transposase gene from a mobile element', *PNAS* 103(21) (2006), p. 8103.

[16] Most of the protein-coding sequences of genes of 'lower' organisms (called prokaryotes), such as bacteria, are continuous. However, in 'higher' organisms (called eukaryotes), including plants and animals, most protein-coding sequences include non-coding sequences which are called introns, with the coding sequences being called exons. When the gene is used to make a protein, all of the gene is copied into RNA, but then the lengths of RNA corresponding to the introns are removed and the exons are joined (spliced) together. This means that the gene must include sequences (splice sites) to identify the exons in the RNA – in addition to the 'start' and 'stop' codons for the protein itself.

8

On the Danger of Locating God's Actions in Shrinking Gaps: A Response to David

GRAEME FINLAY

David writes tellingly of the wonder of life, but we differ in the way we interpret the phenomena of biology. I have divided my response into two sections.

A. Pre-biotic evolution[1]

The research field of *chemical evolution* or *pre-biotic evolution* studies how life might have originated. Central to this is the issue of how the first genetic systems might have arisen. Pre-biotic evolution is not one of the scientific fields that Darwin pioneered,[2] and is a separate issue from that of biological evolution.

The origin of the first living cells is a profound mystery. No credible hypothesis has been suggested. So how should we live with this ignorance?

As a scientist, I have a deep instinct that questions that can be posed in scientific terms should have answers that can be expressed in scientific terms. That is to believe (yes, it is a matter of faith, because the ability to do science depends on unprovable presuppositions)[3] that biological mysteries should *in principle* be open to elucidation in terms of biological processes. The question, 'Can proteins arise in the absence of cells?' can be asked and can, therefore, *in principle* be researched.

Scientists do not entertain the idea that simple chemical precursors spontaneously assorted into proteins in some colossal lottery. Astronomical improbabilities for the random assembly of biological molecules are often put forward, but they do not contribute to the discussion. Rather, scientists seek to discover the consistent patterns by which matter behaves. They search for laws that would describe how chemical precursors might flow along preferred routes (constrained by the nature of physical reality) to form complex biological structures.

As a Christian, I have a deep instinct to see the entire world of biology as the work of God. (Hitherto, I have kept scientific and theological issues separate. But I can do so no longer.) I attribute *all* biological processes to God's wisdom and continuous sustaining power – whether they are familiar (and partially understood) or utterly mysterious. The scientific quest to discover the rationality inherent in the universe is a search for the rationality which comes from God.

Our knowledge of natural law is partial. The current boundaries of our knowledge and ignorance are perpetually changing.[4] We must remain open to the hypothesis that complex molecules and cells were formed via favoured routes as a result of (as yet unknown) lawful, self-organising properties of matter.[5] The Christian physicist Sir Robert Boyd expressed this poetically as follows:[6]

Who is this God …?
… whose plan so shapes the atoms
that they must combine to give dust life …

There may be only one route from simple molecules to living systems, and it will be a formidable challenge to find it among the multitude of false starts.[7] Jesus said that the road to life is narrow and not easily found (Mt. 7:14). God works in particularistic ways in both creation and redemption.

If a molecular sequence of events leading to the origin of life is ever discovered, it will be breathtaking in its elegance, and wholly consistent with the action of an all-wise Creator. Any starkly natural laws that might define chemical evolution express the way science interprets God's dealings with matter.

B. Biological evolution

1. Gene duplication

Gene duplication is an established fact of evolution regardless of what Kimura (quoted by David in chapter 5, p. 108) said in 1983. David made a poor choice in citing the oxygen-carrying proteins (globins) to deny that gene families arise by duplication (chapter 5, p. 108). The generation of the β-globin-γ1 and γ2 genes by a gene duplication event was demonstrated in 1991 (Figure 1).[8] Both the α-globin[9] and β-globin gene families have undergone repeated cycles of gene duplication.

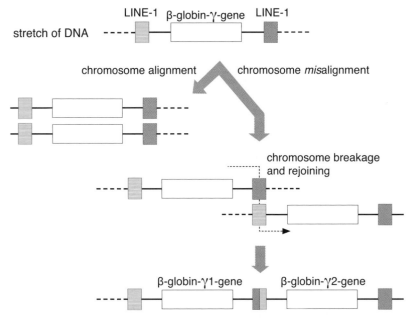

Figure 1   Duplication of a globin gene

An original β-globin-γ gene was sandwiched between two LINE-1 jumping genes (represented by boxes placed along a stretch of DNA). During the production of sex cells, chromosome pairs normally line up alongside each other (left). However, in the instance when gene duplication occurred, the chromosome pair misaligned at stretches of related LINE-1 sequence (right). Breakage and rejoining of the chromosomes (dotted line) generated a new hybrid LINE-1 element and a second β-globin-γ gene. The event occurred in a simian ancestor.[8] This mechanism is called non-allelic homologous recombination.

2. Natural selection

David claimed that there are no examples of evolution involving 'the production of new genes' (chapter 5, pp. 108–9). This is not true (see examples provided in chapter 6, pp. 158–63).

Since I submitted chapter 6, an article was published that showed how the *CDC14Bretro* gene arose by a reverse transcription event (one of those random events orchestrated by jumping genes). The new gene subsequently underwent a sequence of twelve mutations, indicative of natural selection. The outcome was a novel protein with a new function (Figure 2).[10]

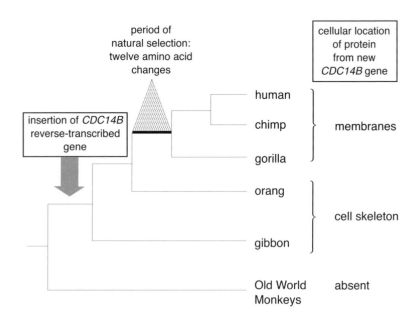

Figure 2   Birth of a novel gene by reverse transcription followed by natural selection

A copy of the CDC14Bretro gene was generated by a reverse transcriptase reaction. This occurred in an ape ancestor. The gene changed minimally for a long time, but 12 mutations occurred in an ancestor of humans, chimps and gorillas (dark line) evincing a period of natural selection. The resulting protein showed a novel location in cells, indicating novel function.[10]

The *XIST* gene controls X chromosome functions in females of all Eutherian mammals. It was generated in an ancestor of Eutherian mammals. It was cobbled together from leftover fragments of an older gene (retained in chickens and marsupials) and a series of ERV and jumping gene insertions.[11]

New proteins are indeed produced via 'series of intermediates'. Far from being 'beyond the bounds of reasonable possibility' (chapter 5, p. 114), the generation of new genes is thoroughly documented. A rationalistic approach to science ('What can I expect?') leads David to declare that the formation of new genes is 'totally out of the question' (chapter 5, p. 99). The empirical approach to science ('What, in fact, has happened?') has shown that gene birth is *in actual fact* commonplace. Time and again what we cannot imagine *before* the event is found to have an elegant and logical explanation when viewed *after* the event. This must be so if the God of biology is the God of redemption (Eph. 3:20–21).

3. Regulation

David rightly raises the issue of *regulatory sequences* that control how genes work (chapter 5, pp. 103, 109). Genome science has revealed that it is not so much genes that are important in evolution (we have a similar number of genes to plants and flies), but the way those genes are *regulated*.[12]

ERVs and jumping genes *repeatedly* have donated stretches of DNA that function to control gene activity (chapter 6, pp. 160–63). Since I submitted chapter 6, the insertion of a piece of retroviral DNA near a member of the GST gene family (*GSTO1*) has been shown to provide novel regulatory function to that gene (Figure 3).[13] David suggests that only an 'extraordinary coincidence' might endow a duplicated gene with new regulatory sequences (chapter 5, p. 103). In fact, such coincidences have occurred *repeatedly* through evolutionary time.

Many stretches of DNA with defined functions (including that of gene regulation) are rapidly evolving; that is, they show a lack of 'evolutionary constraint'.[14] David suggests that this feature is not compatible with an evolutionary interpretation (chapter 5, p. 122). However, these very changes in DNA sequence represent

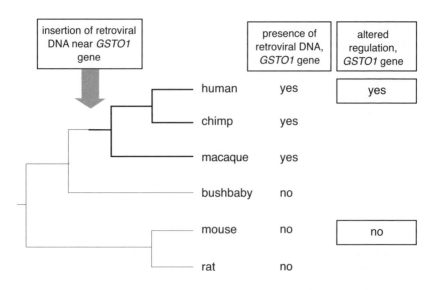

Figure 3   Evolution of a regulatory sequence that controls the *GSTO1* gene

A segment of retroviral DNA was inserted near the GSTO1 gene in an ancestor of humans, chimps and macaques. It contributed a regulatory sequence that controls the activity of the GSTO1 gene. The human gene with the retroviral insert shows altered regulation relative to other members of the gene family, whereas the corresponding mouse gene, which has no insert, does not. This report described many similar instances of ERV-mediated gene regulation.[13]

the alterations in gene regulation that contribute to the evolution of new species. David writes as if the evolution of gene regulation is not compatible with evolution!

4. Homology and the evolution of new structures

David questions the possibility of the eye forming through an evolutionary route (chapter 5, pp. 116, 122). The eye does in fact show a gradation of development, from the light-sensitive cell patch of sea-squirts, to the proto-eye of hagfishes, to the fully formed eye of lampreys (which develops from the hagfish-like proto-eye of lamprey larvae). Lamprey eyes are similar to those of other vertebrates. There is progressive development of the shapes of light-sensitive opsin molecules and in the structure of the cells that contain those molecules. A detailed, plausible and testable outline for eye development constitutes a useful (albeit provisional) working hypothesis. The story so far is typical of how science proceeds.[15]

David questions how certain *Pax* and *Six* genes can be involved in the evolution of eyes as different as insect eyes and our own. *Pax6* genes of distantly related species may trigger the formation of the *specialised cell types* involved in light detection (regardless of the overall anatomy of the eye). It is the *photoreceptor cell type* that is homologous in organisms across the evolutionary spectrum.[16]

Members of the *Pax* and *Six* gene families formed an interactive (and inseparable) partnership very early in animal evolution (Figure 4).[17] The link between *Pax6* and the *Six3* in eye

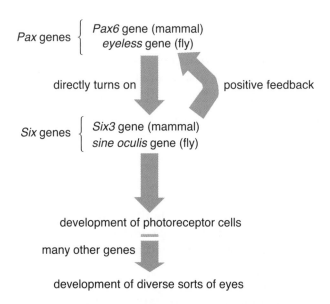

Figure 4   The partnership of *Pax* and *Six* genes in eye development

Triggering of eye development by this gene partnership was established early in evolution. The Pax6 gene product directly activates the Six3 gene in mammals. In the fly the gene equivalents are named eyeless and sine oculis respectively.[15–18]

development is 'a consequence of their common evolutionary history'.[18] Similar correspondences exist between the *Hox* genes and the development of vertebrae.[19] David is creating problems where none exists.

I have previously alluded to the evolution of the placenta (chapter 6, pp. 159–60). A report published subsequently has surveyed the genes involved in generating the placenta. In the early stages of pregnancy the placenta develops in response to the activities of *ancient* genes. This situation reflects altered *regulation* of those genes. But the later stages of placental development are driven by a suite of genes enriched in members that have arisen *recently* (during mammalian history) by duplication.[20]

5. Fossils

David's assertion that new groups always appear suddenly in the fossil record (chapter 5, p. 119) is not true. Issues of *Nature* that were published as I wrote this chapter contain reports describing fossil intermediates in the generation of flatfish (*Heteronectes*; Figure 5)[21] and land creatures (*Ventastega*).[22] Fossils illustrate the evolutionary story just as archaeological artefacts illustrate the biblical story. In both cases the records are fragmentary but illuminating.

6. Common descent

David raises the issue of so-called 'junk' DNA sequences (ERVs and jumping genes). He asserts that if they had functions, they could not be used as markers of common descent because 'if they have a use then this would be a sufficient reason for their existence' (chapter 5, p. 123).

ERVs and jumping genes are markers of evolutionary descent because of the elaborate but haphazard *mechanisms* by which they splice themselves into DNA. It is the *mechanism* of copying-and-pasting, not the *function* of these jumping genes, that proves humans and other mammals have a common ancestor. The director of the Genome Project, Francis Collins (a Christian) has stated that

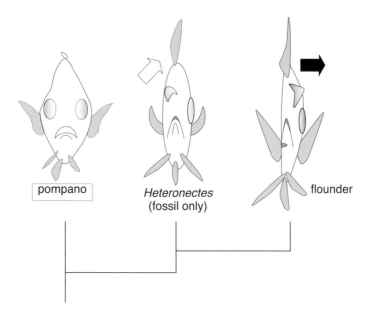

pompano

Heteronectes
(fossil only)

flounder

Figure 5   A fossil intermediate in the evolution of flatfish such as flounder

The evolution of the asymmetrical body shape and eye position in flounder has long been debated. A fossil fish (Heteronectes) demonstrates an intermediate position in which the right eye has shifted leftwards (but not across the midline; open arrow). Subsequently the right eye migrated across the midline (black arrow). The flounder should be rotated 90° in an anti-clockwise direction to picture its actual orientation on the seabed.[21]

jumping genes provide evidence of common ancestry (for example between humans and rodents) that is 'virtually inescapable'.[23]

When jumping genes *initially* invade a new site in the genome, they have no function. What is the 'function' of HTLV-1 (that may cause leukaemia) and of jumping genes (that may cause haemophilia, muscular dystrophy or cancer)? Jumping genes damage DNA and cause mutations, just like radiation and tobacco smoke. When they are first spliced into chromosomal DNA they are indeed junk. But David rightly acknowledges that many ERVs and jumping genes *currently* have vital functions as indicated (chapter 6, pp. 158–63). These functions have arisen *since* the ERVs and jumping genes were spliced into genomes. These potentially destructive agents (junk) have been naturally selected to provide new genes and essential genetic regulatory function. David tells us that these evolutionary innovations are totally impossible! Since David requires that we accept the functionality of at least some jumping genes, he *has to be* a neo-Darwinian.

7. Design

David argues that ID is an *alternative* to natural process as far as the origin of life and of species is concerned. The design inference would be falsified by the discovery of a natural explanation (pp. 124–5).[24] This position requires that God acts in *either* an ID mode *or* a natural law mode. Such an either-or dichotomy sits uneasily with the biblical view that God *always* acts in perfect wisdom ('design') and faithfulness ('law'). Faith in the wisdom of God should motivate us to wait patiently for scientists to come up with a credible scheme of pre-biotic evolution. We impugn God's wisdom by positing that his laws are inadequate to account for complex biological phenomena. Perhaps the basis of the either-or proposition is that when people are baffled by a biological mystery they attribute it to 'design', but when they have started to understand it, they attribute it to 'law'.

The concept of 'design' can tell us nothing about God. If proteins are 'designed' in some *immediate* sense of the word, then what sort of god designed the intricate but devastating cholera toxin and diphtheria toxin molecules? We must accept that God is the source of natural law, and that such laws describe the activity of matter to which God has granted the gift of freedom. The operation of free but lawful process has produced both the wonder of humanity, God's image-bearer, and also the microbes that produce suffering and disease.

Ultimately the ambiguities of nature make sense only in the light of a God who has committed himself to his creation in faithfulness and love. This God has entered into creation, experienced the agonies of death, and triumphed in resurrected glory so that he might transform creation into a new creation from which all suffering and evil will have been removed.

The miracles of Jesus, culminating in his resurrection, are unprecedented events, irreproducible in the context of our current

12 S. Carroll, B. Prud'homme and N. Gompel, 'Regulating evolution', *Scientific American* 298.5 (2008), p. 60.

13 A.B. Conley, J. Piriyapongsa and I.K. Jordan, 'Retroviral promoters in the human genome', *Bioinformatics* 24 (2008), p. 1563.

14 The ENCODE Project Consortium, 'Identification and analysis of functional elements in 1% of the human genome by the ENCODE pilot project', *Nature* 447 (2007), p. 799.

15 T.D. Lamb, S.P. Collin and E.N. Pugh, 'Evolution of the vertebrate eye: opsins, photoreceptors, retina and eye cup', *Nature Reviews Neurobiology* 8 (2007), p. 960.

16 Z. Kozmik, 'The role of Pax genes in eye evolution', *Brain Research Bulletin* 75 (2008), p. 335.

17 D. Hoshiyama, N. Iwabe and T. Miyata, 'Evolution of the gene families forming the *Pax/Six* regulatory network: isolation of genes from primitive animals and phylogenetic analyses', *FEBS Letters* 581 (2007), p. 1639.

18 W.J. Gehring, 'New perspectives on eye development and the evolution of eyes and photoreceptors', *Journal of Heredity* 96 (2005), p. 171.

19 D.M. Wellik, *Hox* patterning of the vertebrate axial skeleton. *Developmental Dynamics* 236 (2007), p. 2454. Regarding the homology of vertebrae, it has been shown that snake vertebrae are induced by the *same* signalling molecules as those of fish, birds and mammals, but that the *timing* of the production of these signals is different (see page 197).

20 K. Knox and J.C. Baker, 'Genomic evolution of the placenta using co-option and duplication and divergence', *Genome Research* 18 (2008), p. 685.

21 M. Friedman, 'The evolutionary origin of flatfish asymmetry', *Nature* 454 (2008), p. 209.

22 P.E. Ahlberg, J.A. Clack, E. Lucsevics et al., '*Ventastega curonica* and the origin of tetrapod morphology', *Nature* 453 (2008), p. 1199.

23 Francis S. Collins, *The Language of God* (New York: Free Press, 2006), pp. 136–8.

24 The demonstration that all mammals are derived from a common ancestor overthrows a *multitude* of design inferences.

situation, and beyond the reach of science. But in the context of the New Creation they flow with utter consistency from God's character and purpose. The lawful behaviour of molecules and organisms in this material world and the lawful resurrection of the body as a phenomenon of the eschaton have a different character, but both manifest the faithfulness of the one redeeming creator God.

Notes

[1] David intended to address the issue of whether novel proteins are generated during biological evolution. However, the scientific literature contains many accounts of how novel proteins are generated during biological evolution. For this reason, I have chosen rather to discuss how we should respond to the profound mystery of how proteins might have been generated during pre-biotic evolution.

[2] K. Padian, 'Darwin's enduring legacy', *Nature* 451 (2008), p. 632.

[3] The presuppositions upon which science depends are derived from the Bible. See for example H. Turner, *The Roots of Science* (Auckland: DeepSight Trust, 1998).

[4] It is not long since the idea of sequencing the human genome was sheer fiction, an implausible pipe dream.

[5] S. Conway Morris, *Life's Solution* (Cambridge: CUP, 2003), ch. 4, especially p. 47.

[6] R.J. Berry, *Real Science, Real Faith* (Eastbourne: Monarch, 1991), pp. 68–9.

[7] Morris, *Solution*, pp. 67, 308–10.

[8] D.H.A. Fitch, W.J. Bailey, D.A. Tagle et al., 'Duplication of the β-globin gene mediated by L1 long interspersed repetitive elements in an early ancestor of simian primates', *Proceedings of the National Academy of Sciences of the USA* 88 (1991), p. 7396.

[9] F.G. Hoffmann, J.C. Opazo and J.F. Storz, 'Rapid rates of lineage-specific gene duplication and deletion in the α-globin gene family', *Molecular Biology and Evolution* 25 (2008), p. 591.

[10] L. Rosso, A.C. Marques, M. Weier et al., 'Birth and rapid subcellular adaptation of a hominoid-specific CDC14 protein', *PLoS Biology* 6 (2008), p. e140.

[11] E.A. Elisaphenko, N.N. Kolesnikov, A.I. Shevchenko et al., 'A dual origin of the *Xist* gene from a protein-coding gene and a set of transposable elements', *PLoS ONE* 3 (2008), p. e2521.

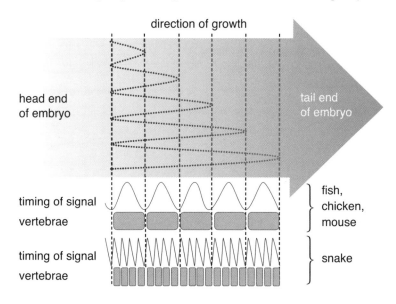

Vertebrate vertebrae

Vertebrate embryos grow in a head-to-tail direction. During this growth, pulses of signalling molecules (FGF8 and WNT3A) are generated, each associated with the appearance of a new vertebra. The vast increase in the number of vertebrae in snakes arises because the pulses of FGF8 + WNT3A occur at a higher frequency relative to the growth rate of the embryo. Same genes, different regulation, vastly different body plan. See C. Gomez, E.M. Ozbudak, J. Wunderlich et al., 'Control of segment number in vertebrate embryos', Nature 454 (2008), p. 335.

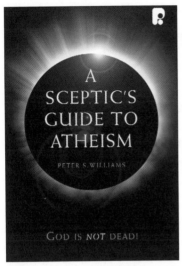

A Sceptic's Guide to Atheism

Peter S. Williams

Atheism has become militant in the past few years with its own popular mass media evangelists such as Richard Dawkins and Daniel Dennett. In this readable book Christian apologist Peter S. Williams considers the arguments of 'the new atheists' and finds them wanting. Williams explains the history of atheism and then responds to the claims that:

- 'belief in God causes more harm than good' ● 'religion is about blind faith and science is the only way to know things' ● 'science can explain religion away' ● 'there is not enough evidence for God' ●'the arguments for God's existence do not work'

Williams argues that belief in God is more intellectually plausible than atheism.

'The new atheism is like the Titanic leaving Southampton. Richard Dawkins, Daniel Dennett, and her other captains proclaim her unsinkable. In this insightful book, Peter Williams shows that a carefully articulated, philosophically grounded faith is to the new atheism what hitting an iceberg was to the Titanic. The lesson is clear and urgent: get off while you still can!' – **William A. Dembski**, Senior Fellow, Discovery Institute, Seattle, author of *The Design Inference*

'A coherent, well-reasoned defense of Christian Theism that challenges the best atheist attacks. As Williams concludes, he has seen nothing that comes close to undermining the Christian faith.' – **Gary R. Habermas**, Distinguished Research Professor, Liberty University, USA

Peter S. Williams is a Christian philosopher and apologist working for the Damaris Trust, UK. He is the author of several books, including *The Case for Angels* and *I Wish I Could Believe in Meaning: a Response to Nihilism*.

978-1-84227-617-4

Think God, Think Science

Conversations on Life, the Universe and Faith

Michael Pfundner in discussion with Ernest Lucas

Has science killed God? How, if at all, are we to 'think God' in the scientific twenty-first century? That question is at the heart of this introductory yet intelligent book in which Michael Pfundner talks to biblical scholar and bio-chemist, Ernest Lucas. The conversation engages three broad areas:

- *The Sky*: as our scientific understanding of the universe – its vastness, its age, and its origins – has increased, have the stars stopped declaring the glory of God?
- *The Cell*: What place is there for a good creator amidst the random genet-ic mutations and brutal processes of neo-Darwinian evolution? How can mere 'naked apes' think of themselves as being made in the image of God? Did Genesis get it wrong?
- *The Faith*: Has the recent work of historians and archaeologists under-mined traditional Christian belief in the historical reliability of the gospels and in Jesus' resurrection?

Ernest Lucas argues that modern science is fully compatible with Christian theology and Scripture.

> This is a wonderfully inspiring book! An immensely valuable – and read-able – contribution to the field.' – **John Bryant**, Professor of Genetics, Exeter University

Ernest Lucas is Vice-Principal and Tutor in Biblical Studies, Bristol Baptist College; Michael Pfunder is Bible & Church Development Officer, Bible Society, UK.

978-1-84227-609-9